How
Learning
Works

How Learning Works

Seven Research-Based Principles for Smart Teaching

Susan A. Ambrose, Michael W. Bridges,
Michele DiPietro, Marsha C. Lovett,
Marie K. Norman

Foreword by Richard E. Mayer

JOSSEY-BASS
A Wiley Imprint
www.josseybass.com

Published by Jossey-Bass
A Wiley Imprint

989 Market Street, San Francisco, CA 94103-1741—www.josseybass.com

The book is based on the seven "Theory and Research-based Principles of Learning," which are used with permission of Carnegie Mellon University's Eberly Center for Teaching Excellence.

Figures created by Judy Brooks.

Readers should be aware that Internet Web sites offered as citations and/or sources for further information may have changed or disappeared between the time this was written and when it is read.

Limit of Liability/Disclaimer of Warranty: While the publisher and author have used their best efforts in preparing this book, they make no representations or warranties with respect to the accuracy or completeness of the contents of this book and specifically disclaim any implied warranties of merchantability or fitness for a particular purpose. No warranty may be created or extended by sales representatives or written sales materials. The advice and strategies contained herein may not be suitable for your situation. You should consult with a professional where appropriate. Neither the publisher nor author shall be liable for any loss of profit or any other commercial damages, including but not limited to special, incidental, consequential, or other damages.

Jossey-Bass books and products are available through most bookstores. To contact Jossey-Bass directly call our Customer Care Department within the U.S. at 800-956-7739, outside the U.S. at 317-572-3986, or fax 317-572-4002.

Jossey-Bass also publishes its books in a variety of electronic formats. Some content that appears in print may not be available in electronic books.

Library of Congress Cataloging-in-Publication Data

How learning works : seven research-based principles for smart teaching /
Susan A. Ambrose . . . [et al.] ; foreword by Richard E. Mayer. – 1st ed.
     p. cm. – (The Jossey-Bass higher and adult education series)
  Includes bibliographical references and index.
  ISBN 978-0-470-48410-4 (cloth)
  1. Effective teaching–Case studies. 2. Educational innovations–Case studies. 3. School improvement programs–Case studies. 4. Learning, Psychology of–Case studies. I. Ambrose, Susan A. II. Title: Seven research-based principles for smart teaching.
  LB1025.3.H68 2010
  371.102–dc22

                      2010003939

Printed in the United States of America
FIRST EDITION

HB Printing   10 9 8 7 6 5 4 3 2 1

THE JOSSEY-BASS HIGHER AND ADULT EDUCATION SERIES

CONTENTS

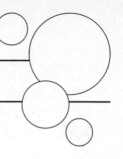

Appendices

LIST OF FIGURES, TABLES, AND EXHIBITS

Figures

Tables

Exhibits

To the faculty and graduate instructors of Carnegie Mellon, whose dedication to student learning continues to inspire us.

FOREWORD: APPLYING THE SCIENCE OF LEARNING TO COLLEGE TEACHING

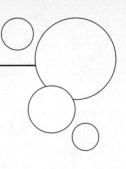

In 1899, the famous American psychologist, William James published a little book called *Talks to Teachers*, in which he sought to explain how to apply psychology to education—that is, he sought to use what he called "the science of the mind's workings" to generate practical advice for classroom teachers. At the time, the book was not much of a success, largely for two reasons: (a) there was a lack of research evidence on how learning works (that is, the science of learning), and (b) there was a lack of research-based principles concerning how to help people learn (that is, the science of instruction).

Much has happened in the learning sciences in the past 100 years, particularly in the last few decades. We finally have the makings of a research-based theory of how people learn that is educationally relevant (that is, the science of learning) and a set of evidence-based principles for how to help people learn that is grounded in cognitive theory (that is, the science of instruction). Indeed, these are exciting times if you are interested in fulfilling William James's mission of applying the science of learning to education.

The book you are holding—*How Learning Works: Seven Research-Based Principles for Smart Teaching*—is the latest advancement in the continuing task of applying the science of learning to education—particularly, college teaching. The authors are experts in helping college teachers understand how research in the science of learning can improve their teaching. If you are interested in what research in the science of learning and instruction has to say for you as a college teacher, then this book is for you.

The book is organized around seven learning principles—each a gem that is based on research evidence from the science of learning and the science of instruction. The principles concern the role of the student's prior knowledge, motivation, and developmental level, as well as opportunities for the student to practice, receive feedback, and learn to become a self-directed learner. Each chapter focuses on one of the principles, such as "Students' prior knowledge can help or hinder learning." Each chapter begins with a concrete scenario in college teaching that exemplifies the principle being highlighted in the chapter, provides a clear statement and rationale for the principle, summarizes the underlying research and its implications, and offers specific advice on how to apply the principle.

Consider the following scenario: You are teaching a course in your field. Based on years of study and work, you are an expert in your field—but you are certainly not an expert in how to teach others about your field. In fact, you have almost no training in how to teach. Yet a fundamental part of your job involves college teaching. You have devised a teaching style that works for you, but you wonder whether there is any way to base what you are doing on scientific principles of learning and teaching. This description fits many college teachers.

The book you are holding is based on the idea that you wish to consider taking an evidence-based approach to college teaching—that is, you wish to inform your instructional decisions with research evidence and research-based theory. Why should you take an evidence-based approach? You could base your instructional choices on fads, ideology, opinions, expert advice, or habit—but these approaches may not be ideal if your goal is to be an effective teacher. Admittedly, advice from experts and your own personal experience can be useful aids to you in planning instruction, but they may be incomplete. In taking an evidence-based approach, you seek to add to your knowledge base by discovering what works and how it works. In short, it is helpful to understand what the science of learning has to offer you in your role as a college teacher.

Where should you look for help in improving your college teaching? Consider three common choices:

Sources that are too hard—You could try to digest research articles in the field of learning and instruction, but you might find them somewhat tedious and perhaps daunting. This approach is too hard because it focuses on scientific evidence without much focus on how to apply the evidence to teaching.

Sources that are too soft—You could read self-help guides that offer practical advice that is not necessarily based on research evidence or research-based theory. This approach is too soft because it focuses on practical advice without supporting evidence or theory to back up the advice.

Sources that are just right—You could read this book, which synthesizes empirical research evidence and research-based learning theory into practical advice for how to improve your college teaching. In short, the strength of this book is that it combines research evidence and practical advice to produce an evidence-based approach to improving your college teaching. If you are interested in what the science of learning has to contribute to your college teaching, then this book is for you.

What should you look for in this book? In reading this book, I suggest that you look to make sure that it meets four basic criteria for applying the science of learning to your college teaching:

Theory-grounded: the advice is grounded in a research-based theory of how people learn

Evidence-based: the advice is supported by empirical research evidence showing how to help people learn

Relevant: the advice has clear and practical implications for how to improve your teaching

Clear: the advice is understandable, concrete, and concise

As you read about each of the seven basic learning principles in this book, you will find advice that is grounded in learning theory, based on research evidence, relevant to college teaching, and easy to understand. The authors have extensive knowledge and experience in applying the science of learning to college teaching, and they graciously share it with you in this organized and readable book.

I congratulate you for your interest in improving your teaching and commend you for taking the important step of reading this book. If you want to improve your teaching, it is useful to understand what research says about how learning works and about how to foster learning. In light of these goals, I welcome you to the feast of evidence-based advice you will find in this volume.

Richard E. Mayer
University of California, Santa Barbara

ACKNOWLEDGMENTS

Writing this book was a significant undertaking, which we would not have been able to complete without the help of many friends and colleagues. Although many faculty colleagues across disciplines and institutions have found these principles helpful and encouraged us to publish them, it was Rich Mayer who, after seeing a presentation of our learning principles, convinced us to share them with the larger education community. Little did he know that his encouragement would lead to more work for him! We are thrilled and grateful to Rich for writing the Foreword to this book.

We are forever in debt to Judy Brooks, our talented graphic designer, who cheerfully endured our endless wordsmithing, listening carefully, and asking insightful questions, in order to help us put our ideas into images for the figures in this book. Judy, we salute you! We also cannot express enough thanks to Hilary Franklin, a Ph.D. student working with us, who read every chapter with her characteristic precision and intelligence and provided invaluable feedback that forced us to recognize and address our own "expert blind spots." Aimee Kane joined our group late in the writing process, and yet we cannot imagine how we functioned before she became our colleague. Her thoughtful and reflective responses to the chapters added a fresh and indispensable perspective and left an indelible mark on the finished product. We were also extremely lucky to have had the help of our former colleague Anne Fay throughout the early phases of planning and writing the book. Her ability to remember and access every research study she has ever read was truly awe inspiring. In addition, our "internal" editor, Lisa Ritter, applied her exacting standards and patience to the job of copy editing the manuscript, thus freeing us to continue revising ad infinitum; we thank her for a job well done.

We are also thankful for an outstanding set of colleagues, both at Carnegie Mellon and at other universities in the United States and abroad, who were willing to take time from their busy schedules to read and provide insightful feedback on different chapters. These colleagues include Vincent Aleven, Ryan Baker, Rebecca Freeland, Scott Kauffman, Edmund Ko, Ken Koedinger, Norma Ming, Matt Ouellett, Ido Roll, and Christian Schunn.

Finally, we would never have embarked upon this endeavor in the first place if it were not for the thousands of faculty members and graduate students with whom we have worked over the years. We are humbled by your ongoing dedication to your students and by your willingness to share your stories and experiences, open up your courses to us, and reflect thoughtfully on and refine your teaching practice. We continue to learn and benefit from our interactions with you, and we hope this book provides something useful in return.

ABOUT THE AUTHORS

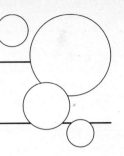

Susan A. Ambrose is associate provost for education, director of the Eberly Center for Teaching Excellence, and teaching professor in the Department of History at Carnegie Mellon. She received her doctorate in American history from Carnegie Mellon in 1986 and has been at the Eberly Center since its inception. Her major responsibilities include identifying and responding to changing educational needs that impact faculty and graduate students, maintaining overall operation of the Eberly Center, and overseeing the Intercultural Communication Center and the Office of Academic Development. Susan Ambrose has been a visiting scholar for the American Society of Engineering Education and the National Science Foundation, and was awarded an American Council on Education fellowship to study leadership styles of two university presidents. She has coauthored three books and published more than twenty-five chapters, articles, and commissioned reports in such areas as faculty satisfaction, engineering education, teaching and learning, and women in science and engineering. In recent years she has received funding from the National Science Foundation, the Alfred P. Sloan Foundation, the Fund for the Improvement of Postsecondary Education, the Lilly Endowment, the Carnegie Corporation of New York, the Eden Hall Foundation, and the ALCOA Foundation. She also teaches courses on immigration, particularly Mexican and Asian immigration to the United States.

Michael W. Bridges is the director of faculty development at University of Pittsburgh Medical Center (UPMC) St. Margaret Hospital, where he works with family practice residents and fellows. He received his doctorate in social psychology from Carnegie Mellon in 1997. He has applied his background in the psychology of personality and motivation to help develop courses across a broad range of topics and disciplines. He has also provided survey research consultation to numerous clients, including Carnegie Mellon's Deliberative Polling Program, a campuswide first year experience called Big Questions and Fathom Designs. His research interests include the role of motivation in goal-directed behavior, the relation between stress and disease, and the role of personality in traumatic life events. He teaches courses in personality and stress and coping.

Michele DiPietro is associate director for graduate programs at the Eberly Center for Teaching Excellence and instructor in the Department of Statistics at Carnegie Mellon. He received his doctorate in statistics from Carnegie Mellon in 2001 and has been at the Eberly Center since 1998. He is responsible for all the graduate students and future faculty programs of the Eberly Center, including teaching workshops, individual consultations, and the Documentation of Teaching Development program. His scholarly interests include the application of learning sciences to enhance college teaching, faculty development, diversity in the classroom, student ratings of instruction, teaching in times of tragedies, academic integrity, and statistics education. He has served on the board of directors of the Professional and Organizational Development Network in Higher Education, the premiere faculty development organization in North America, and was the chair of its 2006 conference, "Theory and Research for a Scholarship of Practice." He has received funding from the National Science

Foundation. His freshman seminar "The Statistics of Sexual Orientation" has been featured in a variety of media, including *The Chronicle of Higher Education*.

Marsha C. Lovett is associate director for faculty development at the Eberly Center for Teaching Excellence and associate teaching professor in the Department of Psychology at Carnegie Mellon. The question that drives her work is how people learn. She has studied this question from various perspectives, as a graduate student, postdoctoral researcher, and assistant professor in Carnegie Mellon's Psychology Department. Her research combines computational and mathematical modeling, controlled experiments, and classroom observation. She has studied learning in several disciplines, including geometry, physics, linear algebra, programming, and statistics, at the high school and college levels. She designed and developed *StatTutor*, a computer-based tutor that helps students learn the skills of data analysis. Her teaching has included undergraduate and graduate courses on research methods, the analysis of verbal data, and the nature of expertise. At the Eberly Center, Lovett applies theoretical and empirical principles from cognitive psychology to help instructors improve their teaching. She has published more than thirty research articles on learning and instruction and is co-editor of the book *Thinking with Data*. In recent years, she has received funding from the National Science Foundation, the Office of Naval Research, and the Spencer Foundation.

Marie K. Norman is a teaching consultant and research associate at the Eberly Center for Teaching Excellence, and adjunct professor of anthropology in the history department at Carnegie Mellon. She received her doctorate from the University of Pittsburgh's Department of Anthropology in 1999, where her research, funded by a Fulbright doctoral studies grant, focused on the effects of tourism on caste relations in Nepal. At the Eberly Center, Marie Norman consults with junior and senior faculty who want to improve their teaching, helps run the Wimmer Faculty Fellows Program, and conducts a variety of workshops and seminars on teaching and learning. She is particularly interested in cross-cultural issues in the classroom. In addition to her work with the Eberly Center, she teaches courses on medical anthropology, gender, tourism, and South Asia. She has served on the faculty of the University of Pittsburgh's Semester at Sea Program (2004), is an academic advisor for the Bachelor of Humanities and Arts Program at Carnegie Mellon, and co-edits the journal *Ethnology*. Norman is committed to applying anthropological approaches to practical problems, and has worked as a consultant on research studies for St. Margaret's Hospital, Allegheny College, and Fathom Designs.

How
Learning
Works

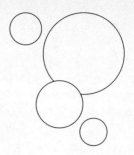

Introduction: Bridging Learning Research and Teaching Practice

Learning results from what the student does and thinks and only from what the student does and thinks. The teacher can advance learning only by influencing what the student does to learn.

HERBERT A. SIMON,[1] one of the founders of the field of Cognitive Science, Nobel Laureate, and University Professor (deceased) at Carnegie Mellon University

As the quotation above suggests, any conversation about effective teaching must begin with a consideration of how students learn. Yet instructors who want to investigate the mechanisms and conditions that promote student learning may find themselves caught between two kinds of resources: research articles with technical discussions of learning, or books and Web sites with concrete strategies for course design and classroom pedagogy. Texts of the first type focus on learning but are often technical, inaccessible, and lack clear application to the classroom, while texts of the second type are written in accessible language but often leave instructors without a clear sense of why (or even whether) particular strategies promote learning. Neither of these genres offers what many instructors really need—a model of student learning that enables them to make sound teaching decisions. In other words, instructors need a bridge between research and practice, between teaching and learning.

We wrote this book to provide such a bridge. The book grew out of over twenty-nine years of experience consulting with faculty colleagues about teaching and learning. In these consultations, we encountered a number of recurring problems that spanned disciplines, course types, and student skill levels. Many of these problems raised fundamental questions about student learning. For example: Why can't students apply what they have learned? Why do they cling so tightly to misconceptions? Why are they not more engaged by material *I* find so interesting? Why do they claim to know so much more than they actually know? Why do they continue to employ the same ineffective study strategies?

As we worked with faculty to explore the sources of these problems, we turned to the research on learning, and from this research we distilled seven principles, each of which crystallizes a key aspect of student learning. These principles have become the foundation for our work. Not only have we found them indispensable in our own teaching and in our consultations with faculty, but as we have talked and worked with thousands of faculty from around the world, we have also found that the principles resonate across disciplines, institution types, and cultures, from Latin America to Asia. In our experience, these principles provide instructors with an understanding of student learning that can help them (a) see *why* certain teaching approaches are or are not supporting students' learning, (b) generate or refine teaching approaches and strategies that more effectively foster student learning in specific contexts, and (c) transfer and apply these principles to new courses.

In this book, we offer these principles of learning, along with a discussion of the research that supports them, their implications for teaching, and a set of instructional strategies targeting each principle. Before briefly summarizing the full set of principles and discussing the characteristics they share and some ways that this book can be used, we begin by discussing what we mean by learning.

WHAT IS LEARNING?

Any set of learning principles is predicated on a definition of learning. In this book, we define learning as a *process* that leads to *change*, which occurs as a result of *experience* and increases the potential for improved performance and future learning (adapted from Mayer, 2002). There are three critical components to this definition:

1. Learning is a *process*, not a product. However, because this process takes place in the mind, we can only infer that it has occurred from students' products or performances.
2. Learning involves *change* in knowledge, beliefs, behaviors, or attitudes. This change unfolds over time; it is not fleeting but rather has a lasting impact on how students think and act.
3. Learning is not something done *to* students, but rather something students themselves do. It is the direct result of how students interpret and respond to their *experiences*—conscious and unconscious, past and present.

OUR PRINCIPLES OF LEARNING

Our seven principles of learning come from a perspective that is developmental and holistic. In other words, we begin with the recognition that (a) learning is a developmental process that intersects with other developmental processes in a student's life, and

(b) students enter our classrooms not only with skills, knowledge, and abilities, but also with social and emotional experiences that influence what they value, how they perceive themselves and others, and how they will engage in the learning process. Consistent with this holistic perspective, readers should understand that, although we address each principle individually to highlight particular issues pertaining to student learning, they are all at work in real learning situations and are functionally inseparable.

In the paragraphs below, we briefly summarize each of the principles in the order in which they are discussed in the book.

Students' prior knowledge can help or hinder learning.

Students come into our courses with knowledge, beliefs, and attitudes gained in other courses and through daily life. As students bring this knowledge to bear in our classrooms, it influences how they filter and interpret what they are learning. If students' prior knowledge is robust and accurate and activated at the appropriate time, it provides a strong foundation for building new knowledge. However, when knowledge is inert, insufficient for the task, activated inappropriately, or inaccurate, it can interfere with or impede new learning.

*How students organize knowledge influences how they learn
and apply what they know.*

Students naturally make connections between pieces of knowledge. When those connections form knowledge structures that are accurately and meaningfully organized, students are better able to retrieve and apply their knowledge effectively and efficiently. In contrast, when knowledge is connected in inaccurate or random ways, students can fail to retrieve or apply it appropriately.

> *Students' motivation determines, directs, and sustains what they do to learn.*

As students enter college and gain greater autonomy over what, when, and how they study and learn, motivation plays a critical role in guiding the direction, intensity, persistence, and quality of the learning behaviors in which they engage. When students find positive value in a learning goal or activity, expect to successfully achieve a desired learning outcome, and perceive support from their environment, they are likely to be strongly motivated to learn.

> *To develop mastery, students must acquire component skills, practice integrating them, and know when to apply what they have learned.*

Students must develop not only the component skills and knowledge necessary to perform complex tasks, they must also practice combining and integrating them to develop greater fluency and automaticity. Finally, students must learn when and how to apply the skills and knowledge they learn. As instructors, it is important that we develop conscious awareness of these elements of mastery so as to help our students learn more effectively.

> *Goal-directed practice coupled with targeted feedback enhances the quality of students' learning.*

Learning and performance are best fostered when students engage in practice that focuses on a specific goal or criterion, targets an appropriate level of challenge, and is of sufficient quantity and frequency to meet the performance criteria. Practice must be coupled with feedback that explicitly communicates about some aspect(s) of students' performance relative to specific target criteria, provides information to help students progress in meeting those criteria, and is given at a time and frequency that allows it to be useful.

> *Students' current level of development interacts with the social, emotional, and intellectual climate of the course to impact learning.*

Students are not only intellectual but also social and emotional beings, and they are still developing the full range of intellectual, social, and emotional skills. While we cannot control the developmental process, we can shape the intellectual, social, emotional, and physical aspects of the classroom climate in developmentally appropriate ways. In fact, many studies have shown that the climate we create has implications for our students. A negative climate may impede learning and performance, but a positive climate can energize students' learning.

> *To become self-directed learners, students must learn to monitor and adjust their approaches to learning.*

Learners may engage in a variety of metacognitive processes to monitor and control their learning—assessing the task at hand, evaluating their own strengths and weaknesses, planning their approach, applying and monitoring various strategies, and reflecting on the degree to which their current approach is working. Unfortunately, students tend not to engage in these processes naturally. When students develop the skills to engage these processes, they gain intellectual habits that not only improve their performance but also their effectiveness as learners.

WHAT MAKES THESE PRINCIPLES POWERFUL?

The principal strength of these seven principles is that they are based directly on research, drawing on literature from cognitive, developmental, and social psychology, anthropology, education, and diversity studies, and research targeting not only higher education but also K–12 education. Although, of course, this is not an exhaustive review and any summary of research necessarily simplifies a host of complexities for the sake of accessibility, we believe that our discussions of the research underlying each principle are faithful to the scholarship and describe features of learning about which there is widespread agreement. Indeed, several of our principles converge with those that others have delineated (Pittsburgh Science of Learning Center, 2009; American Psychological Society, 2008), a convergence that we believe attests to their salience.

Not only are these principles research-based, but as we have shared them with colleagues over the years, we have found that they are

- *Domain-independent:* They apply equally well across all subject areas, from biology to design to history to robotics; the fundamental factors that impact the way students learn transcend disciplinary differences.

- *Experience-independent:* The principles apply to all educational levels and pedagogical situations. In other words, although the pedagogical implications of a principle will be somewhat different for first-year undergraduate students in a lab environment as opposed to graduate students in a studio environment, the principle still applies.
- *Cross-culturally relevant:* Although the research we identified has been conducted primarily in the Western world, faculty colleagues in other countries have resonated with the principles, finding them relevant to their own classes and students. However, it is important to bear in mind that culture can and does influence how the principles should be applied as instructors design and teach their courses.

INTENDED AUDIENCES

This book is intended for anyone interested in understanding more about how students learn and in applying that information to improve instruction. This includes—but is not limited to—faculty members, graduate students, faculty developers, instructional designers, and librarians. It also includes K–12 educators. In addition, the principles outlined here are valuable for instructors at all experience levels. They can help new and inexperienced instructors understand the components of effective course design and classroom pedagogy. They can help experienced instructors troubleshoot problems or adapt effective strategies to suit new courses or student populations. They can also help highly successful and experienced instructors reflect on what makes their approaches and methods effective. Finally, these principles can enable faculty members to better support student learning without having to rely on outside experts (a benefit that is particularly valuable for faculty at campuses without teaching and learning centers).

HOW TO READ THIS BOOK

Each chapter in this book begins with stories that represent teaching situations that we hope will strike readers as familiar. Although the instructors described in these stories are fictional, the scenarios are authentic, representing composites of real problems we have encountered over many years of consulting with faculty. We analyze these stories to identify the core problems or issues involved and use them to introduce the learning principle relevant to those problems. Then we discuss the principle in relation to the research that underlies it. Finally, we provide a set of strategies to help instructors design instruction with that principle in mind.

Because all of these principles combine to influence learning, no one principle stands alone. Consequently, the chapters can be read in any order. Moreover, the book can be read in conjunction with our Web site, which provides additional strategies, applications, sample materials, and resources. The URL is http://www.cmu.edu/teaching.

NOTE

1. Herb Simon was a university professor at Carnegie Mellon University and had joint appointments in the departments of psychology and computer science. While at Carnegie Mellon, Herb played a major role in the development of the Graduate School of Industrial Administration (renamed the Tepper School of Business in 2004), the Department of Psychology, the School of Computer Science, and the College of Humanities and Social Sciences. He was one of the founding fathers of the fields of cognitive psychology and artificial intelligence, and won the Nobel Prize in Economics in 1978 and the National Medal of Science in 1986. For many years (until his death), Herb served as a member of the Advisory Committee to the Eberly Center for Teaching Excellence. He was often heard paraphrasing this quote from Elliott Dunlap Smith, a past president of Carnegie Mellon University.

CHAPTER 1

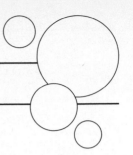

How Does Students' Prior Knowledge Affect Their Learning?

But They Said They Knew This!

I recently taught Research Methods in Decision Sciences for the first time. On the first day of class, I asked my students what kinds of statistical tests they had learned in the introductory statistics course that is a prerequisite for my course. They generated a fairly standard list that included T-tests, chi-square, and ANOVA. Given what they told me, I was pretty confident that my first assignment was pitched at the appropriate level; it simply required that students take a data set that I provided, select and apply the appropriate statistical test from those they had already learned, analyze the data, and interpret the results. It seemed pretty basic, but I was shocked at what they handed in. Some students chose a completely inappropriate test while others chose the right test but did not have the foggiest idea how to apply it. Still others could not interpret the results. What I can't figure out is why they told me they knew this stuff when it's clear from their work that most of them don't have a clue.

Professor Soo Yon Won

Why Is This So Hard for Them to Understand?

Every year in my introductory psychology class I teach my students about classic learning theory, particularly the concepts of positive and negative reinforcement. I know that these can be tough concepts for students to grasp, so I spell out very clearly that *reinforcement* always refers to increasing a behavior and *punishment* always refers to decreasing a behavior. I also emphasize that, contrary to what they might assume, *negative reinforcement* does not mean punishment; it means removing something aversive to increase a desired behavior. I also provide a number of concrete examples to illustrate what I mean. But it seems that no matter how much I explain the concept, students continue to think of negative reinforcement as punishment. In fact, when I asked about negative reinforcement on a recent exam, almost 60 percent of the class got it wrong. Why is this so hard for students to understand?

Professor Anatole Dione

WHAT IS GOING ON IN THESE STORIES?

The instructors in these stories seem to be doing all the right things. Professor Won takes the time to gauge students' knowledge of statistical tests so that she can pitch her own instruction at the appropriate level. Professor Dione carefully explains a difficult concept, provides concrete examples, and even gives an explicit warning about a common misconception. Yet neither instructor's strategy is having the desired effect on students' learning and performance. To understand why, it is helpful to consider the effect of students' prior knowledge on new learning.

Professor Won assumes that students have learned and retained basic statistical skills in their prerequisite course, an assumption that is confirmed by the students' self-report. In actuality, although students have some knowledge—they are able to identify and describe a variety of statistical tests—it may not be sufficient for Professor Won's assignment, which requires them to determine when particular tests are appropriate, apply the right test for the problem, and then interpret the results. Here Professor Won's predicament stems from a mismatch between the knowledge students have and the knowledge their instructor expects and needs them to have to function effectively in her course.

In Professor Dione's case it is not what students do *not* know that hurts them but rather what they *do* know. His students, like many of us, have come to associate positive with "good" and negative with "bad," an association that is appropriate in many contexts, but not in this one. When students are introduced to the concept of negative reinforcement in relation to classic learning theory, their prior understanding of "negative" may interfere with their ability to absorb the technical definition. Instead of grasping that the "negative" in negative reinforcement involves removing something to get a positive change (an example would be a mother who promises to quit nagging if her son will clean his room), students interpret the word "negative" to imply a negative response, or punishment. In other words, their prior knowledge triggers an inappropriate association that ultimately intrudes on and distorts the incoming knowledge.

WHAT PRINCIPLE OF LEARNING IS AT WORK HERE?

As we teach, we often try to enhance our students' understanding of the course content by connecting it to their knowledge and experiences from earlier in the same course, from previous courses, or from everyday life. But sometimes—like Professor Won—we overestimate students' prior knowledge and thus build new knowledge on a shaky foundation. Or we find—like Professor Dione—that our students are bringing prior knowledge to bear that is not appropriate to the context and which is distorting their comprehension. Similarly, we may uncover misconceptions and inaccuracies in students' prior knowledge that are actively interfering with their ability to learn the new material.

Although, as instructors, we can and should build on students' prior knowledge, it is also important to recognize that not all prior knowledge provides an equally solid foundation for new learning.

> **Principle:** *Students' prior knowledge can help or hinder learning.*

Students do not come into our courses as blank slates, but rather with knowledge gained in other courses and through daily life. This knowledge consists of an amalgam of facts, concepts, models, perceptions, beliefs, values, and attitudes, some of which are accurate, complete, and appropriate for the context, some of which are inaccurate, insufficient for the learning requirements of the course, or simply inappropriate for the context. As students bring this knowledge to bear in our classrooms, it influences how they filter and interpret incoming information.

Ideally, students build on a foundation of robust and accurate prior knowledge, forging links between previously acquired and new knowledge that help them construct increasingly complex and robust knowledge structures (see Chapter Two). However, students may not make connections to relevant prior knowledge spontaneously. If they do not draw on relevant prior knowledge— in other words, if that knowledge is *inactive*—it may not facilitate the integration of new knowledge. Moreover, if students' prior knowledge is *insufficient* for a task or learning situation, it may fail to support new knowledge, whereas if it is *inappropriate* for the context or *inaccurate*, it may actively distort or impede new learning. This is illustrated in Figure 1.1.

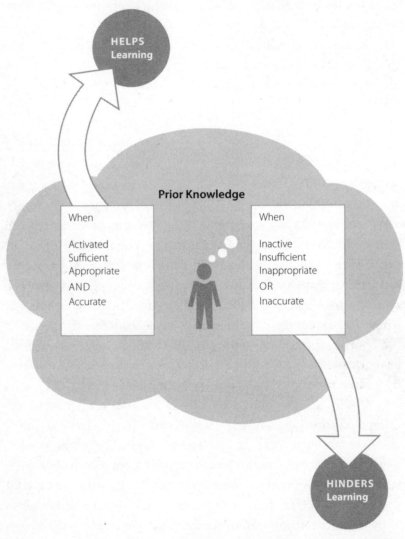

Figure 1.1. Qualities of Prior Knowledge That Help or Hinder Learning

Understanding what students know—or think they know—coming into our courses can help us design our instruction more appropriately. It allows us not only to leverage their accurate knowledge more effectively to promote learning, but also to identify and fill gaps, recognize when students are applying what they know inappropriately, and actively work to correct misconceptions.

WHAT DOES THE RESEARCH TELL US ABOUT PRIOR KNOWLEDGE?

Students connect what they learn to what they already know, interpreting incoming information, and even sensory perception, through the lens of their existing knowledge, beliefs, and assumptions (Vygotsky, 1978; National Research Council, 2000). In fact, there is widespread agreement among researchers that students *must* connect new knowledge to previous knowledge in order to learn (Bransford & Johnson, 1972; Resnick, 1983). However, the extent to which students are able to draw on prior knowledge to *effectively* construct new knowledge depends on the nature of their prior knowledge, as well as the instructor's ability to harness it. In the following sections, we discuss research that investigates the effects of various kinds of prior knowledge on student learning and explore its implications for teaching.

Activating Prior Knowledge

When students can connect what they are learning to accurate and relevant prior knowledge, they learn and retain more. In essence, new knowledge "sticks" better when it has prior knowledge to stick to. In one study focused on recall, for example, participants with variable knowledge of soccer were presented with scores from

15

different soccer matches and their recall was tested. People with more prior knowledge of soccer recalled more scores (Morris et al., 1981). Similarly, research conducted by Kole and Healy (2007) showed that college students who were presented with unfamiliar facts about well-known individuals demonstrated twice the capacity to learn and retain those facts as students who were presented with the same number of facts about unfamiliar individuals. Both these studies illustrate how prior knowledge of a topic can help students integrate new information.

However, students may not spontaneously bring their prior knowledge to bear on new learning situations (see the discussion of transfer in Chapter Four). Thus, it is important to help students activate prior knowledge so they can build on it productively. Indeed, research suggests that even small instructional interventions can activate students' relevant prior knowledge to positive effect. For instance, in one famous study by Gick and Holyoak (1980), college students were presented with two problems that required them to apply the concept of convergence. The researchers found that even when the students knew the solution to the first problem, the vast majority did not think to apply an analogous solution to the second problem. However, when the instructor suggested to students that they think about the second problem in relation to the first, 80 percent of the student participants were able to solve it. In other words, with minor prompts and simple reminders, instructors can activate relevant prior knowledge so that students draw on it more effectively (Bransford & Johnson, 1972; Dooling & Lachman, 1971).

Research also suggests that asking students questions specifically designed to trigger recall can help them use prior knowledge to aid the integration and retention of new information (Woloshyn, Paivio, & Pressley, 1994). For example, Martin and Pressley (1991) asked Canadian adults to read about events that had occurred in various Canadian provinces. Prior to any instructional intervention, the researchers found that study participants often failed to use their relevant prior knowledge to logically situate events in the provinces where they occurred, and thus had difficulty remembering specific facts. However, when the researchers asked a set of "why" questions (for example, "Why would Ontario have been the first place baseball was played?"), participants were forced to draw on their prior knowledge of Canadian history and relate it logically to the new information. The researchers found that this intervention, which they called *elaborative interrogation*, improved learning and retention significantly.

Researchers have also found that if students are asked to generate relevant knowledge from previous courses or their own lives, it can help to facilitate their integration of new material (Peeck, Van Den Bosch, & Kruepeling, 1982). For example, Garfield and her colleagues (Garfield, Del Mas, & Chance, 2007) designed an instructional study in a college statistics course that focused on the concept of variability—a notoriously difficult concept to grasp. The instructors first collected baseline data on students' understanding of variability at the end of a traditionally taught course. The following semester, they redesigned the course so that students were asked to generate examples of activities in their own lives that had either high or low variability, to represent them graphically, and draw on them as they reasoned about various aspects of variability. While both groups of students continued to struggle with the concept, post-tests showed that students who had generated relevant prior knowledge outperformed students in the baseline class two to one.

Exercises to generate prior knowledge can be a double-edged sword, however, if the knowledge students generate is inaccurate or inappropriate for the context (Alvermann, Smith, & Readance, 1985). Problems involving inaccurate and inappropriate prior knowledge will be addressed in the next two sections.

17

Implications of This Research   Students learn more readily when they can connect what they are learning to what they already know. However, instructors should not assume that students will immediately or naturally draw on relevant prior knowledge. Instead, they should deliberately activate students' prior knowledge to help them forge robust links to new knowledge.

Accurate but Insufficient Prior Knowledge

Even when students' prior knowledge is accurate and activated, it may not be sufficient to support subsequent learning or a desired level of performance. Indeed, when students possess *some* relevant knowledge, it can lead both students and instructors to assume that students are better prepared than they truly are for a particular task or level of instruction.

In fact, there are many different types of knowledge, as evidenced by a number of typologies of knowledge (for example, Anderson & Krathwohl, 2001; Anderson, 1983; Alexander, Schallert, & Hare, 1991; DeJong & Ferguson-Hessler, 1996). One kind of knowledge that appears across many of these typologies is *declarative knowledge*, or the knowledge of facts and concepts that can be stated or declared. Declarative knowledge can be thought of as "knowing what." The ability to name the parts of the circulatory system, describe the characteristics of hunter-gatherer social structure, or explain Newton's Third Law are examples of declarative knowledge. A second type of knowledge is often referred to as *procedural knowledge*, because it involves knowing how and knowing when to apply various procedures, methods, theories, styles, or approaches. The ability to calculate integrals, draw with 3-D perspective, and calibrate lab equipment—as well as the knowledge of when these skills are and are not applicable—fall into the category of procedural knowledge.

Declarative and procedural knowledge are not the same, nor do they enable the same kinds of performance. It is common, for instance, for students to know facts and concepts but not know how or when to apply them. In fact, research on science learning demonstrates that even when students can state scientific facts (for example, "Force equals mass times acceleration"), they are often weak at applying those facts to solve problems, interpret data, and draw conclusions (Clement, 1982). We see this problem clearly in Professor Won's class. Her students know *what* various statistical tests are, but this knowledge is insufficient for the task Professor Won has assigned, which requires them to select appropriate tests for a given data set, execute the statistical tests properly, and interpret the results.

Similarly, studies have shown that students can often perform procedural tasks without being able to articulate a clear understanding of what they are doing or why (Berry & Broadbent, 1988; Reber & Kotovsky, 1997; Sun, Merrill, & Peterson, 2001). For example, business students may be able to apply formulas to solve finance problems but not to explain their logic or the principles underlying their solutions. Similarly, design students may know how to execute a particular design without being able to explain or justify the choices they have made. These students may have sufficient procedural knowledge to function effectively in specific contexts, yet lack the declarative knowledge of deep features and principles that would allow them both to adapt to different contexts (see discussion of transfer in Chapter Three) and explain themselves to others.

Implications of This Research   Because *knowing what* is a very different kind of knowledge than *knowing how* or *knowing when*, it is especially important that, as instructors, we are clear in our own minds about the knowledge requirements of different tasks and

19

that we not assume that because our students have one kind of knowledge that they have another. Instead, it is critical to assess both the amount and nature of students' prior knowledge so that we can design our instruction appropriately.

Inappropriate Prior Knowledge

Under some circumstances, students draw on prior knowledge that is inappropriate for the learning context. Although this knowledge is not necessarily inaccurate, it can skew their comprehension of new material.

One situation in which prior knowledge can distort learning and performance is when students import everyday meanings into technical contexts. Several studies in statistics, for example, show how commonplace definitions of terms such as *random* and *spread* intrude in technical contexts, distorting students' understandings of statistical concepts (Del Mas & Liu, 2007; Kaplan, Fisher, & Rogness, 2009). This seems to be the problem for Professor Dione's students, whose everyday associations with the terms *positive* and *negative* may have skewed their understanding of *negative reinforcement.*

Another situation in which inappropriate prior knowledge can impede new learning is if students analogize from one situation to another without recognizing the limitations of the analogy. For the most part, analogies serve an important pedagogical function, allowing instructors to build on what students already know to help them understand complex, abstract, or unfamiliar concepts. However, problems can arise when students do not recognize where the analogy breaks down or fail to see the limitations of a simple 'analogy for describing a complex phenomenon. For example, skeletal muscles and cardiac muscles share some traits; hence, drawing analogies between them makes sense to a point. However, the differences in how these two types of muscles func-

tion are substantial and vital to understanding their normal operation, as well as for determining how to effectively intervene in a
health crisis. In fact, Spiro and colleagues (Spiro et al., 1989)
found that many medical students possess a misconception about
a potential cause of heart failure that can be traced to their failure
to recognize the limitations of the skeletal muscle-cardiac muscle
analogy.

Knowledge from one disciplinary context, moreover, may
obstruct learning and performance in another disciplinary context
if students apply it inappropriately. According to Beaufort (2007),
college composition courses sometimes contribute to this phenomenon by teaching a generic approach to writing that leaves
students ill-prepared to write well in particular domains. Because
students come to think of writing as a "one size fits all" skill, they
misapply conventions and styles from their general writing classes
to disciplinary contexts in which they are not appropriate. For
example, they might apply the conventions of a personal narrative
or an opinion piece to writing an analytical paper or a lab report.
Beaufort argues that without remediation, this intrusion of inappropriate knowledge can affect not only students' performance
but also their ability to internalize the rhetorical conventions and
strategies of the new discipline.

Furthermore, learning can also be impeded when linguistic
knowledge is applied to contexts where it is inappropriate (Bartlett,
1932). For example, when many of us are learning a foreign language, we apply the grammatical structure we know from our
native language to the new language. This can impede learning
when the new language operates according to fundamentally
different grammatical rules, such as a subject-object-verb
configuration as opposed to a subject-verb-object structure
(Thonis, 1981).

Similarly, misapplication of cultural knowledge can—and
often does—lead to erroneous assumptions. For example, when

21

Westerners draw on their own cultural knowledge to interpret practices such as veiling in the Muslim world, they may misinterpret the meaning of the veil to the women who wear it. For instance, Westerners may assume that veiling is a practice imposed by men on unwilling women or that Muslim women who veil do so to hide their beauty. In fact, neither of these conclusions is necessarily accurate; for instance, some Muslim women voluntarily choose to cover—sometimes against the wishes of male family members—as a statement of modern religious and political identity (Ahmed, 1993; El Guindi, 1999). By the same token, some women think of the veil as a way to accentuate, not conceal, beauty (Wikan, 1982). Yet if Westerners interpret these practices through the lens of their own prior cultural knowledge and assumptions, they may emerge with a distorted understanding that can impede further learning.

Research suggests that if students are explicitly taught the conditions and contexts in which knowledge is applicable (and inapplicable), it can help them avoid applying prior knowledge inappropriately. Moreover, if students learn abstract principles to guide the application of their knowledge and are presented with multiple examples and contexts in which to practice applying those principles, it not only helps them recognize when their prior knowledge is relevant to a particular context (see Chapter Four on transfer), but also helps them avoid misapplying knowledge in the wrong contexts (Schwartz et al., 1999). Researchers also observe that making students explicitly aware of the limitations of a given analogy can help them learn not to approach analogies uncritically or stretch a simple analogy too far (Spiro et al., 1989).

Another way to help students avoid making inappropriate associations or applying prior knowledge in the wrong contexts is to deliberately activate their relevant prior knowledge (Minstrell, 1989, 1992). If we recall Professor Dione's course from the story at the beginning of the chapter, we can imagine a potential application for this idea. When presented with the counterintuitive concept of negative reinforcement, Professor Dione's students drew on associations (of positive as desirable and negative as undesirable) that were interfering with their comprehension. However, if Professor Dione had tried activating a different set of associations—namely of positive as adding and negative as subtracting—he may have been able to leverage those associations to help his students understand that positive reinforcement involves adding something to a situation to increase a desired behavior whereas negative reinforcement involves subtracting something to increase a desired behavior.

Implications of This Research   When learning new material, students may draw on knowledge (from everyday contexts, from incomplete analogies, from other disciplinary contexts, and from their own cultural or linguistic backgrounds) that is inappropriate for the context, and which can distort their interpretation of new material or impede new learning. To help students learn where their prior knowledge is and is not applicable, it is important for instructors to (a) clearly explain the conditions and contexts of applicability, (b) teach abstract principles but also provide multiple examples and contexts, (c) point out differences, as well as similarities, when employing analogies, and (d) deliberately activate relevant prior knowledge to strengthen appropriate associations.

Inaccurate Prior Knowledge

We have seen in the sections above that prior knowledge will not support new learning if it is insufficient or inappropriate for the task at hand. But what if it is downright wrong? Research indicates that inaccurate prior knowledge (in other words, flawed ideas, beliefs, models, or theories) can distort new knowledge by

23

predisposing students to ignore, discount, or resist evidence that conflicts with what they believe to be true (Dunbar, Fugelsang, & Stein, 2007; Chinn & Malhotra, 2002; Brewer & Lambert, 2000; Fiske & Taylor, 1991; Alvermann, Smith, & Readance, 1985). Some psychologists explain this distortion as a result of our striving for internal consistency. For example, Vosniadou and Brewer (1987) found that children reconcile their perception that the earth is flat with formal instruction stating that the earth is round by conceiving of the earth as a pancake: circular but with a flat surface. In other words, children—like all learners—try to make sense of what they are learning by fitting it into what they already know or believe.

Inaccurate prior knowledge can be corrected fairly easily if it consists of relatively isolated ideas or beliefs that are not embedded in larger conceptual models (for example, the belief that Pluto is a planet or that the heart oxygenates blood). Research indicates that these sorts of beliefs respond to refutation; in other words, students will generally revise them when they are explicitly confronted with contradictory explanations and evidence (Broughton, Sinatra, & Reynolds, 2007; Guzetti, Snyder, Glass, & Gamas, 1993; Chi, 2008). Even more integrated—yet nonetheless flawed—conceptual models may respond to refutation over time if the individual inaccuracies they contain are refuted systematically (Chi & Roscoe, 2002).

However, some kinds of inaccurate prior knowledge—called *misconceptions*—are remarkably resistant to correction. Misconceptions are models or theories that are deeply embedded in students' thinking. Many examples have been documented in the literature, including naïve theories in physics (such as the notion that objects of different masses fall at different rates), "folk psychology" myths (for example, that blind people have more sensitive hearing than sighted people or that a good hypnotist can command total obedience), and stereotypes about groups

24

of people (Brown, 1983; Kaiser, McCloskey, & Proffitt, 1986; McCloskey, 1983; Taylor & Kowalski, 2004).

Misconceptions are difficult to refute for a number of reasons. First, many of them have been reinforced over time and across multiple contexts. Moreover, because they often include accurate—as well as inaccurate—elements, students may not recognize their flaws. Finally, in many cases, misconceptions may allow for successful explanations and predictions in a number of everyday circumstances. For example, although stereotypes are dangerous oversimplifications, they are difficult to change in part because they fit aspects of our perceived reality and serve an adaptive human need to generalize and categorize (Allport, 1954; Brewer, 1988; Fiske & Taylor, 1991).

Research has shown that deeply held misconceptions often persist despite direct instructional interventions (Ram, Nersessian, & Keil, 1997; Gardner & Dalsing, 1986; Gutman, 1979; Confrey, 1990). For example, Stein and Dunbar conducted a study (described in Dunbar, Fugelsang, & Stein, 2007) in which they asked college students to write about why the seasons changed, and then assessed their relevant knowledge via a multiple choice test. After finding that 94 percent of the students in their study had misconceptions (including the belief that the shape of the earth's orbit was responsible for the seasons), the researchers showed students a video that clearly explained that the tilt of the earth's axis, not the shape of the earth's orbit, was responsible for seasonal change. Yet in spite of the video, when students were asked to revise their essays, their explanations for the seasons did not change fundamentally. Similarly, McCloskey, Caramazza, and Green (1980) found that other deeply held misconceptions about the physical world persist even when they are refuted through formal instruction.

Results like these are sobering. Yet the picture is not altogether gloomy. To begin with, it is important to recognize that

25

conceptual change often occurs gradually and may not be immediately visible. Thus, students may be moving in the direction of more accurate knowledge even when it is not yet apparent in their performance (Alibali, 1999; Chi & Roscoe, 2002). Moreover, even when students retain inaccurate beliefs, they can learn to inhibit and override those beliefs and draw on accurate knowledge instead. Research indicates, for instance, that when people are sufficiently motivated to do so, they can consciously suppress stereotypical judgments and learn to rely on rational analysis more and stereotypes less (Monteith & Mark, 2005; Monteith, Sherman, & Devine, 1998). Moreover, since consciously overcoming misconceptions requires more cognitive energy than simply falling back on intuitive, familiar modes of thinking, there is research to suggest that when distractions and time pressures are minimized, students will be more likely to think rationally and avoid applying misconceptions and flawed assumptions (Finucane et al., 2000; Kahnemann & Frederick, 2002).

In addition, carefully designed instruction can help wean students from misconceptions through a process called *bridging* (Brown, 1992; Brown & Clement, 1989; Clement, 1993). For example, Clement observed that students often had trouble believing that a table exerts force on a book placed on its surface. To help students grasp this somewhat counterintuitive concept, he designed an instructional intervention for high school physics students that started from students' accurate prior knowledge. Because students did believe that a compressed spring exerted force, the researchers were able to analogize from the spring to foam, then to pliable wood, and finally to a solid table. The intermediate objects served to bridge the difference between a spring and the table and enabled the students to extend their accurate prior knowledge to new contexts. Using this approach, Clement obtained significantly greater pre- to posttest gains compared to traditional classroom instruction. In a similar vein, Minstrell's research (1989) shows that students can be guided away from misconceptions through a process of reasoning that helps them build on the accurate facets of their knowledge as they gradually revise the inaccurate facets.

Implications of This Research It is important for instructors to address inaccurate prior knowledge that might otherwise distort or impede learning. In some cases, inaccuracies can be corrected simply by exposing students to accurate information and evidence that conflicts with flawed beliefs and models. However, it is important for instructors to recognize that a single correction or refutation is unlikely to be enough to help students revise deeply held misconceptions. Instead, guiding students through a process of conceptual change is likely to take time, patience, and creativity.

WHAT STRATEGIES DOES THE RESEARCH SUGGEST?

In this section we offer (1) a set of strategies to help instructors determine the extent and quality of students' prior knowledge, relative to the learning requirements of a course. We then provide strategies instructors can employ to (2) activate students' relevant prior knowledge, (3) address gaps in students' prior knowledge, (4) help students avoid applying prior knowledge in the wrong contexts, and (5) help students revise and rethink inaccurate knowledge.

Methods to Gauge the Extent and Nature of Students' Prior Knowledge

Talk to Colleagues As a starting point for finding out what prior knowledge students bring to your course, talk to colleagues

27

who teach prerequisite courses or ask to see their syllabi and assignments. This can give you a quick sense of what material was covered, and in what depth. It can also alert you to differences in approach, emphasis, terminology, and notation so that you can address potential gaps or discrepancies. Remember, though, that just because the material was taught does not mean that students necessarily learned it. To get a better sense of students' knowledge, as well as their ability to apply it, you might also ask your colleagues about students' proficiencies: for example, what concepts and skills did students seem to master easily? Which ones did they struggle with? Did students seem to hold any systematic and pervasive misconceptions? This kind of information from colleagues can help you design your instructional activities so they effectively connect to, support, extend, and, if needed, correct, students' prior knowledge.

Administer a Diagnostic Assessment   To find out what relevant knowledge students possess coming into your course, consider assigning a short, low-stakes assessment, such as a quiz or an essay, at the beginning of the semester. Students' performance on this assignment can give you a sense of their knowledge of prerequisite facts and concepts, or their competence in various skills. For example, if your course requires knowledge of a technical vocabulary and basic calculus skills, you could create a short quiz asking students to define terms and solve calculus problems. You can mark these assignments individually to get a sense of the skill and knowledge of particular students, or simply look them over as a set to get a feel for students' overall level of preparedness. Another way to expose students' prior knowledge is by administering a concept inventory. Concept inventories are ungraded tests, typically in a multiple-choice format, that are designed to include incorrect answers that help reveal common misconceptions. Developing a concept inventory of your own can be time-intensive, so check the Internet to see whether there are inventories already available in your discipline that would suit your needs. A number of concept inventories have been widely used and have high validity and reliability.

Have Students Assess Their Own Prior Knowledge   In some fields and at some levels of expertise, having students assess their own knowledge and skills can be a quick and effective—though not necessarily foolproof—way to diagnose missing or insufficient prior knowledge. One way to have students self-assess is to create a list of concepts and skills that you expect them to have coming into your course, as well as some concepts and skills you expect them to acquire during the semester. Ask students to assess their level of competence for each concept or skill, using a scale that ranges from cursory familiarity ("I have heard of the term") to factual knowledge ("I could define it") to conceptual knowledge ("I could explain it to someone else") to application ("I can use it to solve problems"). Examine the data for the class as a whole in order to identify areas in which your students have either less knowledge than you expect or more. In either case, this information can help you recalibrate your instruction to better meet student needs. See Appendix A for more information about student self-assessments.

Use Brainstorming to Reveal Prior Knowledge   One way to expose students' prior knowledge is to conduct a group brainstorming session. Brainstorming can be used to uncover beliefs, associations, and assumptions (for example, with questions such as "What do you think of when you hear the word *evangelical*?"). It can also be used to expose factual or conceptual knowledge ("What were some of the key historical events in the Gilded Age?" or "What comes to mind when you think about environmental ethics?"), procedural knowledge ("If you were going to do a

29

research project on the Farm Bill, where would you begin?"), or contextual knowledge ("What are some methodologies you could use to research this question?"). Bear in mind that brainstorming does not provide a systematic gauge of students' prior knowledge. Also, be prepared to differentiate accurate and appropriately applied knowledge from knowledge that is inaccurate or inappropriately applied.

Assign a Concept Map Activity To gain insights into what your students know about a given subject, ask them to construct a concept map representing everything that they know about the topic. You can ask students to create a concept map (see Appendix B), representing what they know about an entire disciplinary domain (for example, social psychology), a particular concept (for instance, Newton's third law), or a question (for example, "What are the ethical issues with stem cell research?"). Some students may be familiar with concept maps, but others may not be, so be sure to explain what they are and how to create them (circles for concepts, lines between concepts to show how they relate). There are a number of ways to construct concept maps, so you should give some thought to what you are trying to ascertain. For instance, if you are interested in gauging students' knowledge of concepts as well as their ability to articulate the connections among them, you can ask students to generate both concepts and links. But if you are primarily interested in students' ability to articulate the connections, you can provide the list of concepts and ask students to arrange and connect them, labeling the links. If there are particular kinds of information you are looking for (for example, causal relationships, examples, theoretical orientations) be sure to specify what you want. Review the concept maps your students create to try to determine gaps in their knowledge, inappropriate links, and the intrusion of lay terms and ideas that may indicate the presence of naïve theories or preconceptions.

Look for Patterns of Error in Student Work   Students' misconceptions tend to be shared and produce a consistent pattern of errors. You (or your TAs or graders) can often identify these misconceptions simply by looking at students' errors on homework assignments, quizzes, or exams and noting commonalities across the class. You can also keep track of the kinds of problems and errors that students reveal when they come to office hours or as they raise or answer questions during class. Paying attention to these patterns of error can alert you to common problems and help you target instruction to correct misconceptions or fill gaps in understanding. Some instructors use classroom response systems (also called "clickers") to quickly collect students' answers to concept questions posed in class. Clickers provide an instant histogram of students' answers and can alert instructors to areas of misunderstanding that might stem from insufficient prior knowledge.

Methods to Activate Accurate Prior Knowledge

Use Exercises to Generate Students' Prior Knowledge Because students learn most effectively when they connect new knowledge to prior knowledge, it can be helpful to begin a lesson by asking students what they already know about the topic in question. This can be done any number of ways, such as by asking students to brainstorm associations or create a concept map. Once students have activated relevant prior knowledge in their heads, they are likely to be able to integrate new knowledge more successfully. However, since activities like this can generate inaccurate and inappropriate as well as accurate and relevant knowledge, you should be prepared to help students distinguish between them.

Explicitly Link New Material to Knowledge from Previous Courses   Students tend to compartmentalize knowledge by course, semester, professor, or discipline. As a result, they may not recognize the relevance of knowledge from a previous course to a new learning situation. For example, students who have learned about the concept of variability in a statistics course often do not bring that knowledge to bear on the concept of volatility in a finance course both because of the difference in terminology and because they do not see the link between the two contexts. However, if you make the connection between variability and volatility explicit, it allows students to tap into that prior knowledge and build on it productively.

Explicitly Link New Material to Prior Knowledge from Your Own Course   Although we often expect students to automatically link what they are learning to knowledge gained earlier in the same course, they may not do so automatically. Thus, it is important for instructors to highlight these connections. Instructors can help students activate relevant prior knowledge by framing particular lectures, discussions, or readings in relation to material learned previously in the semester. For example, in a literary theory course, the professor might begin class by saying, "In Unit 2 we discussed feminist theory. Today we are going to talk about a school of thought that grew out of feminist theory.") Sometimes all it takes to activate students' relevant prior knowledge is a slight prompt, such as: "Think back to the research design Johnson used in the article from last week" or "Where have we seen this phenomenon before?" Students can also be encouraged to look for connections within course materials in other ways. For example, the instructor can ask students to write reflection papers that connect each reading to other readings and to larger themes in the course. Also, discussions provide an ideal opportunity to elicit students' knowledge from earlier in the semester and to link it to new material.

Use Analogies and Examples That Connect to Students' Everyday Knowledge   Examples or analogies that draw on students' everyday lives and the wider world make new material more understandable and create more robust knowledge representations in students' minds. For example, an instructor could draw on students' memories from childhood and experiences with younger siblings to help them understand concepts in child development. Similarly, an instructor could use students' experiences with the physical world to introduce concepts such as force and acceleration. Analogies are also useful for connecting new knowledge to prior knowledge. For example, students' experience with cooking can be enlisted to help them understand scientific processes such as chemical synthesis (just as in cooking, when you mix or heat chemicals, you need to know when precision is and is not critical). Students often show more sophisticated reasoning when working in familiar contexts, and we can build on their knowledge from these contexts as we explore new material.

Ask Students to Reason on the Basis of Relevant Prior Knowledge   Often students have prior knowledge that could help them reason about new material and learn it more deeply. Thus, it can be useful to ask students questions that require them to use their prior knowledge to make predictions about new information before they actually encounter it. For example, before asking students to read an article from the 1970s, you might ask them what was going on historically at the time that might have informed the author's perspective. Or when presenting students with a design problem, you might ask them how a famous designer, whose work they know, might have approached the problem. This requires students not only to draw on their prior knowledge but also to use it to reason about new knowledge.

33

Methods to Address Insufficient Prior Knowledge

Identify the Prior Knowledge You Expect Students to Have The first step toward addressing gaps in students' prior knowledge is recognizing where those gaps are. This requires identifying in your own mind the knowledge students will need to have to perform effectively in your course. To identify what the prior knowledge requirements are for your class, you might want to begin by thinking about your assignments, and ask yourself, "What do students need to know to be able to do this?" Often instructors stop short of identifying all the background knowledge students need, so be sure to continue asking the question until you have fully identified the knowledge requirements for the tasks you have assigned. Be sure to differentiate declarative (knowing what and knowing why) from procedural knowledge (knowing how and knowing when), recognizing that just because students know facts or concepts does not mean they will know how to use them, and just because students know how to perform procedures does not mean that they understand what they are doing or why. (See "Strategies to Expose and Reinforce Component Skills" in Chapter Four.)

Remediate Insufficient Prerequisite Knowledge If prior knowledge assessments (as discussed in previous strategies) indicate critical gaps in students' prior knowledge relative to the learning requirements of your course, there are a number of possible responses depending on the scale of the problem and the resources and options available to you and to your students. If only a few students lack important prerequisite knowledge, one option that might be open to you is simply to advise them against taking the course until they have the necessary background. Alternatively, if a small number of students lacks prerequisite knowledge but seem capable of acquiring it on their own, you might consider providing these students with a list of terms they should know and skills they should have and letting them fill in the gaps on their own time. If a larger number of students lacks sufficient prior knowledge in a key area, you might decide to devote one or two classes to a review of important prerequisite material or (if it is applicable) ask your teaching assistant to run a review session outside class time. If a sizable proportion of your class lacks knowledge that is a critical foundation for the material you planned to cover, you may need to revise your course altogether so that it is properly aligned with your students' knowledge and skills. Of course, if your course is a prerequisite for other courses, such fundamental revisions may have broader implications, which may need to be addressed at a departmental level through a discussion of objectives and course sequencing.

Methods to Help Students Recognize Inappropriate Prior Knowledge

Highlight Conditions of Applicability   It is important to help students see when it is and is not appropriate to apply prior knowledge. For example, a statistics instructor might explain that a regression analysis can be used for quantitative variables but not for qualitative variables, or a biology instructor might instruct students to save their expressive writing for other courses and instead write lab reports that focus on conciseness and accuracy. If there are no strict rules about when prior knowledge is applicable, another strategy is to present students with a range of problems and contexts and ask them to identify whether or not a given skill or concept is applicable and to explain their reasoning.

Provide Heuristics to Help Students Avoid Inappropriate Application of Knowledge   One strategy to help students avoid applying their prior knowledge inappropriately is to provide them

35

with some rules of thumb to help them determine whether their knowledge is or is not relevant. For example, when students are encountering different cultural practices and might be tempted to assess them according to their own cultural norms, you might encourage them to ask themselves questions such as "Am I making assumptions based on my own cultural knowledge that may not be appropriate here? If so, what are those assumptions, and where do they come from?" By the same token, if you know of situations in which students frequently get confused by the intrusion of prior knowledge (for example, students' understanding of negative reinforcement in the second story at the beginning of this chapter), you might want to provide them with a rule of thumb to help them avoid that pitfall. For example, an instructor teaching classical learning theory could advise his students, "When you see 'negative' in the context of negative reinforcement, think of subtraction."

Explicitly Identify Discipline-Specific Conventions It is important to clearly identify the conventions and expectations of your discipline so that students do not mistakenly apply the conventions of other domains about which they know more. For example, students may have experience with writing from a science course (lab reports), from a history course (analytical paper), or from an English course (personal narrative), so when they take a public policy course they may not know which set of knowledge and skills is the appropriate one to build on. It is important to explicitly identify the norms you expect them to follow. Without explicit guidance, students may analogize from other experiences or fields that they feel most competent in, regardless of whether the experiences are appropriate in the current context.

Show Where Analogies Break Down Analogies can help students learn complex or abstract concepts. However, they can be problematic if students do not recognize their limits. Thus, it is important to help students recognize the limitations of a given analogy by explicitly identifying (or asking students to identify) where the analogy breaks down. For example, you might point out that although the digestive system is similar to plumbing in that it involves tube-like organs and various kinds of valves, it is far more complex and sensitive than any ordinary plumbing system.

Methods to Correct Inaccurate Knowledge

Ask Students to Make and Test Predictions   To help students revise inaccurate beliefs and flawed mental models ask them to make predictions based on those beliefs and give them the opportunity to test those predictions. For example, physics students with an inaccurate understanding of force could be asked to make predictions about how forces will act on stationary versus moving objects. Being confronted with evidence that contradicts students' beliefs and expectations can help them see where their knowledge or beliefs are incorrect or inadequate, while motivating them to seek knowledge that accounts for what they have seen. Predictions can be tested in experiments, in or outside a laboratory environment, or through the use of computer simulations.

Ask Students to Justify Their Reasoning   One strategy to guide students away from inaccurate knowledge is to ask them to reason on the basis of what they believe to be true. When students' reasoning reveals internal contradictions, it can bring them to the point where they seek accurate knowledge. A caveat to this approach is that students may not necessarily see those internal contradictions. Moreover, if their attitudes and beliefs are very deeply held (for example, religious beliefs that defy logical argument), these contradictions may have little effect.

37

Provide Multiple Opportunities for Students to Use Accurate Knowledge Misconceptions can be hard to correct in part because they have been reinforced through repeated exposure. Thus, replacing inaccurate knowledge with accurate knowledge requires not just introducing accurate knowledge but also providing multiple opportunities for students to use it. Repeated opportunities to apply accurate knowledge can help counteract the persistence of even deeply held misconceptions.

Allow Sufficient Time It is easier for students to fall back on deeply held misconceptions than to employ the reasoning necessary to overcome them. Therefore, when you are asking students to use new knowledge that requires a revision or rethinking of their prior knowledge, it can be helpful to minimize distractions and allow a little extra time. This can help students enlist the cognitive resources necessary to identify flaws in their knowledge or reasoning and instead to consciously employ more thoughtful, critical thinking.

SUMMARY

In this chapter we have examined the critical role of prior knowledge in laying the groundwork for new learning. We have seen that if students' prior knowledge has gaps and insufficiencies it may not adequately support new knowledge. Moreover, if prior knowledge is applied in the wrong context, it may lead students to make faulty assumptions or draw inappropriate parallels. In addition, inaccurate prior knowledge—some of which can be surprisingly difficult to correct—can both distort students' understanding and interfere with incoming information. Consequently, a critical task for us as instructors is to assess what students know and believe so we can build on knowledge that is accurate and relevant, fill in gaps and insufficiencies where they exist, help students recognize when they are applying prior knowledge inappropriately, and help students revise inaccurate knowledge and form more accurate and robust mental models.

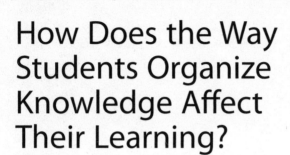

CHAPTER 2

How Does the Way Students Organize Knowledge Affect Their Learning?

That Didn't Work Out the Way I Anticipated

For the past 12 years, I've taught the introductory Art History course. I present the material using a standard approach. That is, I begin with an introductory description of key terms and concepts, including a discussion of the basic visual elements (line, color, light, form, composition, space). Then, for each of the remaining 40 class sessions, I show slides of important works, progressing chronologically from prehistoric Europe to rather recent pieces. As I go, I identify important features that characterize each piece and point out associations among various movements, schools, and periods. I give a midterm and a final exam during which I present slides and ask students to identify the title of the work, the artist, the school, and the period in which it was produced. While the students seem to enjoy the class sessions, they complain about the amount of material they must memorize for the exams. I know there are a lot of individual pieces, but they naturally cluster by period, school, and technique. Once you categorize a work according to those groupings, it should be fairly easy to remember. Nevertheless, the students seem to

40

be having a lot of difficulty in my exams identifying even some of the most important pieces.

Professor Rachel Rothman

There Must Be a Better Way!

Anatomy and Physiology is one of the core courses required for our nursing, pre-med, and pharmacy students. The course is organized around the major systems of the body and requires students to identify and describe the location and function of the major organs, bones, muscles, and tissues in the body. On the whole, students attend the lectures and labs consistently, and most of them appear to work really hard. Indeed, I often find them in the student lounge poring over their notes or quizzing each other in order to memorize all the individual structures. With a lot of work, they learn to identify most of the parts of the human body and can describe the role of each part in its body system. However, when asked to explain the relationships among parts or higher-order principles that cut across systems, the students often fall apart. For example, on the last exam I asked them to identify and describe all the structures involved in the regulation of blood pressure. To my surprise, most of the students were unable to answer the question correctly. I just don't get it—they know all the parts, but when it comes to how those parts fit together, they have a really difficult time.

Professor Anand Patel

WHAT IS GOING ON IN THESE TWO STORIES?

Although the content of the courses in these two stories differs substantially, the two instructors have similar goals. They want their students to develop a deep, functional understanding of a

41

multifaceted, complex domain. In the first story, the domain is the accumulated corpus of artistic expression created by humans over the past 30,000 years. In the second story, the domain is the complex array of organs, systems, and interacting parts that make up the human body. Each domain comprises many individual elements, and each element—be it a bone in the wrist or Picasso's *Guernica*—is related to other elements in important ways. Knowing about these elements but also having a meaningful picture of how they are related to each other is critical to deep understanding. In each of the stories, however, the students appear to lack a sufficiently coherent, organized representation of the material, which impedes their learning and performance.

In the first story, Professor Rothman provides her students with the concepts and vocabulary to analyze the visual elements in works of art and to make connections across various artists, schools, and periods. Then, for the rest of the semester she presents works of art in chronological order, referring to the key features of each piece of art she presents. It appears, however, that mentioning these features in relation to individual works was not sufficient to enable her students to see deeper relationships and make broader connections among clusters of works. That is, while these relationships and comparisons are natural to Professor Rothman, providing her with an easy way to group and organize the factual information, her students may not have made the same connections. Instead, they may have latched onto chronology as the prominent organizing principle for the material and hence organized their knowledge along a time line. Because this chronological structure for organizing knowledge entails remembering a great number of isolated facts, without any other overarching organizational structure to facilitate information retrieval and use, these students may be struggling (and largely failing) to memorize what they need to know for the exam.

In the second story, Professor Patel's students have knowledge of the individual parts of the human body, but this knowledge does not translate into an understanding of how those parts are functionally related to one another. One reason for this may be that students have organized their knowledge much the same way as a standard Anatomy and Physiology textbook: according to the major body systems (for example, the skeletal system, the digestive system, the circulatory system). If Professor Patel's students have organized their knowledge around discrete parts of the body, it could have several effects on their ability to use this information. If these students were asked to name the major bones of the hand or the function of the pancreas, they would probably have little difficulty, since such questions mesh well with how they have organized the information. However, to answer Professor Patel's question about how various structures work together to regulate blood pressure, these students would need an alternative way to organize their knowledge—one including the functional relationships that cut across multiple systems, not simply parts in isolation. In other words, the way these students have organized their knowledge facilitates one kind of use, but it is not sufficiently flexible to support the demands of all the tasks they face.

WHAT PRINCIPLE OF LEARNING IS AT WORK HERE?

As experts in our fields, we create and maintain, often unconsciously, a complex network that connects the important facts, concepts, procedures, and other elements within our domain. Moreover, we organize our domain knowledge around meaningful features and abstract principles. In contrast, most of our students have not yet developed such connected or meaningful ways of organizing the information they encounter in our courses. Yet how they organize their knowledge has profound implications for their learning, a point that is highlighted in our next principle.

> **Principle:** *How students organize knowledge influences how they learn and apply what they know.*

When we talk about the way people organization their knowledge (or, for the sake of simplicity, their *knowledge organizations*), we are not talking about particular pieces of knowledge, but rather how those pieces are arranged and connected in an individual's mind. Knowledge can be organized in ways that either do or do not facilitate learning, performance, and retention.

As an illustration, consider two students who are asked to identify the date when the British defeated the Spanish Armada (National Research Council, 2001). The first student tells us that the battle happened in 1588, and the second says that he cannot remember the precise date but thinks it must be around 1590. Given that 1588 is the correct answer for this historical date, the first student appears to have more accurate knowledge. Suppose, however, that we probe the students further and ask how they arrived at their answers. The first student then says that he memorized the correct date from a book. In contrast, the second students says that he based his answer on his knowledge that the British colonized Virginia just after 1600 and on the inference that the British would not dare organize massive overseas voyages for colonization until navigation was considered safe. Figuring that it took about 10 years for maritime traffic to be properly organized, he arrived at his answer of 1590.

These students' follow-up answers reveal knowledge organizations of different quality. The first student has learned an isolated fact about the Spanish Armada, apparently unconnected in his mind to any related historical knowledge. In contrast, the second student seems to have organized his knowledge in a much more interconnected (and causal) way that enabled him to reason about the situation in order to answer the question. The first student's sparse knowledge organization would likely not offer much support for future learning, whereas the second student's knowledge organization would provide a more robust foundation for subsequent learning.

Although the two students in this example are both relative novices, the differences in their knowledge organizations correspond, in very rough terms, to the differences between novices and experts. As illustrated in Figure 2.1, novice and expert knowledge

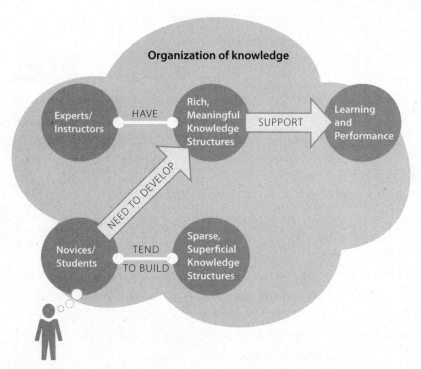

Figure 2.1. Differences in How Experts and Novices Organize Knowledge

organizations tend to differ in two key ways: the degree to which knowledge is sparsely versus richly connected, and the extent to which those connections are superficial versus meaningful. Although students often begin with knowledge organizations that are sparse and superficial, effective instruction can help them develop more connected and meaningful knowledge organizations that better support their learning and performance. Indeed, the second student in the example above shows progression in this direction.

WHAT DOES THE RESEARCH TELL US ABOUT KNOWLEDGE ORGANIZATION?

As a starting point for understanding how knowledge organizations differ and the consequences of those differences, it helps to consider how knowledge organizations develop. This is addressed in the section below. The remaining sections then elaborate on two important ways that experts' and novices' knowledge organizations differ and review research that suggests how novices can develop knowledge organizations that better facilitate learning.

Knowledge Organization: Form Fits Function

People naturally make associations based on patterns they experience in the world. For instance, we tend to build associations between events that occur in temporal contiguity (for example, a causal relationship between flipping the switch and a light turning on), between ideas that share meaning (for example, a conceptual relationship between fairness and equality), and between objects that have perceptual similarities (for example, a category-member relationship between a ball and a globe). As these associations build up over time, larger and more complex structures emerge that reflect how entire bodies of knowledge are organized in a person's mind.

The way people organize their knowledge tends to vary as a function of their experience, the nature of their knowledge, and the role that that knowledge plays in their lives. As a case in point, consider how people in different cultures classify family members. The terms they use provide a window into how a culture organizes standard kinship knowledge. In the United States, for example, we typically employ different terms to distinguish our parents from their siblings (in other words, "mother" and "father" are distinguished from "uncle" and "aunt"). This linguistic distinction—which seems natural and inevitable to many of us—corresponds to the special role of the nuclear family in U.S. society. However, in a number of cultures that are organized around extended families, mother/aunt and father/uncle share the same kinship term (for example, Levi-Strauss, 1969; Stone, 2000). This is because mothers and aunts (and similarly, fathers and uncles) occupy similar functional roles in these children's lives. As an example in the other direction, notice that most people in the United States do not use different kinship terms for paternal versus maternal uncles (and aunts). Because these categories of family members do not have functionally distinct roles in family life, there is no need to distinguish them linguistically. However, in some cultures maternal and paternal uncles and aunts have divergent roles (for example, the disciplinarian paternal uncle versus the indulgent maternal uncle), and in those cases a linguistic distinction is made, indicating these relatives are in functionally different categories. As this example suggests, in cultures that need to distinguish among particular categories of family members, the language—and, by inference, typical knowledge organizations—will reflect that need for differentiation. This points to the fact that knowledge organizations develop in the

47

context of use, thus providing ways of grouping and classifying knowledge that serve practical functions.

This example of kinship terminology highlights the point that no organizational structure is necessarily better or more "correct" than another. Instead, it is more appropriate to think of knowledge organizations as well or poorly matched to a given situation. After all, a system of organizing kinship that collapses "father" and "uncle" into a single category would be potentially confusing in a society in which the difference between these types of family members mattered, but reasonable in a society in which the difference was unimportant. In fact, research has found that the usefulness of knowledge organizations depends on the tasks they need to support. In a study by Eylon and Reif (1984), high school students learned material on a topic in modern physics. Half of the students learned the material according to a historical framework, and the other half learned the same material but according to physics principles. Then the two groups of students were asked to complete various tasks that drew upon what they had just learned. These tasks fell into two categories: tasks that required accessing information according to historical periods versus according to physical principles. Not surprisingly, students performed better when their knowledge organization matched the requirements of the task, and they performed worse when it mismatched.

A similar mismatch between knowledge organization and task demands is likely to be part of the problem Professor Patel describes in the second story at the beginning of this chapter. The students in the Anatomy and Physiology course appear to have organized their knowledge of anatomy around separate body systems. Whereas this mode of knowledge organization would facilitate performance on tasks that emphasize intra-system relationships, it may not help students answer questions focused on functional relationships that involve the interaction of systems.

Implications of This Research   Because knowledge organizations develop to support the tasks being performed, we should reflect on what activities and experiences students are engaging in to understand what knowledge organizations they are likely to develop. And because knowledge organizations are most effective when they are well matched to the way that knowledge needs to be accessed and used, we should consider the tasks students will be asked to perform in a given course or discipline in order to identify what knowledge organizations would best support those tasks. Then we can foster the ways of organizing knowledge that will promote students' learning and performance.

Experts' Versus Novices' Knowledge Organizations: The Density of Connections

One important way experts' and novices' knowledge organizations differ is in the number or density of connections among the concepts, facts, and skills they know. Figure 2.2 shows a variety of organizational structures that differ in regard to the connections that exist among pieces of knowledge. In each panel, pieces of knowledge are represented by nodes, and relationships between them are represented by links.

If we look at panels A and B, we see knowledge organizations that are fairly typical of novices in that they show few connections among nodes. The sparseness of links among components in panel A, for instance, probably indicates that the students have not yet developed the ability to recognize relationships among pieces of knowledge. This kind of organization might be found in a situation in which students absorb the knowledge from each lecture in a course without connecting the information to other lectures or recognizing themes that cut across the course as a whole. Such relatively disconnected knowledge organizations can impede student learning in several ways. First, if students lack a

49

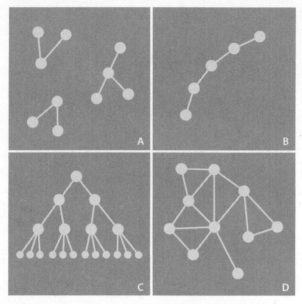

Figure 2.2. Examples of Knowledge Organizations

strongly connected network their knowledge will be slower and more difficult to retrieve (Bradshaw & Anderson, 1982; Reder & Anderson, 1980; Smith, Adams, & Schorr, 1978). Moreover, if students do not make the necessary connections among pieces of information, they may not recognize or seek to rectify contradictions. For example, DiSessa (1982) has repeatedly shown that students whose knowledge of physics is disconnected and lacks coherence can simultaneously hold and use contradictory propositions about the movement of physical objects without noticing the inconsistencies.

Panel B of Figure 2.2 is similar to panel A in that it has relatively sparse connections, but its connections are arranged in the form of a chain of associations. Although this structure affords the sequential access of information (potentially useful for remembering the stanzas of a poem or the steps of a procedure), it can lead to difficulties if one link in the chain is broken, or if some deviation from the specified sequence is required (Catrambone, 1995, 1998). Moreover, the more nodes linked in such a simple chain, the slower and more difficult it is on average to traverse from one piece of knowledge to another. Professor Rothman's students are a case in point: because their knowledge of art history appears to be organized along a time line, they must try to remember each work of art in relation to the one before and after it on the time line, a potentially difficult memory task.

In contrast, panels C and D correspond to knowledge organizations that are more typical of experts. Panel C shows knowledge that is organized hierarchically, indicating an understanding of how various pieces of information fit within a complex structure. An example would be the way an expert distinguishes theoretical schools within her discipline, the scholars whose work falls within each of these schools, and the particular books and articles that exemplify each scholar's work. However, because not all information can be represented as a set of tidy, discrete hierarchies, panel D shows an even more highly connected knowledge structure with additional links that indicate cross-referencing or suggest where strict hierarchies might break down.

These more complex and highly connected knowledge structures allow experts to access and use their knowledge more efficiently and effectively. Indeed, research has shown that experts tend to automatically process information in coherent chunks based on their prior knowledge and then use these chunks to build larger, more interconnected knowledge structures. The power of such highly connected knowledge organizations is illustrated in a classic study by Ericsson, Chase, and Faloon (1980). This study (and others that followed it, such as Ericsson & Staszewski, 1989) documented how college students with ordinary memories could develop an ability to recall amazingly long sequences of digits by organizing what they were learning into a multilevel hierarchical structure, much like that in panel C.

Because these students happened to be competitive runners, they were able to translate four-digit subsequences into famous running times (for example, the digits "3432" might be remembered as "34:32, the world record for . . ."). This strategy, called *chunking*, enabled four digits to be remembered instead of a single, familiar chunk of knowledge. This initial strategy for organizing the to-be-remembered digits increased their ability to recall from seven digits to almost thirty. But what really boosted their memory performance was organizing these four-digit chunks into larger groups consisting of three or four chunks, and then organizing these multichunk groups hierarchically into higher-level groupings, up to the point where one participant was able to recall up to 100 digits without any external memory aids! In other words, by creating a highly organized knowledge structure for remembering digits, they were able to develop exceptional memory ability and recall a great deal of information.

Although the study above focuses on simple recall, it nevertheless suggests that organizing knowledge in a sophisticated, interconnected structure—as experts tend to do—can radically increase one's ability to access that information when one needs it. Professor Rothman (from the first story at the beginning of this chapter) serves as a good illustration. Her own expert knowledge of art history appears to be arranged in an interconnected, hierarchical structure—much like the organization in Figure 2.2, panel C—with links among facts (for example, dates, artists' names, and the titles of various works) and related knowledge (of artistic movements and historical periods, among other things). This hierarchical organization of knowledge allows her to access the information she needs easily. The only problem is that she expects her students—who lack an analogous organizational structure—to be able to do the same. Instead, they struggle to remember an unwieldy set of isolated facts without an organizational structure to hold them.

Although students may not possess the highly connected knowledge organizations that their instructors possess, they can develop more sophisticated knowledge organizations over time. Indeed, research suggests that when students are provided with a structure for organizing new information, they learn more and better. For example, one classic study (Bower et al., 1969) demonstrated that students who were asked to learn a long list of items (various minerals) performed 60 to 350 percent better when they were given category information to help them organize the items into a hierarchy (metals versus stones as the main categories and several subcategories under each). Similarly, students show greater learning gains when they are given an *advance organizer*, that is, a set of principles or propositions that provide a cognitive structure to guide the incorporation of new information (Ausubel, 1960, 1978). Indeed, researchers have demonstrated improvements in students' comprehension and recall from advance organizers that rely on familiar structures when they are presented in writing (Ausubel & Fitzgerald, 1962), orally (Alexander, Frankiewicz, & Williams, 1979), or pictorially (Dean & Enemoh, 1983). These studies indicate that when students are provided with an organizational structure in which to fit new knowledge, they learn more effectively and efficiently than when they are left to deduce this conceptual structure for themselves.

In fact, if we think back to the first story at the beginning of the chapter, we can see applications for these approaches in Professor Rothman's class. Professor Rothman's students needed to learn and retrieve a great deal of factual information, yet probably lacked a hierarchical knowledge organization to help them organize this information for efficient retrieval and use. As a result, they found the memorization task overwhelming. But imagine if Professor Rothman had provided her students with an organizational framework that helped them develop more connections among pieces of knowledge, such as by giving them a template for identifying the characteristics of important artistic schools and movements and categorizing each artist and work in relation to them. With their factual knowledge connected in more—and more meaningful—ways, the students may have found the memorization task less daunting and may have performed better on Professor Rothman's exams and ultimately learned more art history.

Implications of This Research   As experts in our disciplines, we have developed highly connected knowledge organizations that help us retrieve and use information effectively. But we cannot reasonably expect students to have organized their knowledge in equally sophisticated ways. Instead, it is important that we recognize the difference between expert and novice knowledge structures and provide structures that highlight to our students how we organize disciplinary knowledge and draw on it to perform particular tasks.

Experts' Versus Students' Knowledge Structures: The Nature of the Connections

Novices not only have more sparse knowledge organizations compared to experts, but the basis for their organizational structures also tends to be superficial. This affects their ability to remember and use what they learn effectively (Chi & VanLehn, 1991; Hinsley, Hayes, & Simon, 1977; Ross, 1987, 1989). Chi and colleagues (1989) demonstrated this in a study in which they asked physics novices and experts to group various problem descriptions into categories. The novices grouped problems according to the superficial "looks" of their diagrams—for example, putting all the problems with pulleys in one group and all the problems with ramps in another group. This way of organizing the different problems around surface features did not reflect the structural relationships among problems, and thus did not facilitate successful problem solving for the novices. In contrast, the experts in this study organized the problems based on deeper and more meaningful features, such as the physical laws involved in solving each problem. Moreover, when talking through the rationale for their groupings, the experts revealed that sorting each of these problems into a category naturally triggered in their minds the solution template for how "problems like this" are solved. Thus, the experts' organizations were based on a set of deep features that directly related to how they would go about solving the problems.

Experts' ability to classify information in more meaningful—and thus more practically useful—ways than novices is linked to their ability to recognize meaningful patterns. For example, DeGroot (1965) conducted a landmark study in which he showed novice and master chess players a chess board midgame and asked them to generate possible next moves. While both masters and novices considered a roughly equivalent number of possible moves, there were significant differences in the quality of plays they considered: novices tended to choose from among a seemingly random set of options, whereas experts spent their time weighing the pros and cons of a very select set of high-quality moves. From the large amount of research on chess expertise (see also Gobet & Charness, 2006; Chase & Simon, 1973a, 1973b), it is clear that this difference stems from experts' vast experience analyzing chess situations and assessing possible strategies. As the result of this experience, they possess a highly developed knowledge organization that allows them to immediately recognize meaningful board configurations and zero in on a set of high-quality moves.

Indeed, experts' ability to see and instinctively respond to patterns not only helps them solve problems but also enhances their memory. Further research on chess has shown that experts can glance at a chessboard from a particular chess game situation and then take an empty board and replicate the exact positions of fifteen or more of the pieces they just saw (Chase & Simon, 1973a, 1973b). This is not a result of superior memory, but rather a reflection of the deep and intricate set of relationships they can see among pieces and that they automatically use during play. This ability among experts to immediately recognize and respond to patterns is not limited to chess but has been demonstrated among experts in many domains (Egan & Schwartz, 1979; Lesgold, et al., 1988; Soloway, Adelson, & Ehrlich, 1988). In one study, for example, skilled electronics technicians and novices were briefly shown symbolic drawings of complex circuit diagrams and then asked to reconstruct the drawings from memory (Egan & Schwartz, 1979). The experts were able to reconstruct a far greater number of elements in the diagrams, even after seeing them for just a few seconds. The researchers attributed this superior recall to two things: the experts' ability to successfully characterize the entire diagram (as "some kind of power supply," for example) and also to identify parts of each drawing that corresponded to recognizable features, such as amplifiers. They were then able to perceive the visual information from the diagrams in terms of these meaningful configurations and use that knowledge organization to help them remember what they had seen.

In addition to organizing their knowledge around meaningful features and patterns, experts have the benefit of flexibly using *multiple* knowledge organizations. A paleontologist's knowledge of dinosaurs, for example, would not be organized around a single organizational hierarchy, but rather would include an interwoven web of classifications and connections based on geological age, habitat, eating habits, relation to modern-day reptiles, strategies for self-protection, and so on. Likewise, a historian could draw on his or her knowledge in a way that is organized around theories, methodologies, time periods, topic areas, historical figures, or combinations of these. Novices, on the other hand, tend not to have as many alternative organizations to tap into. This difference between novice and expert representations is illustrated in the second story at the beginning of this chapter. As an expert in his field, Professor Patel moves flexibly among multiple ways of representing the human body, such as according to body system *and* according to common functions or higher-order principles. Thus, Professor Patel can use his knowledge in multiple ways, tapping into different knowledge organizations according to the need. His students, however, are more limited.

Obviously, developing the kinds of meaningfully connected knowledge organizations that experts possess takes time and experience. Most of our students are far from attaining that level of expertise. However, even novice students learn and remember more when they can connect information in meaningful ways. In one study that helps to illustrate this point, Bradshaw and Anderson (1982) asked college students to learn various facts about historical figures. They found that students learned the most when they were presented with facts that could be meaningfully related to one another. In other words, it was easier for students to learn and retain multiple facts with a causal dimension (for example: Isaac Newton became emotionally unstable and insecure as a child, Newton's father died when he was born, and Newton's mother remarried and left him with his grandfather) as compared to a single, isolated fact. However, students only showed this advantage when there was a relationship among the multiple facts that allowed students to make meaningful connections. Thus, the learning advantage did not apply when the multiple facts were unrelated (for example: Isaac Newton became emotionally unstable and insecure as a child, Newton was appointed

57

warden of the London mint, and Newton attended Trinity College in Cambridge). Research has also shown that there are instructional approaches that can help students organize their knowledge meaningfully around deep, rather than superficial, features of the domain. For example, studies have shown that when students are given problems that are already solved and are asked to explain the solution to themselves—thereby focusing on the principles that guide the solution—they are better able to solve new problems (Chi et al., 1989). Research also suggests that guiding students through a process of analogical reasoning helps students to see past superficial similarities and instead focus on deeper connections and relationships (for example, Gentner, Loewenstein, & Thompson, 2003; McDaniel & Donnelly, 1996). Similarly, when students are presented with and analyze contrasting cases, they are better prepared to learn from a lecture or reading assignment (Schwartz & Bransford, 1998). By engaging in such processes, students tend to build more effective knowledge organizations and learn and perform more effectively.

Implications of This Research One implication of this research is to realize that, as experts in our domain, we may organize our knowledge in a way that is quite different from how our students organize theirs, and that our knowledge organization plays a significant role in our "expert performance." Given that students are likely to come up with knowledge organizations that are superficial and/or do not lend themselves to abstraction or problem solving, this suggests that, at least initially, we need to provide students with appropriate organizing schemes or teach them how to abstract the relevant principles from what they are learning. In addition, it means that we need to monitor how students are processing what they are learning to make sure it gets organized in useful ways.

WHAT STRATEGIES DOES THE RESEARCH SUGGEST?

The following strategies offer ways for instructors to assess their own knowledge organizations relative to students' and help students develop more connected, meaningful, and flexible ways of organizing their knowledge.

Strategies to Reveal and Enhance Knowledge Organizations

Create a Concept Map to Analyze Your Own Knowledge Organization   It can be difficult for experts to recognize how they organize their own knowledge, and thus difficult for them to communicate this organization to students. One way to make your own knowledge organization apparent to yourself is to create your own concept map. Concept mapping is a technique that helps people represent their knowledge organizations visually. (See Appendix B for more information on what concept maps are and how to create them.) Once you have produced your own concept map, the central organizing principles and key features you use should be easier for you to recognize. You can then walk your students through your own concept map as a way of orienting them to the organizational structures in your domain and to illustrate the principles and features around which you want your students to organize their own knowledge.

Analyze Tasks to Identify the Most Appropriate Knowledge Organization   Different tasks draw on different kinds of knowledge organizations. For example, a paper that asks students to analyze the theoretical perspectives of different authors may

59

require students to organize their knowledge around theories and the ways they shape research and writing, whereas a paper that requires students to analyze the impact of a historic event demands that they organize their knowledge around economic, political, and social factors. Thus, it can be helpful to analyze the tasks assigned to determine what kind of knowledge organization would best facilitate learning and performance. Then you might consider providing your students with a skeletal outline or template for organizing their knowledge. For example, in the case of the theoretical paper described above, you might give students an empty table in which you ask them to identify different theoretical schools in one column, describe the key characteristics of each school in the next column, and list scholars whose work would fall into each in another column (including, perhaps, a column to list ways in which each scholars' work does not conform to the theoretical norm).

Provide Students with the Organizational Structure of the Course   Do not assume that your students, especially those who are new to the content area, will see the logical organization of the material you are presenting. They may not see basic relationships or category structures. Therefore, providing students with a view of the "big picture" that presents the key concepts or topics in your course and highlights their interrelationships can help students see how the pieces fit together. This organizational structure can be communicated in your syllabus in various ways: some instructors represent it visually (for example, through a flow chart or diagram) whereas others communicate it verbally. In addition to presenting and explaining this organization early in a course, periodically remind students of the larger organizational framework and situate particular class days within it (for example, "If you'll remember, the first unit of this course focused on developing basic negotiation skills. Today we will be starting the second unit, in which we will see how those skills apply to real world work situations.")

Explicitly Share the Organization of Each Lecture, Lab, or Discussion   Because students' knowledge organization guides their retrieval and use of information, it is especially beneficial to help students create a useful organization as they are learning. To this end, providing an outline, agenda, or visual representation of each lecture, lab, or discussion session can give students a framework for organizing the information they are about to learn. Not all outlines or agendas are equally effective for helping students develop meaningful and connected knowledge organizations, so be sure that the organizational structure you provide captures the critical concepts or principles around which you want students to organize the information from the class. (For example, an agenda that includes headings such as "Introduction," "Lecture," "Discussion," and "Recap" is considerably less useful than an agenda entitled "Three rules to guide ethnographic fieldwork, the reasons for these rules, and a discussion of their limitations.")

Use Contrasting and Boundary Cases to Highlight Organizing Features   To help students develop more sophisticated and nuanced ways of organizing knowledge, it can be useful to present contrasting cases, or two items that share many features but differ in critical ways. Although cases are often used in teaching, they tend to be most effective when presented not in isolation but rather with some compare-and-contrast analysis. A simple example would be a comparison of sharks and dolphins, which have many similarities but represent different classes of animals. Presenting two such cases together makes the differing features more salient and helps students develop deeper and more finely articulated knowledge structures (for example, instead of organizing animals superficially by habitat, they begin to organize them according to

61

other features: vertebrate versus nonvertebrate, warm-blooded versus cold-blooded, live births versus egg-laying, and so forth). Along the same lines, highlighting boundary cases or anomalies (or otherwise commonly misclassified items) can help students identify the salient features of a particular category and develop more nuanced knowledge organizations. For example, the platypus, as an egg-laying mammal, defies some aspects of mammalian classification while possessing other mammalian attributes. Pointing out cases like this focuses students on the critical elements of a particular classification scheme. The use of anomalies also alerts students to the limitations of taxonomies themselves, which can encourage them to develop alternative knowledge organizations.

Explicitly Highlight Deep Features   In order to help students develop more meaningful and less superficial knowledge organizations, highlight the deep features of problems, designs, theories, and examples. One way to do this is to provide examples of problems that share deep features but differ superficially, or examples of problems that are superficially similar but operate on different structural principles. The use of such comparisons can help students become more adept at identifying underlying features and principles and thus teach them to organize their knowledge more meaningfully.

Make Connections Among Concepts Explicit   As you introduce a new concept (or design, theory, example, or problem), explicitly connect it to others students have learned (for example, "You may remember encountering a similar situation in the case study we read last week"). The connections you draw do not always have to be similarities; they can also be contrasts or discrepancies (for example: "What makes this artist's work so different from other abstract expressionists?"). In addition to pointing out these connections yourself, it is important to ask questions that require students to make these connections themselves (for example: "Where have we seen this theoretical orientation before?" "What aspects of this case are similar to or different from the labor management case we discussed yesterday?" "What characteristics of this artist's work are reminiscent of the Bauhaus approach?").

Encourage Students to Work with Multiple Organizing Structures To enable more flexible application of knowledge, students need to develop multiple knowledge organizations that they can draw on as appropriate. One way to help students develop multiple representations is to ask them to categorize a set of items according to more than one organizational schema; for example, you might ask students to classify plants first on the basis of their evolutionary histories and then on the basis of native habitat. This classification task could then be followed by questions that illuminate the implications of organizing knowledge one way or the other. For example, a taxonomy based on evolutionary history might be useful for paleontological analysis, but not for designing a green roof. Giving students practice organizing their knowledge according to alternative schemata or hierarchies helps them see that different organizations serve different purposes and thus builds more robust and flexible knowledge organizations.

Ask Students to Draw a Concept Map to Expose Their Knowledge Organizations Asking students to create concept maps gives you a window not only into how much students know about a particular subject, but also how they are organizing and connecting their knowledge. Concept maps are a visual representation of a knowledge domain (see Appendix B for more information on what concept maps are and how to create them). A concept-mapping activity can be used at the beginning of a course—to reveal students' prior knowledge organization—and then in an ongoing manner to monitor how that organization changes with time and experience. Concept maps, whether graded or ungraded, can help you diagnose problems in students' knowledge organization; for example, if they have miscategorized pieces of knowledge, inappropriately linked unrelated concepts or failed to connect related concepts, or assigned an item to a superordinate position that belongs in a subordinate position, and so on.

Use a Sorting Task to Expose Students' Knowledge Organizations Another way to expose students' knowledge organizations is to ask them to sort different problems, concepts, or situations into categories. This method reveals how students organize their knowledge without requiring them to identify their sorting criteria explicitly. One example of a sorting task is presenting students with a set of problems that have some superficial and some deep features in common, and asking them to group the problems according to similarities. If students group projects on the basis of superficial similarities, it is an indication that they do not recognize the deep features that would help them develop more meaningful and flexible knowledge organizations.

Monitor Students' Work for Problems in Their Knowledge Organization One way to detect problems in students' organization of knowledge is to pay attention to the patterns of mistakes they make in their work for your course. For example, do students frequently mix up two conceptual categories (such as confusing theories and methodologies or force and acceleration problems)? Do they apply a formula, strategy, or solution in a consistently inappropriate way? If so, it is possible that students are making inappropriate connections or categorizations that are impeding their learning and performance.

SUMMARY

In this chapter, we have reviewed research pointing to the fact that it is not just *what* you know but *how you organize* what you know that influences learning and performance. Knowledge organizations that include more interconnections and that are based on deep and meaningful features tend to be effective in supporting learning and performance. Another key aspect of effective knowledge organizations is that they are well matched to the task(s) at hand. For this reason, rich and meaningful knowledge organizations are very helpful. Experts often take advantage of these aspects of their knowledge organizations. However, students—especially ones who are new to a discipline—tend to have knowledge organizations that are sparsely interconnected and that are based on superficial features. These students can benefit from instruction that helps them to see important relationships and build more connections among the pieces of knowledge they are learning, thus leading them to develop more flexible and effective knowledge organizations.

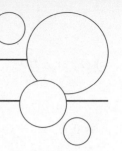

CHAPTER 3

What Factors Motivate Students to Learn?

My Students Are Going to Love This—NOT

This past semester, I finally got to teach a course that relates directly to my area of interest. I put in a lot of time and energy this summer preparing materials and was really excited going into the semester. I used a number of seminal readings in Continental Philosophy and assigned a research project based on primary documents from the nineteenth and twentieth centuries. I thought that students would be excited by the topic and would appreciate reading some of the classic works. But it did not turn out the way I had hoped, and I was really disappointed by their work. With the exception of the two philosophy majors and the one student who "needed an A to get into graduate school," they were not at all interested in the readings and hardly participated in the discussions. In addition, they were not particularly inspired or creative in choosing research topics. Overall, they made little progress across the semester. I guess when it comes right down to it, most students do not much care about philosophy.

Professor Tyrone Hill

A Third of You Will Not Pass This Course

My colleague who usually teaches Thermodynamics was on leave for the semester, and I was assigned to take his place. I knew it would not be easy to teach this course: it has a reputation for being really hard, and engineering students only take it because it is required for the major. On top of that, my colleague had warned me that many students stop coming to lectures early on in the semester, and those who come to class often do not come prepared. It seemed clear that I needed a way to motivate students to work hard and keep up with the material. I recalled that when I was a student, any suggestion by the professor that I might not be up to the challenge really got me fired up and eager to prove him wrong. So I told my students on the first day of class, "This is a very difficult course. You will need to work harder than you have ever worked in a course and still a third of you will not pass." I expected that if my students heard that, they would dig in and work harder to measure up. But to my surprise, they slacked off even more than in previous semesters: they often did not come to class, they made lackluster efforts at the homework, and their test performance was the worst it had been for many semesters. And this was after I gave them fair warning! This class had the worst attitude I have ever seen and the students seemed to be consumed by an overall sense of lethargy and apathy. I am beginning to think that today's students are just plain lazy.

Professor Valencia Robles

WHAT IS GOING ON IN THESE STORIES?

In both of these stories, students fail to acquire and demonstrate the level of understanding the professors desire. In both cases, a lack of engagement with the material seems to be at the root of the problem. To their credit, Professor Hill and Professor Robles both think hard about how to motivate their students, yet they make the common—and often flawed—assumption that their students would be motivated in much the same ways that they themselves were as students. When their students are *not* similarly motivated, the instructors conclude that they are apathetic or lazy.

However, a closer examination of these instructors' approaches and their unintended consequences reveals other likely explanations for student disengagement. Because Professor Hill is so passionate about the course content and finds it so inherently interesting, it does not occur to him that the features of the course that excite him most—the seminal readings and working with primary sources—do not hold the same value for his students. As a consequence, they approach the work half-heartedly and never successfully master the material. Professor Robles, for her part, hopes to recreate the highly competitive classroom environment that had motivated her as a student. However, her warnings about the difficulty of the material and the students' limited chances of passing may fuel preexisting negative perceptions about the course, compromise her students' expectations for success, and undermine their motivation to do the work necessary to succeed.

Although these two stories deal with slightly different issues, the concept of motivation lies at the core of each.

WHAT PRINCIPLE OF LEARNING IS AT WORK HERE?

Motivation refers to the personal investment that an individual has in reaching a desired state or outcome (Maehr & Meyer, 1997). In the context of learning, motivation influences the direction, intensity, persistence, and quality of the learning behaviors in which students engage.

> **Principle:** *Students' motivation generates, directs, and sustains what they do to learn.*

The importance of motivation, in the context of learning, cannot be overstated (Ames, 1990). As students enter college and gain greater autonomy over what, when, and how they study and learn, motivation plays a critical role in guiding their behaviors. In addition, because there are many competing goals that vie for their attention, time, and energy, it is crucial to understand what may increase or decrease students' motivations to pursue specific goals related to learning.

As we can see in the first story, if students do not find the content of the course interesting or relevant, they may see little or no value in mastering it and may fail to engage in the behaviors required for deep learning. Similarly, in the second story, if students do not expect to be successful in a course, they may disengage from the behaviors necessary for learning. Imagine how differently these two stories might have been if the students in Professor Hill's class saw value in learning to use primary sources and the students in Professor Robles' class expected their hard work to result in strong performance and good grades!

As these stories demonstrate, there are two important concepts that are central to understanding motivation: (1) the *subjective value* of a goal and (2) the *expectancies*, or expectations for successful attainment of that goal. Although many theories have been offered to explain motivation, most position these two concepts at the core of their framework (Atkinson, 1957, 1964; Wigfield & Eccles, 1992, 2000). As Figure 3.1 illustrates,

69

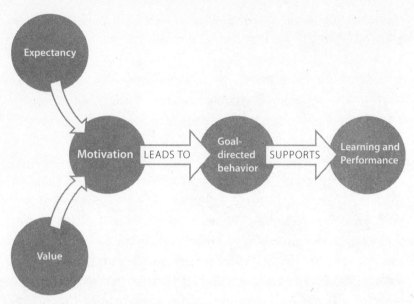

Figure 3.1. Impact of Value and Expectancy on Learning and Performance

expectancies and values interact to influence the level of motivation to engage in goal-directed behavior.

WHAT DOES THE RESEARCH TELL US ABOUT MOTIVATION?

Goals provide the context in which values and expectancies derive meaning and influence motivation. Hence, we begin with a brief discussion of goals.

Goals

To say that someone is motivated tells us little unless we say what the person is motivated to do. Thus, goals serve as the basic organizing feature of motivated behavior (Ryan, 1970; Mitchell, 1982; Elliot & Fryer, 2008). In essence, they act as the compass that guides and directs a broad range of purposeful actions, including those that relate to a person's intellectual and creative pursuits, social and interpersonal relationships, identity and self-concept, needs for safety and material possessions, and desires to be productive and competent in the world (Ford, 1992). Moreover, a number of goals are often in operation simultaneously. This is certainly true for college students who may, in any given moment, seek to acquire knowledge and skills, make new friends, demonstrate to others that they are intelligent, gain a sense of independence, and have fun.

When considering the ways that our students' goals influence their learning behaviors, it is worth noting that students' goals for themselves may differ from our goals for them. This mismatch was true in the first story at the beginning of this chapter. Professor Hill wanted his students to acquire an understanding of Continental Philosophy through the use and appreciation of primary sources. This goal clearly did not match his students' goals for themselves. A more general form of mismatch often occurs when we want our students to pursue learning for its own sake but they are motivated primarily by *performance goals* (Dweck & Leggett, 1988). Performance goals involve protecting a desired self-image and projecting a positive reputation and public persona. When guided by performance goals, students are concerned with normative standards and try to do what is necessary to demonstrate competence in order to appear intelligent, gain status, and acquire recognition and praise. Elliot and colleagues (Elliot, 1999; Elliot & McGregor, 2001) make a further distinction among performance goals. They suggest that goals focused on performance may take two forms: *performance-approach goals* and *performance-avoidant goals*. Students with performance-approach goals focus on attaining competence by meeting normative standards. Students with performance-avoidance goals, on the other hand, focus on avoiding incompetence by meeting standards. They suggest that the cognitive framework with which students approach learning is different for those with an approach versus avoidance orientation, and results of research suggest that performance-approach goals are more advantageous to learning than performance-avoidance goals (Elliot & McGregor, 2001; Cury et al., 2006).

When guided by *learning goals*, in contrast to performance goals, students try to gain competence and truly learn what an activity or task can teach them. As you can imagine, if we want our students to gain the deep understanding that comes from exploration and intellectual risk-taking (a learning goal) but they want only to do what is necessary to get a good grade (a performance goal), we may not obtain the kinds of learning behaviors and outcomes that we desire. Indeed, most research suggests that students who hold learning goals, as compared to those who hold performance goals (particularly performance-avoidance goals), are more likely to use study strategies that result in deeper understanding, to seek help when needed, to persist when faced with difficulty, and to seek out and feel comfortable with challenging tasks. (For more discussion on learning versus performance goals, see Barron & Harackiewicz, 2001; Harackiewicz, Barron, Taucer, Carter, & Elliot, 2000; Miller, Greene, Montalvo, Ravindran, & Nichols, 1996; Somuncuoglu & Yildirim, 1999; McGregor & Elliot, 2002).

Students may also have other goals that conflict with our goals as instructors. *Work-avoidant goals* (Meece & Holt, 1993), for example, involve the desire to finish work as quickly as possible with as little effort as possible. Students guided primarily by work-avoidant goals may show little interest in learning and appear alienated, discouraged, or disengaged. It is important to remember, however, that work-avoidant goals are often context-specific, such that a student who works very hard in one context may avoid work in another. For example, a dedicated engineering student may do as little as possible in Professor Hill's course if he does not see how the knowledge and perspectives from Continental Philosophy apply to his broader intellectual and professional growth and development.

Even though students' goals may not correspond exactly to our goals for them, these two sets of goals (ours and theirs) do not always conflict. In fact, when some of their goals align with ours, powerful learning situations tend to result. Imagine, for example, if the engineering student mentioned above came to see that being able to develop, present, and evaluate a logical argument could help him become a more effective engineer (for example, by helping him defend an engineering design choice to a client or to communicate engineering limitations to colleagues). With his own goals and his philosophy professor's goals in closer—and therefore more productive—alignment, his motivation to pursue learning goals may be strengthened.

Moreover, if an activity satisfies more than one goal, the motivation to pursue that activity is likely to be higher than if it satisfies only one goal. Relevant to this point is the fact that *affective goals* and *social goals* can play an important role in the classroom (Ford, 1992). For instance, if a student's goals in an industrial design project course include learning and applying fundamental design principles (a learning goal), making friends (a social goal), and engaging in stimulating activity (an affective goal), then allowing the student to work on the course project as part of a group provides her the opportunity to satisfy multiple goals at the same time and potentially increases her motivation. This point is further supported by research demonstrating that students who hold multiple types of goals are more successful than those with just one type of goal (Valle et al., 2003).

It is also possible, of course, that students hold a number of conflicting goals. For example, a student may have the goal of doing well on an upcoming psychology exam for which there is an evening study session scheduled. At the same time, he may also have the goal of bonding with his peers via intramural sports and consequently feel a pull to be at an intramural registration meeting held at the same time as the study session. To complicate matters even more, he may have the goal of remaining healthy and, since he has been experiencing a scratchy throat and other symptoms of a cold, may think it is wise to go straight to bed without attending the study session or intramural registration meeting. Given this range of competing goals, which one does he choose? There are some important variables that can provide insight into which goal the student will be motivated to pursue. Remember that value and expectancies interact to influence motivation. In the next section, we discuss value and in the following, expectancies.

Value

A goal's importance, often referred to as its *subjective value*, is one of the key features influencing the motivation to pursue it. Indeed, the lack of perceived value among Professor Hill's students almost certainly contributed to their lack of motivation, described in this chapter's first story. The issue here is quite simple. People are motivated to engage in behaviors to attain goals that have a high relative value. Thus, when confronted with multiple goals (such as going to a study session, attending a registration meeting, or fending off a cold by going to bed early), a student will be more motivated to pursue the goal that has the highest value to him.

Value can be derived from a number of different sources. Wigfield and Eccles (1992, 2000) suggest three broad determinants of subjective value for achievement-related activities and goals. The first is *attainment value*, which represents the satisfaction that one gains from mastery and accomplishment of a goal or task. For instance, a student may receive great satisfaction from solving complex mathematical theorems and consequently work for many hours simply to demonstrate her ability to solve them. Similarly, people often spend hours playing video games in order to reach higher levels of mastery.

A second source of value is *intrinsic value*, which represents the satisfaction that one gains simply from doing the task rather than from a particular outcome of the task. This form of value is operating when students work tirelessly to design and build a beautifully crafted stage set, spend hours writing a computer program, or work hard to understand the complex interplay of variables that regulate blood flow to tumor cells simply because they love it. At its core, this value is intimately tied to the specific content of the goal or activity and is the source of what researchers have traditionally call *intrinsic motivation*.

A final source of value, one that Eccles and Wigfield call *instrumental value*, represents the degree to which an activity or goal helps one accomplish other important goals, such as gaining what are traditionally referred to as *extrinsic rewards*. Praise, public recognition, money, material goods, an interesting career, a high-status job, or a good salary are all longer-term goals that may provide instrumental value to shorter-term goals. For example, students who study business only because of the salary and prestige they expect a job in business will bring are motivated to study and attend their classes by the instrumental value the classes provide toward their desired salary and status.

Most of the students in Professor Hill's Continental Philosophy course appeared to have been unable to find any of the three sources of value. Like the two philosophy majors, for whom the content of the course held intrinsic value, and the student for whom a good grade in the course was instrumental toward getting into graduate school, a single source of value may motivate behavior. However, in many cases, sources of value operate in combination. Indeed, the distinction between the traditional concepts of intrinsic and extrinsic motivation is rarely as dichotomous as theory posits. For instance, by working hard in a course, a biology student may derive value from multiple sources, including solving challenging problems (attainment value), engaging her fascination with biological processes (intrinsic value), and advancing her chances of getting into a good medical school (instrumental value). Consequently, it is important not to think of these sources of value as necessarily conflicting but as potentially reinforcing. In fact, a task that initially holds only instrumental value to a student (something he does primarily to earn a grade or satisfy a requirement) can come to have intrinsic value as he develops knowledge and competence in the subject area (Hidi & Renninger, 2006).

Expectancies

Although one must value a desired outcome in order to be motivated to pursue it, value alone is insufficient to motivate behavior. People are also motivated to pursue goals and outcomes that they believe they can successfully achieve. Conversely, if they do not expect to successfully achieve a desired goal or outcome, they will not be motivated to engage in the behaviors necessary to achieve it. Motivational theorists refer to these expectations as *expectancies*. Here we describe two forms of expectancies that help inform our understanding of motivated behavior.

To be motivated to pursue specific goals, students must hold positive *outcome expectancies*. Outcome expectancies reflect the belief that specific actions will bring about a desired outcome (Carver & Scheier, 1998). A student holds positive outcome expectancies when he thinks, "If I do all the assigned readings and participate in class discussions, I will be able to learn the material well enough to solve problems on the exam and achieve a passing grade." In this case, there is a positive outcome expectancy linking the student's behavior and the desired outcome. In contrast, negative outcome expectancies involve a belief that specific actions have no influence on a desired outcome. For example, a student may think, "No matter how hard I work in this course, I won't get a good grade." This dynamic was likely to be at work among some of Professor Robles' students in the story at the beginning of this chapter. Professor Robles warned her students that a third of them were likely to fail, even after working harder than they had ever worked before. As a result, many of them may have developed negative outcome expectancies; in other words, they began to doubt that hard work would, in fact, result in a passing grade and so lost their motivation. Ironically, what Professor Robles thought would "fire up" her students might have profoundly demotivated them. In order for students to be motivated to engage in the behaviors that result in learning, they must believe that there is a connection between those behaviors and the outcomes they desire.

Whereas positive outcome expectancies are necessary for motivated behavior, they are insufficient on their own. *Efficacy expectancies* are also essential. Efficacy expectancies represent the belief that one is *capable* of identifying, organizing, initiating, and executing a course of action that will bring about a desired outcome (Bandura, 1997). So in order to hold a positive expectancy for success, a student must not only believe that doing the assigned work can earn a passing grade, she must also believe that she is capable of doing the work necessary to earn a passing grade. Thus it is the belief in personal agency that is the potent feature of this expectancy variable and that drives motivation.

What determines a student's expectation for success? One important influence is prior experience in similar contexts. If a student has experienced success in a particular activity in the past, she is more likely to expect success in a similar activity in the future. If she has experienced failure in the past, she is more likely to expect failure in the future. A more complicated analysis of past success and failure suggests, however, that the *reasons* that students identify for their previous successes and failures may be an even more powerful determinant of expectancies. These reasons, or attributions, involve the causal explanations students use to make sense of the outcomes they experience (Weiner, 1986).

When students successfully achieve a goal and attribute their success to internal causes (for example, their own talents or abilities) or to controllable causes (for example, their own efforts or persistence), they are more likely to expect future success. If however, they attribute success to external causes (for example, easy assignments) or uncontrollable causes (for example, luck), they are less likely to expect success in the future. For instance, if a student attributes the good grade she received on a design project to her own creativity (ability) or to the many long hours she spent on its planning and execution (effort), she is likely to expect success on future design assignments. This is because she has attributed her success to relatively stable and controllable features about herself. These same features form the basis for her positive expectations for similar situations in the future.

When a student fails to achieve a goal, however, his motivation is likely to be low if he attributes his failure to a lack of ability (for example, "I am not good at math" or "I am just not a good writer"), especially if he sees his ability as fixed or not amenable to change. On the other hand, even in failure situations, motivation is likely to remain high if a student explains his poor performance in terms of controllable and temporary causes such as inadequate preparation, insufficient effort, or lack of relevant information. Under these circumstances, students can maintain the belief that they are capable of changing their behaviors to achieve a more positive outcome.

Thus, in the context of the classroom, motivation and the effort and persistence that accompany it are highest among students who attribute successful performance to a combination of ability and effort, and poor performance to insufficient effort and inadequate information. These attributions form the basis for the expectation that good performance can be sustained and poor performance can be changed.

How Perceptions of the Environment Affect the Interaction of Value and Expectancies

Value and expectancies do not operate in a vacuum. Indeed, they interact within the broader environmental context in which they exist (see Chapter Six for more on course climate). From a student's point of view, this environment can be perceived along a continuum from supportive to unsupportive (Ford, 1992). Without question, the complex dynamics of the classroom, its tone, the interpersonal forces at play, and the nature and structure of communication patterns all combine to either support or inhibit the students' motivation to pursue a goal. If students perceive the environment as supportive (for example, "The instructor is approachable and several of my classmates seem willing to help me if I run into trouble"), motivation is likely to be enhanced. If students perceive the environment as unsupportive (for example, "This instructor seems hostile to women in engineering"), it can threaten expectations for success and erode motivation.

Thus, our framework for understanding motivation suggests that if a goal is valued *and* expectancies for success are positive *and* the environment is perceived to be supportive, motivation

79

will be highest. However, if there is little value associated with a goal *or* efficacy expectancies for success are negative *or* the environment is not perceived to be supportive, motivation is likely to be lower. So what does this mean for our classrooms and how students behave?

To begin, it is important to realize that we have three important levers (value, efficacy expectancies, and the supportive nature of the environment) with which we can influence motivation. Moreover, if we neglect any of one of the three, motivation may suffer substantially. Based on the work of Hansen (1989) and Ford (1992), Figure 3.2 presents the range of behaviors that result from the interaction of value and expectancies in both supportive and unsupportive environments.

When students care little about a goal and have little confidence in their abilities to successfully achieve that goal, they tend to behave in a *rejecting* manner. This characterizes students in both supportive and unsupportive environments. These students are prone to disengage from learning situations and may experience

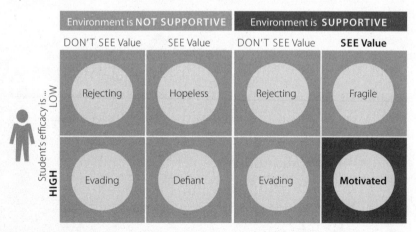

Figure 3.2. Interactive Effects of Environment, Efficacy, and Value on Motivation

apathy, general passivity, alienation, or even a sense of anger if, in the case of a supportive environment, support is perceived as coercive or pressuring.

When students, in both supportive and unsupportive environments, see little value in a goal but are confident in their abilities to successfully achieve it, they may act in an *evading* manner. Since they see the task as doable but unimportant, students often have difficulty paying attention and are frequently preoccupied by social distractions or daydreaming. Often, in an attempt to avoid overt disapproval and pressure from the instructor or the stigma associated with a poor grade, they may do the minimum amount of work that is needed to just get by.

Those students who see value in a goal but lack confidence in their ability to achieve it can manifest two forms of behavior, depending on the nature of the environment. Those that perceive little or no support from the environment tend to be *hopeless*. As such, they appear to have no expectation of success and demonstrate very low levels of motivation, behaving in helpless fashions. Those who do perceive a supportive environment tend to be *fragile*. That is, because they value the task and believe the environment offers support, they want to succeed. However, they are dubious about their own abilities and may try to protect their sense of self-esteem by feigning understanding, avoiding situations that require overt performance, denying difficulty, and making excuses to explain poor performance.

Similarly, depending on their perceptions of the supportive nature of the environment, students who see value in a task and have confidence in their abilities also manifest two forms of behavior. Those that perceive little or no support from the environment may be *defiant*. That is, because the task is important and they are confident of their own abilities, they may take an "I will show you" or "I will prove you wrong" attitude in response to the perceived lack of support from the environment. Those students who perceive the environment to be supportive demonstrate the most *motivated* behavior. In essence, all three levers that influence motivation are aligned in a positive direction. As a consequence, these students seek to learn, integrate, and apply new knowledge and view learning situations as opportunities to extend their understanding.

Implications of This Research

Several important points should be evident thus far. First, value, expectancy, and environment interact to produce an array of distinctive student behaviors. Thus, no single variable is universally deterministic with regard to motivating students. That said, changes in any one dimension can change students' levels of motivation and thus alter their behaviors. For instance, providing support and encouragement to students who tend toward defiance can edge them toward greater motivation. Similarly, by helping "fragile" students build positive beliefs about their chances of success, we may support them to become more highly motivated. Indeed, each of the dimensions in the table represents features of the learning environment over which we, as instructors, can have substantial influence. Finally, if we neglect any single dimension, motivation may suffer substantially. As a case in point, if we fail to address students' perceived lack of value for a given task or goal, at best they are likely to demonstrate an evading pattern of motivation (see the left column of Figure 3.2). Similarly, if students perceive the environment in which they learn as unsupportive, even those who find value in the goal and hold positive efficacy expectancies may fall short of highly motivated behavior. Indeed, when the environment is perceived as unsupportive, the best we can hope for is a defiant pattern of motivation (see the top half of Figure 3.2).

WHAT STRATEGIES DOES THE RESEARCH SUGGEST?

In this section we present a number of strategies that may help you increase the value that students place on the goals and activities that you have identified and created for them, as well as strategies to help you strengthen students' expectancies and create an environment that supports motivation.

Strategies to Establish Value

Connect the Material to Students' Interests   Students are typically more motivated to engage with material that interests them or has relevance for important aspects of their lives. For example, courses on the history of rock 'n' roll, philosophy and the *Matrix* films, the statistics of sexual orientation, how technology can combat global poverty, and how to build virtual reality worlds may strongly connect with students' interests. All of these courses can be rigorous and yet demonstrate high demand because they tap into issues that are important to students.

Provide Authentic, Real-World Tasks   Assign problems and tasks that allow students to vividly and concretely see the relevance and value of otherwise abstract concepts and theories. For example, an economics professor might use a case study of economic instability to illustrate market forces. Analyzing a real-world event provides students with a context for understanding economic theories and their applicability to current situations. Similarly, in an information systems course, the instructor might assign a service-learning project in which students must build a database for an actual client in the community. This kind of authentic task allows students to work within real constraints, interact with real clients, and explore the profession. It might also create possibilities for future internships or jobs.

Show Relevance to Students' Current Academic Lives Students sometimes do not appreciate a current learning experience because they do not see its value relative to their course of study. For instance, psychology students may see little value in taking a math course because they do not realize that the knowledge they acquire will serve them well when they take a required statistics or research methods course. If you make explicit connections between the content of your course and other courses to come, students can better understand the value of each course as a building block for future courses.

Demonstrate the Relevance of Higher-Level Skills to Students' Future Professional Lives Students often focus on specific course content without recognizing how the skills and abilities they develop across courses (for example, quantitative reasoning, public speaking, persuasive writing, teamwork skills) will benefit them in their professional lives. For example, students often complain about being graded on the quality of their writing in lab reports, failing to recognize the importance of written communication skills in a wide range of professions. We can help motivate students by explaining how various skills will serve them more broadly in their professional lives.

Identify and Reward What You Value It is important to explicitly identify for students what you value. This can be done in the syllabus, through feedback, and through modeling. Having identified what you value, be sure to reward it through assessments that are aligned with course objectives. For instance, if you value the quality of group interactions in a project course, you should identify and describe the aspects of such interactions that are important (for example, clear communication, effective resolution of disagreements, consideration of multiple perspectives) and include an evaluation of the group as part of the final grade. Similarly, if you want students to take intellectual or creative risks, identify these features as important and assess students' work based on the extent to which they pushed the limits, whether or not they were ultimately successful.

Show Your Own Passion and Enthusiasm for the Discipline
Your own enthusiasm and passion can be powerful and contagious. Even if students are not initially attracted to or interested in your course, don't be afraid to let your excitement for your discipline show. Your enthusiasm might raise students' curiosity and motivate them to find out what excites you about the subject, leading them to engage more deeply than they had initially planned or discover the value they had overlooked.

Strategies That Help Students Build Positive Expectancies

Ensure Alignment of Objectives, Assessments, and Instructional Strategies   When these three components of a course are aligned—when students know the goals, are given opportunities to practice and get feedback, and are able to show their level of understanding—learning is supported. Students also have a more coherent picture of what will be expected of them and thus are more motivated because they feel more confident and in control of their learning, as well as their grade.

Identify an Appropriate Level of Challenge   Setting challenging but attainable goals is critical for optimally motivating students. However, identifying the appropriate level at which to frame your expectations may be difficult. To do so, you need to know who your students are—in terms of their prior knowledge and experience as well as their future plans and goals. A pre-assessment may be useful in evaluating both prior knowledge and future goals. Examining the syllabi of courses that immediately precede your course in the curricular sequence (when relevant) may also provide insight into your students' prior academic experiences. Syllabi from instructors who have taught the course in the past may also offer clues about the appropriate level at which to frame your expectations. Finally, talk to colleagues about their process for identifying appropriate expectations or ask to observe their classes.

Create Assignments That Provide the Appropriate Level of Challenge   One the one hand, if your course or an assignment is pitched at a level that students do not expect will allow them to be successful with reasonable effort, they will not be motivated to engage with the assignment. On the other hand, if the course or the assignment is too easy, students will not think that it has value or is worth their time to engage with it, deeming it busy work. Consequently, we need to set standards that are challenging but attainable with student effort. Determining these standards is not always easy given that student cohorts differ, so administering diagnostic or early assessments can help you determine the right level for each cohort.

Provide Early Success Opportunities   Expectations for future performance are influenced by past experiences. Hence, early success can build a sense of efficacy. This strategy is incredibly important in courses that are known as "gateway" or "high-risk" courses or for students who come into your course with anxiety for whatever reason. For example, you might incorporate early, shorter assignments that account for a small percentage of the final grade but provide a sense of competence and confidence before you assign a larger project.

Articulate Your Expectations Articulate your course goals clearly to students so that they know what the desired outcomes are. Then make it clear to students what you expect them to do in order to reach those goals. This will help make the connection between a course of action and a desired outcome more concrete and tangible, thus creating a more positive outcome expectancy. Help students set realistic expectations by identifying areas in which they might encounter difficulty and support their sense of agency by communicating your confidence and expectation that they will overcome those challenges and succeed. At the same time, let students know what support they can expect from you in pursuit of those goals (for example, office hours or review sessions).

Provide Rubrics Rubrics are a way of explicitly representing performance expectations and thus can direct students' behaviors toward your intended goals. For example, a rubric for a research paper can identify the components of the task (for example, hypothesis, evidence, conclusion, writing) and the expectations for performance for each component at several levels of sophistication (for example, developing, competent, exemplary). See Appendix C for examples.

Provide Targeted Feedback Because feedback provides information about progress toward a goal, it can have a powerful motivating effect. Feedback is most effective when it is timely and constructive. Timely feedback is close enough in proximity to the performance to have impact and to allow for incorporation of the feedback into the next iteration. Constructive feedback identifies strengths, weaknesses, and suggestions for future action. For more discussion on feedback, see Chapter Five.

Be Fair   Be sure that the standards and criteria used to assess students' work are administered fairly. This is particularly relevant when multiple graders are involved (for example, teaching assistants). If students perceive that their work is being assessed differently from their peers or differently from one time to the next, their expectations for success may be compromised.

Educate Students About the Ways We Explain Success and Failure   To give students a better sense of control over the outcomes that they experience and in turn influence their expectations for success, educate them about the attributions that people make for success and failure. For example, we frequently attribute success to things about us (that is, internalize) and attribute failures to things about the external world (that is, externalize). Help them shape their attribution for success to include appropriate study strategies, good time management, and hard work. Similarly, help them avoid attributing failure to factors such as "not being good with numbers," "not being good with details," or "not being very smart." Rather, help them focus on controllable features, such as the way they studied (for example, how much, when, the nature of their study habits).

Describe Effective Study Strategies   Students may not be able to identify ways in which they should appropriately change their study behaviors following failure. In this case, it is important to discuss effective study strategies to give them alternatives to the behaviors that resulted in poor performance. In doing so, we may help adjust their expectations about being able to successfully obtain their goals.

88

Strategies That Address Value and Expectancies

Provide Flexibility and Control   Where possible, allow students to choose among options and make choices that are consistent with their goals and the activities that they value. One way to give students greater flexibility is to allow them choices in portions of the course content, topics for papers, and questions for class discussion. Flexibility lends a sense of control, which can contribute to a student's expectation of success.

Give Students an Opportunity to Reflect   It is important to give students an opportunity to reflect on assignments. Facilitating their reflection with specific questions can help structure the process to support motivation. For example, asking students "What did you learn from this assignment?" or "What was the most valuable feature of this project?" helps them identify the value of their work. Asking students "What did you do to prepare for this assignment/exam? What skills do you need to work on? How would you prepare differently or approach the assignment differently if you were doing it in the future?" can help them to identify specific strategies that leverage their strengths and overcome their weaknesses, thus bolstering their expectations for future success.

SUMMARY

In this chapter, we have discussed some of the variables that underlie student motivation. We have used the concept of goals as an organizing feature and have argued that students frequently have multiple and diverse goals, many of which may not align with ours. We described a model in which the subjective value that students place on goals and their expectancies of success play a key role in influencing their motivation.

We have described how subjective value, efficacy expectancies, and beliefs about the supportive nature of the environment interact to affect the specific ways in which students behave. Our hope is that by understanding how some of these variables influence motivation and by arming yourself with some practical strategies, you can increase the motivation of your students and improve the quality of learning in your courses.

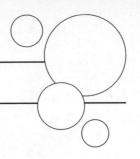

CHAPTER 4

How Do Students Develop Mastery?

A Sum of Their Parts

I worked in industry for over twenty years before coming to academia, and I know how critical teamwork is, so in my Industrial Management course I assign a number of group projects in addition to individual projects. Students generally do well on their individual projects, and since the group assignments and individual assignments require more or less the same content knowledge, you would think that students would do even better on the group projects: after all, there are more people to share the work and generate ideas. Instead, it is just the reverse. Not only do my student groups fail to meet deadlines, but their analyses are also superficial and their projects lack internal coherence. I am not sure what the problem is, but at this point I am tempted to scrap the group projects and go only with individual projects. I just wish someone could explain to me why these groups are *less*, not *more*, than a sum of their parts.

Professor Fritz Solomon

Shouldn't They Know This by Now?

I just came from the second meeting of my acting class, and I have never felt so frustrated. This is an upper-level course, so by the time students get to my course they have already taken a number of courses in speech, voice, and movement. In other words, they *should* have a solid grounding in the fundamentals. Yet they make the most elementary mistakes! To give an example, I assigned students an easy scene from a Tennessee Williams play, something they should be able to handle with ease. And yet, a good proportion of the class mangled the Southern accents, dropped props, or mumbled their lines. Not only that, but they completely disregarded two things I know their instructors have emphasized over and over again in the introductory classes: the importance of doing vocal warm-ups and phonetically transcribing all their lines. How can they not know this stuff by now? I know they have learned it, because I have sat in on some of the first- and second-year classes and have been impressed by their skills. So why do they seem to have forgotten everything when they get to my course?

Professor Pamela Kozol

WHAT IS GOING ON IN THESE STORIES?

The instructors in these two stories believe that their students have the skills and knowledge necessary to perform well on the assigned tasks, yet their students' performance is disappointing, and neither instructor knows why. What is happening in each case that can help explain why these students fail to meet their instructor's expectations?

In fact, the tasks these instructors have assigned may require more from students than the instructors realize, and their students may be less prepared than their instructors assume. In the first story, for example, Professor Solomon expects the quality of group projects to be higher than the quality of individual projects because there are more people "to share the work and generate ideas." This seems like a reasonable assumption and is one that many instructors make. However, it is predicated on the expectation that students will know how to work effectively in groups. In fact, successful teamwork requires not only content skills and knowledge, but also an additional and qualitatively different set of process skills, such as the ability to delegate tasks, coordinate efforts, resolve conflicts, and synthesize the contributions of group members. When students possess the process skills necessary to manage the particular challenges of teamwork, the quality of work they produce in teams may indeed surpass the quality of the work they do individually. But when students lack these key component skills, it can seriously impede their performance.

Professor Kozol's students, in contrast, appear to have the necessary component skills. They have taken classes in and apparently mastered fundamental movement, voice, and speech skills. Yet when assigned a task that requires these skills, their performance is characterized by mistakes and omissions. Why? There are several possible explanations. First, although students have come to Professor Kozol's class with a solid grounding in movement, voice, and speech, they practiced these skills in classes targeting each skill area separately. Consequently, they may not have had sufficient practice using the complete set of skills in combination—especially while acting out an entire scene. If so, it is not the component skills they lack, but rather the ability to integrate them effectively.

Another possible explanation is that Professor Kozol's students did not recognize the relevance of phonetic transcriptions and vocal warm-ups—practices they had learned in previous courses—to the task they were assigned in her class. They may have failed to make this connection if their understanding of the underlying function of these practices was superficial or if they associated them entirely with the contexts (voice and speech classes) in which they had originally learned them. If so, the problem was not that students lacked component skills or that they were unable to integrate them successfully, but that they could not transfer them successfully to a new context and apply them appropriately.

WHAT PRINCIPLE OF LEARNING IS AT WORK HERE?

As the stories above suggest, tasks that seem simple and straightforward to instructors often involve a complex combination of skills. Think back to when you learned to drive. You had to keep in mind a sequence of steps (for example, adjust the mirrors, apply the brakes, turn the key in the ignition, put the car in reverse, check the rear view mirror, release the brake, press the accelerator), a set of facts (for example, traffic rules and laws, the meaning of street signs, the functions of the car's controls and gauges), and a set of skills (for example, accelerating smoothly, parallel parking, performing a three-point turn). You also had to learn how to integrate all of these component skills and knowledge, such as checking your mirror and moving into another lane. Finally, you had to recognize the appropriate context for certain knowledge and skills, such as adapting speed and braking behavior when driving on icy or clear roads.

To an experienced driver, driving is effortless and automatic, requiring little conscious awareness to do well. But for the novice driver it is complex and effortful, involving the conscious and gradual development of many distinct skills and abilities. A similar process exists in the development of mastery in academic contexts, as described in the following principle.

> **Principle:** *To develop mastery, students must acquire component skills, practice integrating them, and know when to apply what they have learned.*

Mastery refers to the attainment of a high degree of competence within a particular area. That area can be narrowly or broadly defined, ranging from discrete skills (for example, using a Bunsen burner) or content knowledge (for example, knowing the names of all U.S. presidents) to extensive knowledge and skills within a complex disciplinary domain (for example, French theater, thermodynamics, or game theory). For students to achieve mastery within a domain, whether narrowly or broadly conceived, they need to develop a set of key component skills, practice them to the point where they can be combined fluently and used with a fair degree of automaticity, and know when and where to apply them appropriately (see Figure 4.1).

WHAT DOES THE RESEARCH TELL US ABOUT MASTERY?

Common sense suggests that having achieved mastery within a domain should position an instructor well to help novices develop mastery. But this is not necessarily the case. In the following sections we examine why expertise can potentially be a problem for teachers; we then explore research relevant to each element of mastery and discuss implications for teaching.

Expertise

Ironically, expertise can be a liability as well as an advantage when it comes to teaching. To understand why, consider the model of

95

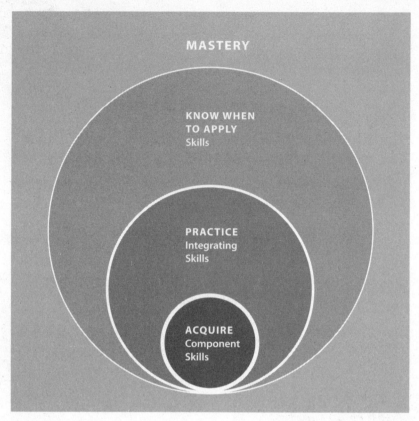

Figure 4.1. Elements of Mastery

mastery offered by Sprague and Stuart (2000) and illustrated in Figure 4.2. It describes a four-stage developmental trajectory from novice to expert focused on two dimensions: competence and consciousness.

As illustrated in the diagram below, novice students are in a state of *unconscious incompetence*, in that they have not yet developed skill in a particular domain, nor do they have sufficient knowledge to recognize what they need to learn. Put simply, they do not know what they do not know. As they gain knowledge and experience, they advance to a state of *conscious incompetence*, where

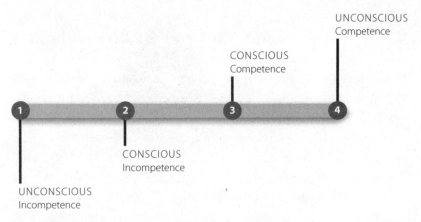

Figure 4.2. Stages in the Development of Mastery

they are increasingly aware of what they do not know and, consequently, of what they need to learn. As their mastery develops, students advance to a state of *conscious competence* wherein they have considerable competence in their domain, yet still must think and act deliberately and consciously. Finally, as students reach the highest level of mastery, they move into a state of *unconscious competence* in which they exercise the skills and knowledge in their domain so automatically and instinctively that they are no longer consciously aware of what they know or do. As this model suggests, while competence develops in a more-or-less linear way, consciousness first waxes and then wanes, so that novices (in stage one) and experts (in stage four) operate in states of relative unconsciousness, though for very different reasons.

It is easy to see why novices lack conscious awareness of what they do not know, but less obvious why experts lack conscious awareness of what they *do* know. Research on expert-novice differences helps to illuminate the issue, however. Experts, by definition, possess vastly more knowledge than novices, but they also organize, access, and apply their knowledge very differently (see

97

Chapter Two on organization of knowledge; Ericsson & Smith, 1991; Ericsson & Lehmann, 1996). For instance, experts organize knowledge into large, conceptual "chunks" that allow them to access and apply that knowledge with facility (Chase & Simon, 1973b; Chase & Ericsson, 1982; Koedinger & Anderson, 1990). Moreover, because experts immediately recognize meaningful patterns and configurations based on their previous experiences, they are able to employ shortcuts and skip steps that novices cannot (DeGroot, 1965; Anderson, 1992; Chase & Simon, 1973a; Koedinger & Anderson, 1990; Blessing & Anderson, 1996). Also, because experts have extensive practice in a narrowly defined area (for example, planning a problem-solving strategy or critiquing a theoretical perspective), they can perform with ease and automaticity tasks that are much more effortful for novices (Smith & Chamberlin, 1992; Lansdown, 2002; Beilock, Wierenga, & Carr, 2002). Finally, experts link specific information to deeper principles and schemas and are consequently better able than novices to transfer their knowledge across contexts in which those principles apply (see Chapter Two; Chi, Feltovich, & Glaser, 1981; Larkin et al., 1980; Boster & Johnson, 1989).

These attributes of expertise are an obvious advantage when instructors are working within their disciplinary domains, but they can be an obstacle to effective teaching. For example, the way instructors chunk knowledge can make it difficult for them to break a skill down so that it is clear to students. Moreover, the fact that instructors take shortcuts and skip steps with no conscious awareness of doing so means they will sometimes make leaps that students cannot follow. In addition, the efficiency with which instructors perform complex tasks can lead them to underestimate the time it will take students to learn and perform these tasks. Finally, the fact that instructors can quickly recognize the relevance of skills across diverse contexts can cause them to overestimate students' ability to do the same.

When expert instructors are blind to the learning needs of novice students, it is known as *expert blind spot* (Nickerson, 1999; Hinds, 1999; Nathan & Koedinger, 2000; Nathan & Petrosino, 2003). To get a sense of the effect of expert blind spot on students, consider how master chefs might instruct novice cooks to "sauté the vegetables until they are done," "cook until the sauce is a good consistency," or "add spices to taste." Whereas such instructions are clear to chefs, they do not illuminate matters to students, who do not know what "done" entails, what a "good consistency" is, or what spices would create a desired taste. Here we see the unconscious competence of the expert meeting the unconscious incompetence of the novice. The likely result is that students miss vital information, make unnecessary mistakes, and function inefficiently. They may also become confused and discouraged. Although they might muddle through on their own, it is unlikely that they will learn with optimal efficiency or thoroughness.

As instructors, we are all susceptible to expert blind spot. However, we can reduce the problems it poses for student learning by becoming more consciously aware of three particular elements of mastery that students must develop: (1) the acquisition of key component skills, (2) practice in integrating them effectively, and (3) knowledge of when to apply what they have learned.

Component Skills

As the driving and cooking examples above suggest, tasks that seem fairly simple to experts can hide a complex combination of component skills. For example, the ability to analyze a case study requires component skills such as the capacity to identify the central question or dilemma of the case, articulate the perspectives of key actors, enumerate constraints, delineate possible courses of action, and recommend and justify a solution. Similarly, problem solving might involve a number of component skills including (but not limited to) representing the problem, determining an appropriate solution strategy, doing the calculations necessary to execute that strategy, and evaluating the result. These component skills are particularly difficult to identify when they involve purely cognitive processes (for example, recognizing, planning, and formulating) that are not directly visible.

If students lack critical component skills—or if their command of those skills is weak—their performance on the overall task suffers (Resnick, 1976). This is demonstrated in a number of studies in which researchers decompose complex tasks, identify weak or missing component skills, and track the effect of those gaps on student performance. Lovett's (2001) research with introductory statistics students, for instance, identified two key skills involved in statistical data analysis: the ability to recognize the relevant variables and the ability to categorize them according to types. Lovett found that when students lacked these component skills, they were less able to choose appropriate forms of analysis and their performance on the overall problem-solving task was compromised (Lovett, 2001). We see a similar phenomenon in the first story at the beginning of the chapter: while Professor Solomon's students possess many of the component skills necessary for their group projects—as evidenced by their performance on individual assignments—their lack of teamwork skills erodes their overall performance.

In order to teach complex skills systematically—without missing pieces—instructors must be able to "unpack" or decompose complex tasks. This can be challenging because of expert blind spot, but there are tangible payoffs for student learning. Indeed, research indicates that when instructors identify and reinforce weak component skills through targeted practice, students' performance on the overall task often improves significantly. For example, Koedinger and Anderson (1990) found that, relative to experts, novice geometry students lacked the ability to plan problem-solving strategies. After assigning students exercises to specifically reinforce this skill within the context of the larger task, the researchers found that students became much more adept problem-solvers (Koedinger & Anderson, 1993). Lovett (2001) found that if beginning students were given a mere 45 minutes of practice identifying statistical problem types, and were given feedback on this particular skill, they were able to select appropriate analyses as adeptly as students who had had a semester-long course. In other words, even a small amount of focused practice on key component skills had a profound effect on overall performance. This same effect is demonstrated in research on cognitive tutors (computer-based tutoring programs), which are designed to detect the component skills that students lack and direct them to exercises that strengthen their abilities in those areas (Anderson et al., 1995; Singley, 1995; Ritter et al., 2007; Anderson, Conrad, & Corbett, 1989).

While we know that students need to practice component skills in order to improve their performance on the complex tasks involving those skills, the question of whether students should practice component skills in isolation or in the context of the whole task is more complicated. The advantage to practicing a component skill in isolation is that it allows students to focus their attention solely on the skill that needs work. Think, for example, of the benefits to a basketball player of drills that emphasize dribbling or shooting. Drilling these component skills in isolation gives players more repeated practice with each skill than they could ever get in the context of a game or scrimmage, and allows them to devote their energy and concentration exclusively to the skill in question. The advantage to practicing the whole task, on the other hand, is that students see how the parts fit into the whole in a context that is authentically complex. Think, for example, how much more difficult it is to shoot under defensive pressure in a game situation than when taking practice shots during a drill!

Whether or not students benefit more from practicing component skills in isolation or in the context of the overall task depends to a large extent on the nature of the task. Although the research results are mixed, it seems generally true that whole-task practice is preferable if the overall task is fairly simple or if components cannot be realistically extracted from the whole (Wightman & Lintern, 1985; Naylor & Briggs, 1963; Teague, Gittelman, & Park, 1994). However, if the task is highly complex and can be easily divided into component parts, students often learn more effectively if the components are practiced temporarily in isolation, and then progressively combined (White & Frederickson, 1990; Wightman & Lintern, 1985; Salden, Paas, & van Merrienboer, 2006). The extent to which isolated practice facilitates learning also depends in part on the skill level of the student. Studies have shown that explicit instruction and isolated practice of component skills, while helpful for novice learners (Clarke, Ayres, & Sweller, 2005), might be counterproductive for advanced learners if they have already integrated these components into a coherent whole (Kalyuga, Ayres, Chandler, & Sweller, 2003). Finally, the extent to which isolated practice is beneficial depends on the learning objectives of the class. For example, if a central objective of a course like Professor Solomon's is to help students build teamwork skills, then it might make sense to focus on specific skills in isolation. One example might be to reinforce students' abilities to reconcile intra-group differences of opinion by having them role-play responses to hypothetical conflicts.

Implications of This Research   In order to build new skills systematically and to diagnose weak or missing skills, instructors must be able to break complex tasks down into their component parts. Decomposing complex tasks helps instructors pinpoint skills that students need to develop through targeted practice. However, in designing practice opportunities to reinforce component skills, instructors should consider whether their learning goals are best accomplished through isolated practice, whole-task practice, or some combination of the two.

Integration

Acquiring component skills does not by itself prepare students to perform complex tasks. This is because mastering complex tasks requires not only the temporary decomposition of subskills and the opportunity to practice them separately, but also their eventual recomposition and the opportunity to practice them in combination. Integrating component skills can be difficult and demanding, as is evidenced in the second story at the beginning of this chapter in which Professor Kozol's students struggle to integrate and use in combination skills they have learned separately.

The performance deficits that Professor Kozol's students exhibit when attempting to combine skills are not unusual. Many studies have shown that people's performance tends to degrade when they are asked to do more than one task at a time (Kahnemann, 1973; Navon & Gopher, 1979; Wickens, 1991). This degradation occurs because performing multiple tasks simultaneously tends to require attention to and processing of a great deal of information, and yet people have a limit to how much they can attend to and process at once. In other words, the total information-processing demands imposed by a given task or set of tasks—also known as *cognitive load*—can easily exceed what people can manage. When people's limit is exceeded, they are left with insufficient attention and other cognitive resources to complete the task effectively. For example, Strayer and Johnston (2001) found that when they asked adults to perform a simulated driving task, various measures of performance (for example, the number of traffic signals obeyed and reaction time for braking at red lights) declined when a cell-phone conversation task was added to the driving task. Furthermore, as the complexity of the cell-phone task increased, driving performance worsened. In other words, although the participants in this study likely had sufficient cognitive resources to perform well on the driving task in isolation, the more resources that were demanded by the secondary (cell phone) task, the fewer resources there were left for driving—leading to worse driving performance.

The same phenomenon often occurs when people perform a single complex task, because complex tasks require people to perform multiple skills in concert, which can similarly overload people's limited cognitive resources. Thinking back to Professor Kozol's acting class, it appears that her students could manage the cognitive load of voice, speech, or movement individually in classes devoted to each of those skill areas. However, the cognitive load of executing and coordinating these skills all at once—while incorporating new acting skills—may have been too much for them to manage, as revealed in their errors and mistakes.

Interestingly, experts do not suffer as much as novices when performing complex tasks or combining multiple tasks. Because experts have extensive practice within a circumscribed domain, the key component skills in their domain tend to be highly practiced and more automated. Each of these highly practiced skills then demands relatively few cognitive resources, effectively lowering the total cognitive load that experts experience. Thus, experts can perform complex tasks and combine multiple tasks relatively easily (Smith & Chamberlin, 1992; Lansdown, 2002; Beilock, Wierenga, & Carr, 2002). This is not because they necessarily have *more* cognitive resources than novices; rather, because of the high level of fluency they have achieved in performing key skills, they

104

can *do* more with what they have. Novices, on the other hand, have not achieved the same degree of fluency and automaticity in each of the component skills, and thus they struggle to combine skills that experts combine with relative ease and efficiency.

Because instructors, as experts, do not experience the same cognitive load as novices, they may have performance expectations for students that are unrealistically high. This can lead to the kind of astonishment and frustration Professor Kozol experiences as her students struggle with an assignment she perceives as easy. For her, combining speech, voice, movement, and other acting skills is not terribly cognitively demanding, so her students' mistakes seem inexplicable. Fortunately, as students gain mastery over time, the knowledge and procedures required for complex tasks become automatized and thus require fewer cognitive resources. Thus, with practice, students gain greater fluency in executing individual subskills and will be better prepared to tackle the complexity of multiple tasks.

How then can we help students manage cognitive load as they learn to perform complex tasks? One method that has proved effective in research studies is to allow students to focus on one skill at a time, thus temporarily reducing their cognitive load and giving them the opportunity to develop fluency before they are required to integrate multiple skills. For example, Clarke, Ayres, and Sweller (2005) found that math students who knew little about spreadsheets learned less and performed less well when they were taught new mathematical concepts in the context of spreadsheets. This is because they had to learn both the spreadsheet skills and the math concepts concurrently, and they became overwhelmed. However, when these students first learned spreadsheet skills and *then* used those skills to learn the mathematics, learning and performance improved. Another method to emerge in the research is to support some aspects of a complex task while students perform the entire task (Sweller & Cooper, 1985; Cooper &

Sweller, 1987; Paas & van Merrienboer, 1994). For example, Sweller and Cooper (1985) demonstrated this with students learning to solve problems in a variety of quantitative fields from statistics to physics. They found that when students were given typical word problems, it was possible for them to solve the problems without actually learning much. This is because the problems themselves were sufficiently demanding that students had no cognitive resources available to learn from what they did. But when students were given "worked-examples" (such as presolved problems) interspersed with problems to solve, studying the worked-examples freed up cognitive resources that allowed students to see the key features of the problem and to analyze the steps and reasons behind problem-solving moves. The researchers found this improved students' performance on subsequent problem solving. This result, called the *worked-example effect,* is one example of a process called *scaffolding,* whereby instructors temporarily relieve some of the cognitive load so that students can focus on particular dimensions of learning. (For more discussion on scaffolding, see Chapter Seven.)

A subtle but important point to mention here is that some reductions in cognitive load promote learning while others do not (Paas, Renkl, & Sweller, 2003, 2004). The key to reducing cognitive load effectively lies in identifying which of the demanding aspects of a task are related to the skills students need to learn and which may be disruptive to (or distracting from) those learning goals. Research has shown that removing extraneous load—that is, aspects of a task that make it difficult to complete but that are unrelated to what students need to learn—is helpful. In contrast, reducing load that is germane to what students need to learn will naturally be counterproductive in that students will not have a chance to practice what they need to learn. To illustrate this distinction between extraneous and germane load, consider engineering students who are having difficulty solving practice problems. They have been introduced to a number of different formulas over the course of the semester and are having trouble keeping them straight. Now, if the instructor's goal is for students to learn to select and apply the appropriate formula for each of the problems, then giving students a sheet listing all the relevant formulas might be a legitimate choice: it would reduce extraneous load because students would no longer have to spend their time and cognitive resources *remembering* the relevant formulas and could focus instead on the skills of selection and application. However, if the instructor's goal is for students to be able to remember the formulas and then apply each one when told to do so, a sheet listing all the formulas would obviously thwart the learning goal.

Implications of This Research Performing complex tasks can be cognitively demanding for students, particularly when they have not yet developed fluency or automaticity in all the component skills. Thus, instructors should have reasonable expectations about the time and practice students will need, not only to develop fluency in component skills but also to learn to integrate those skills successfully. It can be helpful under some circumstances for instructors to strategically lighten aspects of the task that intro-duce extraneous cognitive load so that students can focus their cognitive resources on the aspects of a task most germane to the learning objectives. Several specific ways to do this are discussed in the Strategies section.

Application

As we have seen, mastery requires component skills *and* the ability to integrate them successfully. However, it also requires that students know when and where to use what they have learned. When students acquire skills but do not learn the conditions of their appropriate application, they may fail to apply skills that are relevant to a task or problem, or, alternatively, apply the wrong skill for the context.

The application of skills (or knowledge, strategies, approaches, or habits) learned in one context to a novel context is referred to as *transfer*. Transfer is said to be *near* if the learning context and transfer context are similar, and *far* when the contexts are dissimilar. For example, various dimensions of farness come into play when a student is given a task in his Public Policy course that requires him to apply a statistics formula he learned two semesters previously in Statistics 101. Not only has the knowledge domain changed from statistics to public policy, but so too have the physical and temporal contexts (a new class, two semesters later). If the transfer task were in a different functional context altogether, say outside academia, additional transfer distance would be introduced (for a discussion of different dimensions of transfer, see Barnett & Ceci, 2002).

Far transfer is, arguably, the central goal of education: we want our students to be able to apply what they learn beyond the classroom. Yet most research has found that (a) transfer occurs neither often nor automatically, and (b) the more dissimilar the learning and transfer contexts, the less likely successful transfer will occur. In other words, much as we would like them to, students often do not successfully apply relevant skills or knowledge in novel contexts (Singley & Anderson, 1989; McKeough, Lupart, & Marini, 1995; Thorndike & Woodworth, 1901; Reed, Ernst, & Banerji, 1974; Singley, 1995; Cognition and Technology Group at Vanderbilt, 1994; Singley & Anderson, 1989; Holyoak & Koh, 1987). In this section, we examine why this is the case by exploring issues that can affect transfer negatively and positively.

There are a number of reasons students may fail to transfer relevant knowledge and skills. First, they may associate that knowledge too closely with the context in which they originally learned it and thus not think to apply it—or know how to apply it—outside that context. This is called *overspecificity* or *context dependence* (Mason Spencer & Weisberg, 1986; Perfetto, Bransford, & Franks, 1983). To illustrate: students in a statistics course might perform well on their chapter quizzes but perform poorly on a final exam involving questions of precisely the same type and difficulty, but from a number of different chapters. If students relied on superficial cues to figure out which formula to apply on chapter quizzes (for example, if it is chapter 12, it must be a T-test), then in the absences of these cues, they may have been unable to identify the salient features of each problem and select an appropriate statistical test. Their knowledge, in other words, was overly context dependent and thus not flexible. Context dependence may also account for why students in Professor Kozol's class failed to phonetically transcribe their lines. If they associated phonetic transcription narrowly with the physical context in which they learned it (speech class), it may not have occurred to them to carry this practice over to their acting class.

Second, students may fail to transfer relevant skills, knowledge, or practices if they do not have a robust understanding of underlying principles and deep structure—in other words, if they understand what to do but not why. This might explain some of the problems Professor Kozol encountered in the story at the beginning of this chapter. If Professor Kozol's students understood some of the functions of vocal warm-ups (for example, to prevent vocal strain when singing) but not others (such as to relax the voice for greater emotional expressivity), they might not have recognized the applicability of this practice to the assigned task. In other words, an incomplete understanding of the functions of this practice might have affected their ability to apply it appropriately in new contexts.

Fortunately, much of the same research that documents transfer failure also suggests instructional approaches that can bolster transfer. For example, studies have shown that students are better able to transfer learning to new contexts when they can combine concrete experience within particular contexts and abstract knowledge that crosscuts contexts (Schwartz et al., 1999). A classic study by Schoklow and Judd (in Judd, 1908) illustrates this point. The researchers asked two groups of students to throw darts at a target twelve inches under water. Predictably, the performance of both groups improved with practice. Then one group was taught the abstract principle of refraction, while the other was not. When asked to hit a target four inches under water, the group that knew the abstract principle adjusted their strategies and significantly outperformed the other group. Knowing the abstract principle helped students transfer their experiential knowledge beyond the immediate context in which it was learned and to adjust their strategies for new conditions. Similarly, when students have the opportunity to apply what they learn in multiple contexts, it fosters less context-dependent, more "flexible" knowledge (Gick & Holyoak, 1983).

Structured comparisons—in which students are asked to compare and contrast different problems, cases, or scenarios—have also been shown to facilitate transfer. For example, Loewenstein, Thompson, and Gentner (2003) asked two groups of management students to analyze negotiation training cases. One group analyzed each case individually; the other group was asked to compare cases. The researchers found that the group that compared cases demonstrated dramatically more learning than the group that considered them individually. Why? Because when students were asked to compare cases, they had to recognize and identify the deep features of each case that would make it analogous or non-analogous to other cases. Having identified those deep features, students could link the cases to abstract negotiation principles, which then allowed them to learn more deeply and apply what they learned more effectively. Other methods that

110

have been found to facilitate transfer include analogical reasoning (Gentner, Holyoak, & Kokinov, 2001; Catrambone & Holyoak, 1989; Holyoak & Koh, 1987; Klahr & Carver, 1988), using visual representations to help students see significant features and patterns (Biederman & Shiffrar, 1987), and asking students to articulate causal relationships (Brown & Kane, 1988).

Finally, research indicates that minor prompts on the part of the instructor can aid transfer. In Gick and Holyoak's (1980) study, college students were presented with a passage describing a military conundrum in which an army is trying to capture a fortress and must ultimately divide into small groups, approach from different roads, and converge simultaneously on the fortress. After memorizing this information, students were presented with a medical problem that required a similar solution (the use of multiple laser beams coming from different angles and converging on a tumor). Despite having just encountered the military solution, the large majority of students did not apply what they had learned to the medical problem. Even though the physical, social, and temporal contexts were the same, the knowledge domains (military strategy versus medicine) and functional contexts (storming a fortress versus treating a tumor) were sufficiently different that students did not recognize their analogous structures or think to apply knowledge from one problem to the other. However, when students were asked to think about the medical problem in relation to the military one, they could solve it successfully (Gick & Holyoak, 1980). Similar results have been shown in other studies as well (Perfetto et al., 1983; Klahr & Carver, 1988; Bassok, 1990). A little prompting, in other words, can go a long way in helping students apply what they know.

Implications of This Research   Transfer does not happen easily or automatically. Thus, it is particularly important that we "teach for transfer"—that is, that we employ instructional strategies that reinforce a robust understanding of deep structures and underlying principles, provide sufficiently diverse contexts in which to apply these principles, and help students make appropriate connections between the knowledge and skills they possess and new contexts in which those skills apply. We consider some specific strategies under the heading, "Strategies to Facilitate Transfer," later in this chapter.

WHAT STRATEGIES DOES THE RESEARCH SUGGEST?

The following strategies include those faculty can use to (1) decompose complex tasks so as to build students' skills more systematically and to diagnose areas of weakness, (2) help students combine and integrate skills to develop greater automaticity and fluency, and (3) help students learn when to apply what they have learned.

Strategies to Expose and Reinforce Component Skills

Push Past Your Own Expert Blind Spot   Because of the phenomenon of expert blind spot, instructors may have little conscious awareness of all the component skills and knowledge required for complex tasks. Consequently, when teaching students, instructors may inadvertently omit skills, steps, and information that students need in order to learn and perform effectively. To determine whether you have identified all the component skills relevant for a particular task, ask yourself: "What would students have to know—or know how to do—in order to achieve what I am asking of them?" Keep asking this question as you decompose the task until you have identified all the key component skills. Many instructors stop decomposing the task too soon and thus fail to identify critical component skills their students might lack.

Enlist a Teaching Assistant or Graduate Student to Help with Task Decomposition As experts in our disciplinary domains, we operate in a state of "unconscious competence" that can make it difficult to see the component skills and knowledge that students must acquire to perform complex tasks. Graduate students, on the other hand, tend to be at the *"conscious* competence" stage (see Sprague and Stewart's model as illustrated in Figure 4.2), and thus may be more aware than you are of the necessary component skills. Thus, it can be helpful to ask a teaching assistant or graduate student to help you decompose complex tasks.

Talk to Your Colleagues Another way to overcome expert blind spot is to compare notes with colleagues to see how *they* decompose complex tasks, such as research papers, oral presentations, or design projects. Although your colleagues have their own expert blind spots to overcome, they may have identified skills that you have not. Thus it can be helpful to talk with them and ask to examine their syllabi, assignments, and performance rubrics for ideas. (See Appendix C for information on rubrics.)

Enlist the Help of Someone Outside Your Discipline Also helpful when you are attempting to decompose a complex task is to ask someone outside your discipline to help you review your syllabus, lectures, assignments, and other teaching materials. A person (such as a teaching consultant or colleague outside your discipline) who is intelligent and insightful but does not share your disciplinary expertise *or* its blind spots can help you identify areas in which you may have inadvertently omitted or skipped over important component knowledge or skills.

113

Explore Available Educational Materials   Many, though not all, of the component skills necessary for a particular task are specific to disciplinary context. Depending on your discipline, there may be published work that presents completed task analyses that can help you think about the component skills in your course. Check journals on teaching in your discipline.

Focus Students' Attention on Key Aspects of the Task   If students are expending their cognitive resources on extraneous features of the task, it diverts those resources from the germane aspects of the task. Thus, one way to help students manage cognitive load is to clearly communicate your goals and priorities for particular assignments by telling students where to put their energies—and also where not to. For example, if you assign students in your architecture class a task meant to help them explore a wide range of creative design solutions, you might explicitly instruct them not to spend time getting the details right or making their designs aesthetically pleasing, but rather to generate as many different design solutions as possible. Rubrics that spell out your performance criteria for particular assignments can help students focus their cognitive resources where they best serve your learning objectives. (See Appendix C for more information on and examples of rubrics.)

Diagnose Weak or Missing Component Skills   To assess your students' competence vis-à-vis component skills and knowledge, consider giving a diagnostic exam or assignment early in the semester (see Appendix A for information on developing student self-assessments). If a small number of students lack key skills, you can alert them to this fact and direct them to resources (academic support on campus, tutoring, additional readings) to help them develop these skills on their own. If a large number of students lack key prerequisite skills, you might opt to devote some class time to addressing them or hold an informal review session outside class. You can also assess your students' understanding of subject matter in your own course by analyzing the patterns of mistakes students make on exams, papers, oral presentations, and so on. The information you gain from these kinds of ongoing analyses can help you design instruction to reinforce critical skills, or improve the next iteration of the course.

Provide Isolated Practice of Weak or Missing Skills   Once you have identified important missing skills, create opportunities (such as homework assignments or in-class activities) for students to practice those skills in relative isolation. For example, if students are writing conclusions to their papers that simply restate the topic paragraph or descend into banalities—and you perceive this as an obstacle to achieving one of your learning objectives—you might (1) ask students to read the conclusions of several articles and discuss what makes them compelling or not compelling, (2) have them write a conclusion for an article that is missing one, and (3) critique their conclusions together. Similarly, in a class focused on quantitative problem solving, you might ask students to plan a problem-solving strategy without actually carrying it out. This focuses their energies on one aspect of the task—planning—and builds that particular skill before allowing students to jump into calculations.

Strategies to Build Fluency and Facilitate Integration

Give Students Practice to Increase Fluency   If diagnostic assessments, such as those described above, reveal that students can perform key component skills but they continue to do them inefficiently and with effort, you might want to assign exercises specifically designed to increase students' speed and efficiency. In a language class, for example, this might involve asking students to drill verb conjugations until they come easily. In a quantitative class, it might involve assigning supplementary problem-solving exercises to build automaticity in a basic mathematical skill—vector arithmetic, for example. When providing practice intended to increase automaticity, explain your rationale to your students. For example: "It is important not only that you can do these calculations, but also that you can do them quickly and easily, so that when you are solving a complex problem you do not get bogged down in the basic mathematical calculations. These exercises are to increase your efficiency." You should also be explicit about the level of fluency you expect students to achieve, as illustrated in these examples: "You should practice these to the point that you can solve an entire page of problems in less than fifteen minutes without the use of a calculator" or "You should be able to scan a thirty-page journal article and extract its main argument in less than five minutes."

Temporarily Constrain the Scope of the Task It can be helpful to minimize cognitive load temporarily while students develop greater fluency with component skills or learn to integrate them. One way to do this is by initially reducing the size or complexity of the task. For example, a piano teacher might ask students to practice only the right hand part of a piece, and then only the left hand part, before combining them. If the student still struggles to integrate the two parts successfully, the teacher might ask her to practice only a few measures, until she develops greater fluency at coordinating both hands. Similarly, a typography instructor might give an assignment early in the semester in which students must create a design using only font and font size but no other design elements. Once students have practiced these particular components, the instructor can then add additional

116

elements, such as color or animations, adding to the level of complexity as students gain fluency in the component skills.

Explicitly Include Integration in Your Performance Criteria
As we have seen, integration is a skill in itself. Thus, it is reasonable to include the effective integration of component parts in your performance rubrics for complex tasks. For example, on the rubric for a group project and presentation, you could include the seamless integration of every member's contribution to the project, or a consistent voice, as features of high-quality performance (see Appendix C for information on rubrics). Likewise, on an analytical paper, you could identify the coherence or "flow" of ideas as an important dimension of performance.

Strategies to Facilitate Transfer

Discuss Conditions of Applicability Do not assume that because students have learned a skill that they will automatically know where or when to apply it. It is important to clearly and explicitly explain the contexts in which particular skills are—or are not—applicable (for example, when one might collect qualitative versus quantitative data, use a T-test, or transcribe lines of dialogue phonetically). Of course, there will not always be a single "best" solution or approach, in which case it is helpful to ask students to discuss the pros and cons of different approaches (for example, "What objectives are and are not served by staging a play in a minimalist style?" or "What do you gain and lose by using a questionnaire instead of a face-to-face interview?"). Explicitly discussing the conditions and contexts of applicability can help students transfer what they know more successfully.

Give Students Opportunities to Apply Skills or Knowledge in Diverse Contexts When students practice applying skills

117

across diverse contexts it can help them overcome context-dependence and prepare them better to transfer that skill to novel contexts. So when possible, give students opportunities to apply a particular skill (or knowledge) in multiple contexts. For example, if you are teaching students a set of marketing principles, you might assign multiple case studies to give students the opportunity to apply those principles in the context of very different industries.

Ask Students to Generalize to Larger Principles   To increase the flexibility of knowledge and thus the likelihood of transfer, encourage students to generalize from specific contexts to abstract principles. You can do this by asking questions such as "What is the physical principle that describes what is happening here?" or "Which of the theories we have discussed is exemplified in this article?" Asking students to step back from the details of particular problems or cases and focus on larger principles can help them reflect on and, one hopes, transfer and adapt the skills they are learning to new contexts.

Use Comparisons to Help Students Identify Deep Features
Students may fail to transfer knowledge or skills appropriately if they cannot recognize the meaningful features of the problem. Providing your students with structured comparisons—of problems, cases, scenarios, or tasks—helps them learn to differentiate the salient features of the problem from the surface characteristics. For example, in a physics class you might present two problems in which the surface features are similar (they both involve pulleys) but the physics principles at work are different (coefficient of friction versus gravity). Or you could present two problems in which the surface features are different (one involves a pulley and one involves an inclined plane) but the physics principle is the same. Structured comparisons such as these encourage students to identify and focus on underlying, structural similari-

118

ties and differences and caution them not to be fooled by super-ficial features. This can then help them recognize the deep features of novel problems and thus facilitate successful transfer.

Specify Context and Ask Students to Identify Relevant Skills or Knowledge   Help students make connections between prob-lems they might confront and the skills and knowledge they possess by giving them a context—a problem, case, or scenario—and asking them to generate knowledge and skills (for instance, rules, procedures, techniques, approaches, theories, or styles) that are appropriate to that context. For example, "Here is a statistical problem; which of the tests you know could be used to solve it?" or "Here is an anthropological question you might want to inves-tigate; what particular data-gathering methods could you use to answer it?" Then vary the context by asking "what if" questions, such as "What if this involved dependent variables? Could we still use this test?" or "What if the subjects of your research were chil-dren? Could you still employ that methodology?" It is not always necessary for students to *do* the actual application (apply the sta-tistical test, conduct the ethnographic research) but rather to *think* about the features of the problem in relation to particular applications.

Specify Skills or Knowledge and Ask Students to Identify Contexts in Which They Apply   To further help students make connections between skills and knowledge they possess and appropriate applications, turn the strategy described above around. In other words, specify a particular skill (for instance, a technique, formula, or procedure) or piece of knowledge (for example, a theory or rule) and ask students to generate contexts in which that skill or knowledge would apply. For example, "Give me three statistical problems that a T-test could help you solve" or "Here is a data-gathering method used in ethnographic research;

119

what questions could it be used to investigate?" Again, it is not necessary for students to do the actual application, but rather to think about the applicability of particular skills and knowledge to particular problems.

Provide Prompts to Relevant Knowledge   Sometimes students possess skills or knowledge that are relevant to a new problem or situation but do not think to apply what they know. Small prompts to relevant knowledge and skills (such as "Where have we seen this style of brushwork before?" or "Would this concept be relevant to anything else we have studied?" or "Think back to the bridge example we discussed last week") can help students make connections that facilitate transfer. Over time, prompts from the instructor may become unnecessary as students learn to look for these connections on their own.

SUMMARY

In this chapter we have argued that in order to develop mastery, students must acquire a set of component skills, practice combining and integrating these components to develop greater fluency and automaticity, and then understand the conditions and contexts in which they can apply what they have learned. Students need to have these three elements of mastery taught and reinforced through practice. However, because instructors have often lost conscious awareness of these aspects of expert practice, they may inadvertently neglect them in their instruction. Consequently, it is of particular importance that instructors deliberately regain awareness of these elements of mastery so they can teach their students more effectively.

CHAPTER 5

What Kinds of Practice and Feedback Enhance Learning?

When Practice Does Not Make Perfect ...

I teach a public policy course to juniors, and I believe strong communication skills are essential to moving up the ranks in the public sector. As a result, I require my students to write frequently. The three papers I assign focus on the different types of writing my students will potentially do: a policy briefing, a persuasive memo to their boss, and an editorial for a newspaper. I had expected the students' writing on these assignments to be at least decent because all of our students are required to take two writing courses in their first year. Then, when I saw the serious problems in their first papers, I thought at least I could help them improve. So I have been spending an enormous amount of time grading and writing margin comments throughout their papers, but it does not seem to be doing any good: the second and third assignments are just as bad as the first. As much as I think these assignments are useful because they prepare students for their future professional lives, I am ready to nix them because the students' writing is so poor and my efforts are bringing about little or no improvement.

Professor Norman Cox

They Just Do Not Listen!

Last semester, when I taught Medical Anthropology, the students' research presentations were all glitz and very little substance. So this time, because this project is worth 50 percent of their final grade, I tried to forewarn my students: "Do not be seduced by technology; focus on substantive anthropological arguments and create engaging presentations." And yet, it happened again. Last Tuesday, student after student got up in front of the class with what *they* believed to be engaging presentations—fancy fonts in their PowerPoint slides, lots of pictures swishing on and off the screen, embedded video clips, and so on. It was clear they had spent hours perfecting the visuals. Unfortunately, although their presentations were visually stunning, the content was very weak. Some of the students had not done thorough research, and those who did tended merely to describe their findings rather than craft an argument. In other cases, students' arguments were not supported by sufficient evidence, and most of the images they included were not even connected to the research findings. I thought I was clear in telling them what I wanted and did not want. What is it going to take to make them listen?

Professor Tanya Strait

WHAT IS GOING ON IN THESE STORIES?

In both stories, the professors and their students seem to be putting in time and effort without reaping much benefit. For example, Professor Cox makes lengthy comments on his students' writing but fails to see any improvement across assignments. Professor Strait's students spend an inordinate amount of time on aspects of the presentation that actually matter least to her, despite the guidance she gave them. And both professors are understandably frustrated that students' learning and performance is not up to expectations. A theme running through both stories is that time is being misspent—just the kind of mistake that neither students nor instructors can afford to make.

In the first story, Professor Cox's students probably enter his course with only basic writing skills. Unfortunately, even though the students may begin to develop additional writing skills through the practice they get during the first writing assignment, these new skills are not built upon through the later assignments. Recall that Professor Cox's assignments involve different genres (policy briefing, memo, and editorial). This means they involve somewhat different writing skills to address the distinct goals, audiences, and writing styles specific to each (see Chapter Four). Moreover, even though Professor Cox gives plenty of comments on his students' papers, the students probably have little opportunity to incorporate this feedback into further practice because each subsequent assignment is so different from the previous ones.

In the second story, Professor Strait tells her students that their arguments should have substance and their presentations should be engaging. However, her students seem not to understand what constitutes a substantive anthropological argument based on thorough research or what characteristics she identifies with engaging presentations. Although it is true that Professor Strait's students have spent the bulk of the semester reading and analyzing anthropological arguments, they have had relatively little opportunity to conduct library research and construct arguments of their own. So this partly explains their disconnect. Similarly, although these students have accumulated a good deal of prior experience giving oral presentations, they have not done so earlier in her course, so they mistakenly equate putting glitz in their presentations with what Professor Strait wants. Thus, the students probably have only minimal skill at argument construction and yet great familiarity with applying technical skills to prepare PowerPoint slides (for example, adding animations, pictures, and sound). Thus, it appears that these students are falling back on the more comfortable task of working on visuals at the expense of articulating an argument in their presentations. Professor Strait reasonably assumes that her warnings should be sufficient to guide students, but students often need significantly more guidance and structure than we would expect in order to direct their efforts productively. With only one chance to "get it right" with regard to this large-scale project, these students end up losing a key learning opportunity.

WHAT PRINCIPLE OF LEARNING IS AT WORK HERE?

We all know that practice and feedback are essential for learning. Unfortunately, the biggest constraint in providing sufficient practice and feedback to students is the time it takes—both on the part of students and faculty. Although we cannot control the length of a semester or class period, we can be more *efficient* in designing practice opportunities and giving feedback. Thus, this chapter focuses on ways to "work smarter" by exploring what kinds of practice and feedback are most productive.

It is important to acknowledge that all practice is not equal. In particular, there are more and less effective ways students can practice. Consider two music students who spend the same amount of time practicing a piece after having made several errors in a difficult passage. If one of the students practices for an hour, spending the majority of that time working on the difficult passage and then playing that passage in the context of the whole piece, this student will be likely to show sizeable performance gains. However, if the other student spends the same hour but uses that time to play through the whole piece a few times, much of that time will be spent suboptimally by practicing parts of the piece that were already mastered. This is reminiscent of Professor Strait's students, who seem to spend much of their time on what they already know—how to make fancy PowerPoint slides—only to miss their main chance at practicing less developed skills. In other words, *how* students spend their time on a learning activity (either in or out of class) determines the benefits they gain.

This problem of unproductive practice is even worse when students fail to receive sufficient feedback along the way. Think about the first music student who spent considerable time on the problematic passage rather than playing the whole piece multiple times. Even though this student's approach had greater potential to fix all the errors, this student could have introduced new errors without realizing it because no feedback was provided. In this way, lacking feedback, the first student's practice actually could have entrenched new, bad habits. This example highlights the critical role that feedback plays in keeping learners' practice moving toward improvement. In other words, students need both productive practice *and* effective feedback.

> **Principle**: Goal-directed *practice coupled with* targeted *feedback are critical to learning.*

At one level, this principle states the obvious: practice is important, and feedback is helpful to learning. To be clear about terminology, we define "practice" as any activity in which students engage their knowledge or skills (for example, creating an argument, solving a problem, or writing a paper). We define "feedback" as information given to students about their performance that guides future behavior. However, the full potential of practice and

125

feedback is not realized unless the two are effectively combined. For example, Professor Cox provides an enormous amount of feedback, but it is not coordinated with practice opportunities in which students could incorporate the feedback and refine a repeated set of skills. In contrast, when practice and feedback are focused on the same aspects of students' performance, students have the chance to practice and refine a consistent body of new knowledge and skill. Figure 5.1 depicts this interaction as a cycle: practice produces observed performance that, in turn, allows for

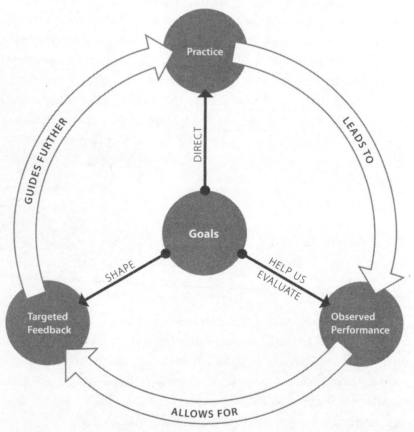

Figure 5.1. Cycle of Practice and Feedback

targeted feedback, and then the feedback guides further practice. This cycle is embedded within the context of learning goals that ideally influence each aspect of the cycle. For example, goals can direct the nature of focused practice, provide the basis for evaluating observed performance, and shape the targeted feedback that guides students' future efforts.

Although practice and feedback ideally go hand in hand—as this chapter's principle and Figure 5.1 indicate—each has a sizeable body of literature. So we discuss the research in two major sections below—one on practice and the other on feedback—and highlight the importance of their coordination.

WHAT DOES THE RESEARCH TELL US ABOUT PRACTICE?

Research has shown that learning and performance are best fostered when students engage in practice that (a) focuses on a specific goal or criterion for performance, (b) targets an appropriate level of challenge relative to students' current performance, and (c) is of sufficient quantity and frequency to meet the performance criteria. The following sections focus on these three characteristics of practice.

Focusing Practice on a Specific Goal or Criterion

Research shows that the amount of time someone spends in *deliberate practice* is what predicts continued learning in a given field, rather than time spent in more generic practice (Ericsson, Krampe, & Tescher-Romer, 2003). One of the key features of deliberate practice is that it involves working toward specific goals. As an illustration of the power of such goal-oriented practice, research shows that world-class musicians spend much of their time

127

engaging in rather demanding practice activities, continually monitoring their performance toward a particular goal, and then, once it is achieved, pushing themselves to strive for a new goal (Ericsson & Lehmann, 1996; Ericsson & Charness, 1994). In contrast, we all know of people who have studied a musical instrument—even spending considerable time practicing it—but who do not achieve a very high level of performance. Ericsson's explanation of these contrasting paths is that those who spend their considerable practice time working deliberately toward a specific goal tend to go on to be expert musicians, whereas those who do not engage in such deliberate practice do not.

Intuitively, it makes sense that having specific goals for practice would be helpful to learning. Goals provide students with a focus for their learning, which leads to more time and energy going to that area of focus. Consistent with this, Rothkopf and Billington (1979) found that students who had specific goals when they were learning from a text paid more attention to passages that were relevant to their goals and hence learned those passages better. Another advantage of having a goal to direct one's learning is that one can monitor (and hence adjust) one's progress toward that goal along the way (see Chapter Seven).

A key challenge in providing goal-directed practice is that instructors often think they are conveying specific goals to students when, in fact, they are not. This is natural because, as experts, we often see things very differently from our students (see Chapter Four), and so we tend not to recognize when our stated goals are unclear to students or when students are likely to misinterpret our criteria. A case in point is Professor Strait, who thought she was being clear by advising her students to focus on "substantive anthropological arguments" and "engaging presentations"—two ideas that carried specific meaning in her field of expertise. However, her students did not share that expertise, so they did not share her sense of the specific goals for their work. Without a clear idea of what Professor Strait wanted, the students "filled in the blanks" based on their prior experience (see Chapter One). Unfortunately, in this case, students' interpretations of the goals led them to spend their time in a way that gave more practice to skills they already had developed (such as creating glitzy PowerPoint presentations) and less practice to skills they needed to develop (such as creating anthropological arguments).

When instructors do not clearly articulate their goals, it is difficult for students to know what (or how) to practice. For example, giving students the goal of "understanding a key concept" tells rather little about the nature or level of understanding students should be trying to attain. In contrast, the goals of "recognizing when a key concept is at issue" or "explaining the key concept to a particular audience" or "applying the key concept to solve problems" are more concrete and directive. Note that these more specifically stated goals share several key features. First, they all are stated in terms of something students *do*, which automatically leads to more concrete specifications that students can more easily interpret correctly. Second, all of these goals are stated in such a way that students' performance can be monitored and measured (by instructors as well as students themselves), which enables the provision of feedback to help students refine their performance or learning. For more information on articulating effective learning goals (also called learning outcomes or objectives), see Appendix D.

The notion of articulating goals in a measureable way still leaves open the question (to students and instructors) of *how much* of a particular measureable quality is enough for the goal to be achieved. Research has shown that clearly specified performance criteria can help direct students' practice and ultimately their learning. For example, Goodrich Andrade (2001) found that creating a rubric (a clear description of the characteristics associated with different levels of performance; see Appendix C) and sharing it with students when an assignment is distributed leads to better outcomes—both in terms of the quality of work produced and students' knowledge of the qualities associated with good work.

An important caveat here, however, is that the goals one specifies must be in accord with what one really wants students to learn. For example, Nelson (1990) studied a case in which students were given detailed specifications for a research paper, such as the requirement to include at least three pieces of evidence supporting their argument. In writing their papers, students took this and other similar prescriptions to heart and included the required pieces of evidence in their writing. An important missing piece, however, was that the paper assignment did not specify higher-level goals such as having a well-organized paper or making a coherent argument. Thus, although these students included the required pieces of evidence in their papers, they tended to fall short on other important criteria. A key implication of this work is that explicitly communicating goals for students' performance can indeed guide their work, but one must be sure that those goals are ones that will support students in what they need to do and learn.

Identifying the Appropriate Level of Challenge for Practice

Specifying goals and criteria is not enough. To ensure that students' practice has a significant effect on learning, the practice they do should be at an appropriate level of challenge and, as necessary, accompanied by the appropriate amount and type of support. An appropriate level of challenge is neither too hard (the student struggles, makes many errors, and possibly gives up) nor too easy (the student completes the goal without much effort and

130

is not pushed to improve). This relates to the notion of deliberate practice mentioned earlier. As it turns out, deliberate practice more specifically is defined as working toward a *reasonable yet challenging goal* (Ericsson, Krampe, & Tesch-Romer, 2003).

Identifying the appropriate level of challenge seems possible, albeit potentially time consuming, to accomplish in one-on-one teaching and learning situations. Indeed, research has shown that the success of one-on-one tutoring is in large part driven by this capacity to tailor instruction to an individual student's needs (Anderson, Corbett, Koedinger, & Pelletier, 1995; Bloom, 1984; Merrill, Reiser, Ranney, & Trafton, 1992). Instructors who, given practical constraints, cannot provide different levels of challenge for individual students will be glad to know that research has also shown benefits from adjusting the difficulty of a practice task to fit students' needs at the group level. In one study, Clarke, Ayres, and Sweller (2005) designed an instructional unit to teach students mathematical concepts and procedures through the use of a spreadsheet application. Instruction was either sequential (focused on learning spreadsheet skills first and then using those skills to learn the mathematics) or concurrent (learning and using these skills simultaneously). They found that, for students with little prior knowledge of spreadsheets, the concurrent learning condition was too demanding; these students showed better mathematics learning and performance in the sequential condition, where the tasks were presented in isolation, making the challenge level more reasonable. Correspondingly, the opposite pattern held for more knowledgeable students. These results reinforce the idea that when novices are given too great a challenge, learning is hampered. This was probably part of the problem faced by Professor Strait's students, who were asked to take on challenges they had not practiced before (doing research in medical anthropology, constructing an argument of their own, and creating an engaging presentation).

Given a particular instructional activity, then, how can one effectively adjust it to target the appropriate level of challenge for different students, particularly those students who might not be quite ready to take on the activity in its full form? Research has shown that adding structure and support—also called *instructional scaffolding*—to a practice activity in or out of class promotes learning when it helps students practice the target skills at an appropriate level of challenge. This relates to Vygotsky's Zone of Proximal Development, which defines the optimal level of challenge for a student's learning in terms of a task that the student cannot perform successfully on his or her own but could perform successfully with some help from another person or group. A research study by Palincsar and Brown (1984) shows the success of this approach in helping students who were learning to read texts actively rather than passively. In particular, the researchers developed a protocol for pairs of students to follow in which students switched back and forth between the role of teacher and student, with the "teacher" asking the "student" a set of questions designed to exercise four strategic subskills of active reading—questioning, clarifying, summarizing, and predicting. These researchers found that when active reading skills were explicitly supported in this way, students' overall comprehension and retention improved markedly.

Research also indicates that instructional support does not need to come directly from another person to be helpful. For instance, Bereiter and Scardamalia developed a set of written prompts to help writing students target their efforts on two oft-neglected stages of the writing process: planning and revision. Because students did not naturally engage in these two stages on their own, following the prompts shifted their attention and effort toward (a) generating, refining, and elaborating their ideas and (b) evaluating their own writing, diagnosing problems, and deciding on revisions. As a result, students' writing process and product showed significant improvements, including a ten-fold increase in the frequency of idea-level revisions (Bereiter & Scardamalia, 1987). This set of research results suggests that if Professor Strait had employed various kinds of instructional scaffolds to support her students in completing their final project presentations, they probably would have spent their practice time more effectively, learned more from it, and lived up to her expectations on the final project presentation.

Another advantage of finding an appropriate challenge level for students' practice is that it can help students remain motivated to sustain their efforts (see Chapter Three). For example, if a challenge is too great, learners may have a negative expectation for success and hence become disengaged and apathetic. In contrast, if students feel that the challenge is reasonable, they will likely hold a positive expectation for success that will increase their tendency to persevere and work hard for the goal. Finally, engaging in a task that is at the right level of challenge for a person's knowledge and skills is one of the key predictors of *flow*—the state of consciousness in which a person is totally engaged in and experiencing deep enjoyment of a particular task (Csikszentmihalyi, 1991).

Accumulating Practice

In addition to identifying the two features that make practice most productive—goal-directed and appropriately challenging—research in this area also reiterates the importance of *time on task.* In other words, even if students have engaged in high-quality practice, they still need a sufficient *quantity* of practice for the benefits to accumulate (Healy, Clawson, & McNamara, 1993; Martin, Klein, & Sullivan, 2007). The idea that the benefits of practice accumulate only gradually may seem obvious, but the practical constraints of time and resources often lead faculty to move from concept to concept or skill to skill rather quickly, giving students no more than a single opportunity to practice each. For example, Professor Cox is giving his students exposure to multiple genres, but this comes at the expense of giving students only a single opportunity to develop their skills at writing in each of the genres he has assigned. If his goal is to simply expose students to the three different genres, without expecting them to gain proficiency in any of them, then the design of his activities is appropriate. But if his goal is for students—by the end of the course—to be able to write in each of the three genres at a professional level, then they would need more time on task.

Generally speaking, both professors and students underestimate the need for practice. Students often assume that when they can perform a task on one occasion in one context, their knowledge is secure when, in fact, it is much more difficult than that (see Chapter Four). It takes much more than one trial to learn something new, especially if the goal is for that new knowledge to be retained across time and transferred to new contexts.

Although it is true that the benefits of practice accrue gradually, it is important to note that the knowledge or skill gained by a given amount of additional practice often depends on where the student is in his or her learning process. As Figure 5.2 indicates, the early and late phases of learning tend to show relatively little effect of practice relative to the middle phase. These flatter portions at both ends of the curve tend to occur for two reasons.

The first reason is that the measures students often use to monitor their learning, such as accuracy, tend to be less sensitive at the extremes. So even though learning may be occurring, students do not see evidence of the change and hence feel like they are at a plateau. For example, consider a student who has just started learning to play the violin. Even though this student may be improving in several ways (better recall of the finger positions for different notes, increased accuracy in placement of the bow),

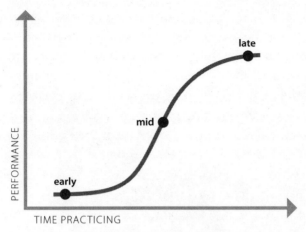

Figure 5.2. Unequal Effects of Practice on Performance

the sound produced may be so poor that improvements are hard to detect. Or imagine a student learning to program in a new computer language. Early on, the student may be making so many errors in programming syntax that it is hard to discern that he or she is formulating increasingly better algorithms. A similar lack of sensitivity to changing performance tends to occur on the upper end of learning because in this later phase students have managed to refine their performance to such a degree that they do not perceive changes, or the changes may occur in aspects of performance to which they are not attending. For example, advanced students may not recognize that they have actually improved in their ability to complete tasks more quickly and with less effort than they could before, or they may not realize that they are now able to reflect on their own processes *while* they complete complex tasks. Thus, because of this phenomenon at the early and late phases of learning, it is all the more important for instructors to highlight for students how their performance is changing or to provide more refined goals and criteria so that students can discern that they are improving.

135

The second reason that the learning curve in Figure 5.2 tends to be flatter at both ends is that the tasks we naturally assign for practice tend to pose too great a challenge for beginning students and too little challenge for accomplished students. As discussed earlier, when students engage in practice that is either too challenging or not challenging enough, their learning is hampered. This reason offers additional support for the notion of setting an appropriate level of challenge for students.

In contrast to the early and late phases of learning, the middle part of the curve in Figure 5.2 is steep, which indicates students are able to see large improvements in performance with additional practice. This is because students in this phase have a foundation of knowledge and skills upon which to build and because they are more likely to be able to detect improvements in their performance. This may also explain why students sometimes appear to "take off" in their development of knowledge and skill only after they have achieved a certain amount of learning.

Implications of This Research

Overall, the implications of the body of research on practice are that to achieve the most effective learning, students need *sufficient* practice that is *focused* on a specific goal or set of goals and is at an *appropriate level of challenge*. Given the constraints of time and resources that we must face, however, it is often difficult or impossible to increase students' practice time (either in or out of the class). Instead, the results in this chapter highlight the benefits of using a given amount of practice time more efficiently by focusing students' efforts on what they need to learn (rather than what they already know or may be more comfortable doing) and setting their goals for performance at a reasonable and productive level of challenge.

WHAT DOES THE RESEARCH TELL US ABOUT FEEDBACK?

Goal-directed practice alone is insufficient to foster students' learning. Goal-directed practice must be coordinated with targeted feedback in order to promote the greatest learning gains. The purpose of feedback is to help learners achieve a desired level of performance. Just as a map provides key information about a traveler's current position to help him or her find an efficient route to a destination, effective feedback provides information about a learner's current state of knowledge and performance that can guide him or her in working toward the learning goal. In other words, effective feedback can tell students *what* they are or are not understanding, *where* their performance is going well or poorly, and *how* they should direct their subsequent efforts.

Taking this map analogy a step further, imagine trying to find your way through a maze without any guiding information as to where you are relative to the entrance or exit; you could wander in circles without even realizing it, waste time, and become confused—even if you ultimately do find your way out of the maze. This situation is akin to the position that students are in without effective feedback. It is not surprising, then, that effective feedback can greatly facilitate students' learning. For example, consider two students who have the same misconception that leads them to solve several problems incorrectly. Suppose, however, that these two students receive feedback on their work at different times and with different content. One student solves all of these problems in a single, large homework assignment and, after submitting the assignment, gets it back a week later with the letter grade "C." He notices from the points marked off that he failed to get full credit for even a single problem, so he infers that he is totally lost on this topic. Suppose the other student is in a course

137

where the instructor includes a bit of problem-solving practice in each class session and then highlights some natural mistakes and how to remediate them after students have a chance to try a couple of problems. This student rather quickly gets some input from the instructor, indicating that in two of the practice problems he was making the same error. Once this is identified, the student is able to correct his understanding and then go on to solve that week's homework problems with this in mind.

Note that based on the different timing and content of the feedback, these two students may take very different paths from this point onward in the course. The first student, not realizing that it was only a single misconception that led to his level of performance, may believe he is unable to learn the current topic and hence skip any opportunities for further practice (for example, not bothering to study for the upcoming exam). The second student, armed with information about where he went wrong, can work on additional problems to strengthen his new understanding of this tricky issue. In other words, feedback at the right time and of the right nature can promote students' learning not only in the present but also in the future.

Consistent with this example, research points to two features of feedback that make students' learning more effective and efficient: content and timing. First, feedback should communicate to students where they are relative to the stated goals and what they need to do to improve. Second, feedback should provide this information when students can make the most use of it, based on the learning goals and structure of activities you have set for them. Like so many aspects of teaching and learning, there is no single approach to feedback that will work across the variety of situations students and instructors encounter. Rather, the content and timing of feedback need to be considered in terms of the learning goals we have for our students, students' incoming level of knowledge and proficiency, and the practical constraints of the course.

Research on what tends to make the content and timing of feedback most effective is discussed in the following two sections.

Communicating Progress and Directing Subsequent Effort

Feedback is most effective when it explicitly communicates to students about some specific aspects of their performance relative to specific target criteria, and when it provides information that helps students progress toward meeting those criteria. This kind of feedback, which informs students' subsequent learning, is often called *formative* feedback. In contrast, *summative* feedback is that which gives a final judgment or evaluation of proficiency, such as grades or scores.

Extending our earlier analogy between using a map to navigate and receiving feedback to learn, consider a more sophisticated navigational aid such as a global positioning system (GPS). A GPS has the capability of tracking a traveler's current position relative to a destination. To be helpful, a GPS needs to communicate more than the fact that the traveler is far away from the destination; ideally, it needs to identify how far the traveler is from the destination and provide directions to help the traveler reach it. Similarly, effective feedback needs to do more than simply tell a student that he or she is wrong; effective feedback involves giving students a clear picture of how their current knowledge or performance differs from the goal and providing information on adjustments that can help students adjust to reach the goal.

Research has long shown that feedback is more effective when it identifies particular aspects of students' performance they need to improve rather than providing a generic evaluation of performance, such as a grade or abstract praise or discouragement (Black & William, 1998; Cardelle & Corno, 1981). As illustrated by the example of the student who received a "C" with no comments on his homework, giving only a letter grade or numerical score tends not to be effective feedback. Although grades and scores provide some information on the *degree to which* students' performance has met the criteria, they do not explain *which aspects* did or did not meet the criteria and *how*. Moreover, feedback that is specific to the processes students are engaging in (for example, helping students to properly approach a problem or to detect their own errors; see Chapter Seven) has been associated with deeper learning (Balzer et al., 1989). In one study, students were learning to solve geometry problems on the computer, with feedback automatically provided whenever the computer detected an error in students' solutions. One group of students received generic messages indicating that they had made an error, and another group received specific information about their errors and how to remediate them. The group with the more targeted feedback significantly outperformed the generic feedback group on a post-test assessing problem-solving skills (McKendree, 1990).

At the other extreme, simply giving students lots of feedback about their performance is also not necessarily an example of effective feedback. This is because too much feedback tends to overwhelm students and fails to communicate which aspects of their performance deviate most from the goal and where they should focus their future efforts. For example, research has shown that too many comments in the form of margin notes on student writing are often counterproductive because students are either overwhelmed by the number of items to consider or because they focus their revision on a subset of the comments that involve detailed, easy-to-fix elements rather than more important conceptual or structure changes (Lamburg, 1980; Shuman, 1979).

Remember Professor Cox's lament of spending so much time making comments on his students' papers but seeing no improvement in later assignments? Providing too much information in his comments may have been part of the reason. In his case, giving fewer comments that addressed one or two top-priority issues probably would have provided his students with more targeted feedback. However, it is important to note that even if Professor Cox had given this kind of targeted feedback, it might not have been fully effective unless his students also had an opportunity to use the feedback in a rewrite or related assignment. The key idea here is that *targeted* feedback gives students prioritized information about how their performance does or does not meet the criteria so they can understand how to improve their future performance.

Indeed, the full benefits of feedback can only be realized when the feedback adequately directs students' subsequent practice *and* when students have the capacity to incorporate that feedback into further practice. Recall that in Professor Cox's course, students had only one opportunity to practice writing in each of the three genres he assigned. Although he may have conceived of this as repeated practice at the general skill of writing, these three assignments probably required rather different subsets of skills (see Chapter Four). So, even if Professor Cox had provided targeted feedback on the first assignment, students might not have benefited much from it unless they had an opportunity to carry it into the next assignment.

How could Professor Cox use feedback in a way that ties in with students' opportunities for further practice? One option is that he could have included more repetition of assignments within the same genre and then asked students to incorporate his feedback into subsequent assignments. Alternatively, he could have asked students to submit a rough draft of each assignment, made targeted comments on those drafts, and then explicitly articulated that the final draft's goal was to address his comments in the revision. This scenario highlights the interaction between feedback and practice. Indeed, one can conceive of the practice that follows targeted feedback as a particularly tailored form of goal-directed practice.

Timing Feedback Appropriately

Whereas the research just discussed involves the content of feedback, it is also important to consider the appropriate timing of feedback. This involves both *how soon* feedback is given (typically, earlier is better) as well as *how often* (typically, more frequently is better). The ideal timing of feedback, however, cannot be determined by any general rule. Rather, it is best decided in terms of what would best support the goals you have set for students' learning. For example, going back to our GPS analogy, it is clear that one of the key features of these devices is that they give feedback *when the driver needs it* to support the goal of reaching a particular destination as quickly as possible.

Generally, more frequent feedback leads to more efficient learning because it helps students stay on track and address their errors before they become entrenched. Ample research supports this conclusion (see Hattie & Timperley, 2007, for a review). However, given practical constraints, this is often difficult. Fortunately, research shows that even minimal feedback on students' writing can lead to better second drafts because the feedback gives students a better sense of what their readers do and do not understand (Traxler & Gernsbacher, 1992). This result highlights that giving even a modest amount of feedback, especially when it is given early, can be helpful. This result also suggests that if Professor Strait had established milestones early in her students' project work, it could have enabled her to offer feedback earlier on in the process, before her students went off track.

This research does not mean, however, that greater frequency of feedback is always better. Again, *timeliness* of the feedback is a significant factor. For example, consider a study in which college students were learning to write mathematical functions in a spreadsheet application (Mathan & Koedinger, 2005). The particular goal for students' learning in this situation was not only that they be able to write these functions accurately but also that they be able to recognize and fix their own errors. Students who received feedback immediately after they made a mistake scored lower on final assessments compared to students who received "delayed" feedback. Although surprising at first, this result makes sense when one realizes that the immediate feedback group was missing the opportunity to practice recognizing and repairing their own errors. In contrast, the students receiving delayed feedback had a chance to fix their own errors so they had more practice at the corresponding skills. That is, when the delayed feedback group made errors, feedback was given only when they (a) showed sufficient signs of not having recognized their error or (b) made multiple failed attempts at fixing their error. In this way, one could argue that even though it was not immediate, their feedback was given in a more timely manner relative to the learning goals at hand.

Implications of This Research

There are three key implications of this research on what makes feedback more effective. The feedback must (1) focus students on the key knowledge and skills you want them to learn, (2) be provided at a time and frequency when students will be most likely to use it, and (3) be linked to additional practice opportunities for students. As we saw in some of the sections above, each of these aspects of feedback must align with the goals you have set for students' learning. It is best to find a type and frequency of feedback that allows students to reap the benefits of feedback while staying actively engaged in monitoring their own learning—in other words, feedback that does not undermine students' progress in becoming independent, self-regulated learners. Giving too little detail in feedback can leave students unclear on what they need to do to improve, whereas giving too much detail can overwhelm them or mislead them as to what aspects are higher priority. Similarly, giving feedback too infrequently can leave students floundering without enough information to direct their learning, whereas giving feedback too frequently can potentially irritate students or lead them to depend on the feedback rather than on themselves.

In addition to balancing the amount and timing of feedback to make it most effective, it is often necessary to pay attention to the practical aspects of giving feedback. For example, the instructor's time in composing or tailoring feedback and the students' time in processing and responding to feedback is a key consideration in guiding how and when to give feedback. We must always consider both the pedagogical and practical consequences of feedback. Also, all feedback need not be tailored to individual students, and it need not all come from the instructor. We discuss a variety of strategies for feedback that are effective and feasible, including peer response, group feedback, and more.

WHAT STRATEGIES DOES THE RESEARCH SUGGEST?

Here we present strategies that can help you provide students with (1) goal-directed practice and (2) targeted feedback. In both cases, the focus is on how to do so in effective and efficient ways.

Strategies Addressing the Need for Goal-Directed Practice

Conduct a Prior Knowledge Assessment to Target an Appropriate Challenge Level Students come into our classes with a broad range of pre-existing knowledge, skills, and competencies. Giving a prior knowledge assessment (such as a survey, pretest, or early ungraded assignment) can help you gauge students' strengths and weaknesses in order to better target their practice at the right level (based on where they are, not where you wish they were). A performance assessment (for example, actual problems to solve or terms to define) will provide the best indication of what students actually know or can do, while a survey asking them about the level of their knowledge (for example, can they define or apply, do they know when to use) will give you a sense of what students *believe* they know or can do. (See Chapter One for additional, related strategies and Appendix A for more information on incorporating student self-assessments.)

Be More Explicit About Your Goals in Your Course Materials
Without specific goals for the course as a whole or for individual assignments, students often rely on their assumptions to decide how they should spend their time. This makes it all the more important to articulate your goals clearly (in your course syllabus and with each specific assignment), so students know what your expectations are and can use them to guide their practice. Students are more likely to use the goals to guide their practice when the goals are stated in terms of what students should be able to *do* at the end of an assignment or the course. (See Appendix D for more information on articulating learning goals.)

145

Use a Rubric to Specify and Communicate Performance Criteria   When students do not know what the performance criteria are, it is difficult for them to practice appropriately and to monitor their progress and understanding. A common approach to communicating performance criteria is through a *rubric—*a scoring tool that explicitly represents the performance expectations for a given assignment. A rubric divides the assigned work into component parts and provides clear descriptions of the characteristics of high-, medium-, and low-quality work associated with each component. (See Appendix C for more information on rubrics.)

Build in Multiple Opportunities for Practice   Because learning accumulates gradually with practice, multiple assignments of shorter length or smaller scope tend to result in more learning than a single assignment of great length or large scope. With the former, students get more opportunity to practice skills and can refine their approach from assignment to assignment based on feedback they receive. For example, this strategy can free you to think beyond the traditional term paper and be more creative in the variety and number of shorter writing assignments you require (for example, a letter, program notes, or a short policy memo). Bear in mind, however, that a single opportunity to practice a given kind of assignment is likely to be insufficient for students to develop the relevant set of skills, let alone to be able to incorporate your feedback on subsequent, related assignments.

Build Scaffolding into Assignments   In order to adjust a task so that it continues to target an appropriate level of challenge for students, provide scaffolding. Scaffolding refers to the process by which instructors give students instructional supports early in their learning, and then gradually remove these supports as students develop greater mastery and sophistication. One way to apply scaffolding to a more complex assignment is to ask students to first practice working on discrete phases of the task and, later, ask students to practice integrating them. (See Chapter Four.)

Set Expectations About Practice   Students can underestimate the amount of time an assignment requires. As a result, it is vital to provide students with guidelines for the amount, type, and level of practice required to master the knowledge or skills at the level you expect. There are at least two ways to help you estimate the time students will need. Some faculty members collect data by asking students, over a number of semesters, how long an assignment took to complete. They can then report to their current students the average and range of time spent by past students. Other faculty members adhere to a general rule of thumb that it takes students approximately three to four times as long as it would take them to complete an assignment. This ratio may vary from situation to situation, however, so it is worthwhile to try multiple strategies for this estimation and to adjust based on one's experience, as necessary.

Give Examples or Models of Target Performance   Building on the previous strategy, it can also be helpful to *show* students examples of what the target performance looks like (such as a model design, an effective paper, or a robust solution to a problem). Sharing samples of past student work can help students see how your performance criteria can be put into practice in an actual assignment. Such examples are even more powerful when you either highlight or annotate for students particular features of the sample assignment that "work."

Show Students What You Do *Not* Want   In addition to sharing exemplary models of target performance, it can be helpful to contrast those with examples of what you do *not* want, by illustrating common misinterpretations students have shown in the past or by explaining why some pieces of work do not meet your assignment goals. For example, in the case of writing or giving presentations, it is often helpful to share samples that are annotated to highlight weak features. Such samples can also be used to give students practice at distinguishing between high- and low-quality work. To get students more actively involved and check their understanding, you can ask students to grade a sample assignment by following a rubric (see Appendix C).

Refine Your Goals and Performance Criteria as the Course Progresses As students move through a course practicing various skills, you may need to add new challenges, refine your goals to meet students' continually changing proficiency, or both. For example, once students have acquired competency with a skill, you may want them to be able to apply that skill more quickly, with less effort, or in more diverse contexts. You need to continually articulate the increasingly sophisticated goals you want students to work toward.

Strategies Addressing the Need for Targeted Feedback

Look for Patterns of Errors in Student Work Within a class, students can often share common errors or misconceptions that only are revealed when you make a concerted effort to look for patterns. For example, you might identify an exam question that many students missed or a homework assignment that was particularly difficult for many students. You may also notice that during your office hours multiple students are asking the same type of question or are making the same kind of mistake. If you are grading student work, you have access to this information and can seek out the patterns of errors. If you have TAs grading, ask them to summarize any major patterns of errors or misconceptions and report these to you. Once you have identified common patterns across students, you can provide feedback to the class as a whole using the following strategies.

Prioritize Your Feedback   The question of exactly what information feedback should include is dependent on many aspects of the course context: your learning objectives (for the course and the particular assignment), level of students, what they most need to improve, and the time you have available. So the key to being efficient while still providing effective feedback is to think carefully about what information will be most useful to students at a particular point in time and to prioritize that information in your feedback. In many cases, it is not necessary or even best to give feedback on all aspects of students' performance but rather focus your feedback on key aspects of the assignment. One way to do this is to offer feedback on a single dimension at a time (for example, one aspect of presenting an argument, one piece of the design process, or one step in problem solving). This strategy avoids overwhelming students with too much feedback and enables them to engage in targeted practice—that is, with a specific goal in mind.

Balance Strengths and Weaknesses in Your Feedback Students are often unaware of the progress they are making, so communicating to them the areas where they are doing well or have improved is just as important as communicating to them the areas where they lack understanding or need further improvement. The positive feedback indicates which aspects of their knowledge and performance should be maintained and built upon, whereas the negative feedback indicates what aspects should be adjusted (and, ideally, how). Moreover, beginning with targeted feedback that is positive can increase students' sense of efficacy

149

and hence enhance their motivation. How you balance positive versus negative feedback for a given class or for a particular student should depend on your priorities and their needs.

Design Frequent Opportunities to Give Feedback   The prerequisite to giving frequent feedback is to provide multiple opportunities for students to practice using their knowledge and skills. More tasks of shorter length or smaller scope provide the frequency of feedback that allows students to refine their understanding. This also makes a more manageable workload for you and your students. As indicated in other strategies in this section, not all feedback needs to be focused on individual students or come from the instructor. These strategies reduce the load on instructors in giving frequent feedback.

Provide Feedback at the Group Level   Not all feedback has to be individual to be valuable. Although you might want to write notes on individual assignments (which takes more time and hence decreases how quickly you can get feedback to students), you might at times identify the most common errors that students committed, provide the group with this list, and discuss those errors. In a similar vein, you can show the group two examples of high-quality performance and discuss the features that make this work "A" level.

Provide Real-Time Feedback at the Group Level   In a classroom situation, especially large lectures, instructors often assume that it is impossible to give effective feedback. However, by posing questions to the class in a format that allows easy collection of their responses, instructors can overcome this challenge. You can collect students' responses quickly in a paper-based way (with color-coded index cards) or with interactive technology (often called personal response systems, or "clickers"). In either case, the instructor poses a question and students respond (either by raising the index card corresponding to their answer or by submitting their answer choices via clicker). The instructor can then easily glean the proportion of correct/incorrect answers (either by scanning the room for the different colors of index cards or viewing the computer screen that tallies the clicker responses). Based on this information, the instructor can decide how to give appropriate feedback to the class as a whole. For example, the instructor may simply indicate that there was a high proportion of incorrect answers and ask students to discuss the question in small groups before polling them again. Alternatively, the instructor might recognize a common misconception in students' responses and provide further explanation or examples, depending on the nature of the misconception.

Incorporate Peer Feedback   Not all feedback has to come from you to be valuable. With explicit guidelines, criteria, or a rubric, students can provide constructive feedback on each other's work. This can also help students become better at identifying the qualities of good work and diagnosing their own problems. Besides the advantages to students, peer feedback allows you to increase the frequency of feedback without increasing your load. Keep in mind, however, that for peer feedback to be effective, you need to clearly explain what it is, the rationale behind it, how students should engage in it, and—as this chapter attests—give students adequate practice with feedback on it for it to reach its potential. (For more information, see Appendix H.)

Require Students to Specify How They Used Feedback in Subsequent Work   Feedback is most valuable when students have the opportunity to reflect on it so they can effectively incorporate it into future practice, performance, or both. Because students often do not see the connection between or among

151

assignments, projects, exams, and so on, asking students to explicitly note how a piece of feedback impacted their practice or performance helps them see and experience the "complete" learning cycle. For example, some instructors who assign multiple drafts of papers require students to submit with each subsequent draft their commented-on prior draft with a paragraph describing how they incorporated the feedback. An analogous approach could be applied to a project assignment that included multiple milestones.

SUMMARY

In this chapter, we have tried to move beyond simple maxims such as "practice makes perfect" or "the more feedback, the better" in order to hone in on the critical features that make practice and feedback most effective. Key features of effective practice include (a) focusing on a specific goal or criterion for performance, (b) targeting an appropriate level of challenge relative to students' current performance, and (c) being of sufficient quantity and frequency so students' skills and knowledge have time to develop. Key features of effective feedback are that it (a) communicates to students where they are relative to the stated goals and what they need to do to improve and (b) provides this information to students when they can make the most use of it. Together, then, practice and feedback can work together such that students are continuing to work toward a focused goal and incorporating feedback received in a way that promotes further development toward the goal. When practice and feedback are carefully designed with all these features in mind, we can prioritize them appropriately and help make the learning-teaching process not only more effective but also more efficient.

CHAPTER 6

Why Do Student Development and Course Climate Matter for Student Learning?

End of Story

Yesterday in my Economics class, we were discussing an article about the cost of illegal immigration to the U.S. economy. The discussion was moving along at a brisk pace when one student, Gloria, began to intervene quite forcefully, saying the reading was biased and didn't represent the situation accurately. Another student, Danielle, responded: "Gloria, why do you always have to bring up race? Why can't we just discuss the figures in the articles without getting so defensive?" A third student, Kayla, who has been pretty quiet up to this point in the semester, said that, as far as she was concerned, illegal immigrants should be arrested and deported, "end of story." Her grandparents were Polish immigrants, she continued, and had come to the U.S. legally, worked hard, and made good lives for themselves, "but now this country is getting sucked dry by Mexican illegals who have no right to be here, and it's just plain wrong." At that point, the rest of the class got really quiet and I could see my three Hispanic students exchange furious, disbelieving looks. Annoyed, Gloria shot back: "Those 'illegals' you're talking about include some people very close to me, and you don't know anything about them." The whole thing erupted in an angry back-and-forth, with Gloria calling Kayla entitled and racist and Kayla looking close to tears. I tried to regain control of the class by asking Gloria to try to depersonalize the discussion and focus on the central economic issues, but when we returned to the discussion I couldn't get anyone to talk. Kayla and Gloria sat silently with their arms folded, looking down, and the rest of the class just looked uncomfortable. I know I didn't handle this situation well, but I really wish my students were mature enough to talk about these issues without getting so emotional.

Professor Leandro Battaglia

No Good Deed Goes Unpunished

There's been a lot of discussion in my department about how to get more female students into Electrical Engineering. This is something I believe is very important, so I've gone out of my way to support and encourage the women in my classes. I know engineering can be an intimidating environment for women, so I always try to provide extra help and guidance to female students when they're working on problem sets in small groups. I've also avoided calling on women in class, because I don't want to put them on the spot. So you can imagine my frustration when a student reported to me a few weeks ago that one of my teaching assistants had made a blatantly derogatory comment during recitation about women in engineering. I've had a lot of problems with this TA, who has very strong opinions and a tendency to belittle people he doesn't agree with, but I was particularly unhappy about this latest news. I chastised the TA, of course, and gave him a stern warning about future misconduct, but unfortunately the damage was already done: one female student in that recitation (who seemed particularly promising) has dropped the course and others have stopped speaking up in class. I braced myself for complaints on the early course evaluations I collected last week, and some students did complain about the sexist TA, but what really baffled me was that they complained about me too! One student wrote that I "patronized" female students while another wrote that the class was "unfair to us guys" since I "demanded more from the men in the course." I have no idea what to make of this and am beginning to think there's simply no way to keep everyone happy.

Professor Felix Guttman

WHAT IS GOING ON IN THESE TWO STORIES?

In both of the stories described above, unanticipated social and emotional dynamics in the classroom have complicated the learning experience. Although Professor Battaglia has assigned a reading that touches on a controversial topic, he expects his students to be able to discuss the material in terms of economic principles rather than personal experience and ethnic identity, which in his mind are mutually exclusive. What begins with an intellectual discussion of the reading quickly devolves into a highly charged emotional exchange about racial issues—in his mind, only marginally related to the course content—culminating in hurt feelings, discomfort, disengagement, and ultimately a complete collapse of the discussion. Professor Battaglia finds himself unable to rein in the chaos. The fracas that arises leaves him feeling helpless and wondering why students are unable to check their emotions at the door.

Professor Guttman's situation, however, is completely unrelated to his course content. Here we see a well-meaning instructor, doing his best to reach out to women, whom he worries (with some reason) may be marginalized in a male-dominated field. He is justifiably upset by the blatantly sexist behavior of his TA and addresses it immediately, yet he is unaware of how his students are perceiving his own behavior. In fact, his attempts to support female students by providing extra help and reduced pressure backfires: to the women in the class, it signals a lack of faith in their competence and abilities, while the men perceive it as just plain unfair to them. As a result, students seem dissatisfied and disaffected, to the point where classroom participation is negatively affected and one promising student has dropped the course altogether.

WHAT PRINCIPLE OF LEARNING IS AT WORK HERE?

Two interacting concepts are at the core of the two stories. The first is that of holistic student development, and the second is of classroom climate. As educators we are primarily concerned with fostering intellectual and creative skills in our students, but we must recognize that students are not only intellectual but also social and emotional beings, and that these dimensions interact within the classroom climate to influence learning and performance. Figure 6.1 summarizes this model. In both stories, emotions and social processes hamper the students' ability to engage productively with the material and to learn.

Students are still developing the full range of social and emotional skills. To some extent, people are always developing in those areas, but two considerations are important when dealing with college students. First, emotional and social processes are particularly salient during this phase of life. In fact, a preponderant body of research documents that the social and emotional

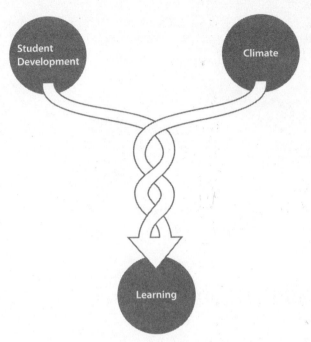

Figure 6.1. Interactive Effect of Student Development and Course Climate on Learning

gains that students make during college are considerably greater than the intellectual gains over the same span of time (Pascarella & Terenzini, 1991). Second, these emotions can overwhelm students' intellect if they have not yet learned to channel them productively.

Although we cannot control the developmental process, the good news is that if we understand it, we can shape the classroom climate in developmentally appropriate ways. Moreover, many studies have shown that the climate we create has implications for learning and performance. A negative climate may impede learning and performance, but a positive climate can energize students' learning (Pascarella & Terenzini, 1991).

> **Principle:** *Students' current level of development interacts with the social, emotional, and intellectual climate of the course to impact learning.*

As shown in Figure 6.1, student development and classroom climate interact with each other to affect learning. However, for expository purposes we review the research on student development and classroom climate separately. The two strands come together in the strategies section, where we provide pedagogical strategies that take both student development and classroom climate into account.

WHAT DOES THE RESEARCH TELL US ABOUT STUDENT DEVELOPMENT?

Just as the holistic movement in medicine calls for doctors to treat patients, not symptoms, student-centered teaching requires us to teach students, not content. Thus, it is important to recognize the complex set of social, emotional, and intellectual challenges that college students face. Recognition of these challenges does not mean that we are responsible for guiding students through all aspects of their social and emotional lives (for instance, we need not and should not be in the business of coaching students in financial planning or matters of the heart). However, by considering the implications of student development for teaching and learning we can create more productive learning environments.

Students between the ages of seventeen and twenty-two are undergoing momentous changes. As they make the transition from high school and learn to manage the intellectual demands of college, they must also learn to live independently from their parents; establish new social networks; negotiate differences with room- and floormates; manage their finances; make responsible decisions about alcohol, drugs, sexuality; and so on. In their courses, but also in their social interactions, they must grapple with ideas and experiences that challenge their existing values and assumptions. They must chart a meaningful course of study, choose a major, and start to view themselves as members of a disciplinary field. As they get ready for graduation, they must decide on jobs or graduate programs and face the exciting, but daunting, prospect of being an adult in the "real world." In other words, in addition to the intellectual challenges students are facing in college, they are also grappling with a number of complex social, emotional, and practical issues.

How can we make sense of all the ways in which students develop? Most developmental models share a basic conceptual framework, so we can start there. Typically, development is described as a response to intellectual, social, or emotional challenges that catalyze students' growth. It should be understood, though, that developmental models depict student development in the aggregate (that is, in broad brushstrokes) and do not necessarily describe the development of individual students. In fact, individual students do not necessarily develop at exactly the same pace. Furthermore, movement is not always in a forward direction. That is, under some circumstances, a student might regress or foreclose further development altogether. In addition, a student can be highly developed in one area (say, intellectual maturity) and less developed in another area (say, emotional maturity). Finally, it should be noted that although some models have been revised in light of changing student demographics, most currently focus on traditional-age, rather than older or returning, students and reflect a Western perspective.

Our approach here is not a complete review of the student development literature (for a broader treatment of student development models, see Evans et al., 1998). Rather, we start with the

Chickering model—a comprehensive model that systematically examines the range of issues students are dealing with in their college years. We then highlight two aspects of student development that we believe have particularly profound implications for the classroom. These are intellectual development and social identity development.

The Chickering Model of Student Development

Chickering (1969) provides a model that tries to systematically account for all the developmental changes students experience through the college years. He groups them in seven dimensions, which he calls vectors. They build on each other cumulatively:

- *Developing competence.* This dimension involves intellectual, physical, and interpersonal competence. Intellectual competence includes everything from developing study skills appropriate for college to developing sophisticated critical thinking and problem-solving abilities. Physical competence involves athletic activities, but also the realization on the part of students that they (and not their parents) are now responsible for their health and well-being. Interpersonal competence includes communication, group, and leadership skills. These three competences together give the individual a general sense of confidence that she can successfully deal with challenges that come her way. As Professor Guttman avoids calling on women in class, he might inadvertently hinder the development of their sense of intellectual and interpersonal competence, because this act highlights an assumption that women would not be able to perform as well on the spot.
- *Managing emotions.* This dimension involves being aware of one's own emotions (including anxiety, happiness, anger, frustration, excitement, depression, and so on) as well as expressing

160

them appropriately. The students in the Economics class are clearly in touch with their own emotions, but have trouble expressing them in a productive way in the discussion, with the result that the discussion does not explore the content fully and everybody's learning is diminished.

- *Developing autonomy.* This dimension involves disengaging from one's parents, relying more on peers, and finally developing personal autonomy. This process happens through the development of emotional independence (freeing oneself from the need for parental approval) and of instrumental independence (ability to deal with challenges on one's own terms). Research on Millennials (those students born in 1982 and after) suggests current students might struggle more with this dimension (Howe & Strauss, 2000). Later on, the challenge becomes how to reincorporate interconnectedness with others so that interdependence is the final goal (Chickering & Reisser, 1993). Again, as Professor Guttman provides extra help to women in small groups he might inadvertently interfere with the development of their sense of autonomy, which can impact their performance.

- *Establishing identity.* This is the pivotal dimension in Chickering's theory. It builds on the preceding vectors and serves as the foundation for the ones that follow. It culminates in the development of a sense of self. It involves comfort with one's own body and appearance, gender and sexual orientation, and racial and ethnic heritage. Students with a well-developed sense of self feel less threatened by new ideas involving beliefs that conflict with their own. In the economics class, some students appear to be working through such challenges, but they are clearly not mature enough yet to consider alternative points of view without their whole sense of identity feeling threatened.

- *Freeing interpersonal relationships.* This dimension involves achieving mature interpersonal relationships. It necessitates an

161

awareness of differences among people and a tolerance of those differences. The development of meaningful intimacy in the context of a romantic relationship is also part of this vector.

· *Developing purpose.* Once identity is achieved, the question is no longer "Who am I?" but "Who am I going to be?" This dimension involves nurturing specific interests and committing to a profession, or a lifestyle, even when it meets with opposition from others (such as parents). The TA's sexist comment might be challenging the women's sense that they belong in engineering. The woman who dropped the course and the other women who stopped speaking up in class are examples of the implications of this dimension for learning and performance. Indeed, many women in traditionally male-dominated fields report being told in college or graduate school that they would never succeed in science because of their gender (Ambrose et al., 1997; Hall, 1982).

· *Developing integrity.* This dimension speaks to the tension between self-interest and social responsibility. When navigated successfully, it culminates with the adoption of a set of internally consistent values that guide and direct behavior. We can understand Gloria's outburst as her trying to gain integrity and speak her own truth.

As we can see, these developmental vectors involve a number of social and emotional as well as intellectual processes. How students negotiate these processes shapes how they will grow personally and interact with one other, the instructor, and the content of their courses. It will also influence their level of engagement, motivation, and persistence, as well as their sense of agency and identity in their chosen field. Developmental processes, in other words, have profound implications for learning.

Even though Chickering's model looks at development very broadly, in a classroom situation we cannot control all those dimensions. Each of the models below focuses on an aspect of particular relevance to the classroom. They describe development as a stage-like process, whereby individuals undergo a series of qualitative shifts in how they think and feel about themselves, others, and their social environment.

Intellectual Development

Intellectual development in the college years has been studied since the 1950s. Although the formulation presented here is that of Perry (1968), it is extended in the work of later researchers who have found very similar developmental trajectories (Belenky et al., 1986; Baxter-Magolda, 1992). Even though these models contain different numbers of stages, all of them describe a student's trajectory from simplistic to more sophisticated ways of thinking. A student's movement forward is usually propelled by a challenge that reveals the inadequacies of the current stage.

In the earlier stages, students' reasoning is characterized by a basic *duality* in which knowledge can easily be divided into right and wrong statements, with little to no room for ambiguity and shades of gray. Kayla's exclamation—"It's just plain wrong!"— exemplifies this way of thinking. Students at this stage of intellectual development believe that knowledge is something absolute, that it is handed down from authorities (the teacher, the textbook), and that the role of students is to receive it and give it back when asked. This is a quantitative view of knowledge, with education seen as a process of amassing piles of "right" facts. The implicit assumption is that all that is knowable is known, and great instructors have the answers to any question. Students in these stages do not recognize different perspectives and are not likely to see discussions as a legitimate way of gaining knowledge about an issue.

Challenged with a sufficient number of questions to which we do not yet know the answers, or with issues for which there is no clear right answer, students move forward to a stage of *multiplicity*. Knowledge now becomes a matter of opinions, and anybody can have an opinion on an issue. Students at a multiplistic stage view evaluation as very subjective and can become frustrated if their opinion does not score them a good grade. At this point they have difficulty seeing how to differentiate among different opinions, as they all seem valid. The instructor might no longer be seen as an authority but only as another perspective among all the possible ones. At first it might be hard to see how this stage represents a move forward, but two important things have happened in this stage. First, students are now more open to differences of opinions because they are no longer fixated on the "right one." This crucial transition is foundational for all further development in later stages. Second, learning can now become personal. They, too, are entitled to their own opinion and can legitimately dialogue and disagree with the instructor or the textbook, which means they can start to construct their own knowledge. Gloria's claim that the readings are biased could not have come from a student in an earlier developmental stage.

With enough insistence that opinions need to be justified with evidence, students progress to stages characterized by *relativism*. Students with this worldview realize that opinions are not all equal, and that indeed their pros and cons can be understood and evaluated according to general and discipline-specific rules of evidence. This transition marks a shift from a quantitative to a qualitative view of knowledge. Instructors become guides and facilitators, expected to provide good models of how to interact with the content in a critical way, which is how the role of the student is now understood. As students hone their analytic and critical skills, they find the empowerment inherent in this stage, but they might also experience some frustration as they realize that all theories are necessarily imperfect or incomplete.

Students who successfully navigate this challenge move to the last set of stages, which are characterized by a sense of *commitment*. While it is true that all theories have pros and cons, learners realize they must provisionally commit to one as a foundation to build on, refining it as they go. In a sense, they have come full circle, as they now choose one theory or approach over the others, but unlike in the dualistic stage, their choice is now nuanced and informed. It is easy to see how this sense of commitment might apply to moral issues as well as cognitive ones. In fact, Kohlberg (1976) and Gilligan (1977) have formulated moral development theories that echo Perry's, in which students move from strongly held but unexamined views about right and wrong to more nuanced, responsible ethical positions where actions are evaluated in context according to a variety of factors. One of the lessons from their work is that moral development cannot be divorced from learning. For example, both Kayla's and Gloria's positions on illegal immigration are indeed as much moral as they are intellectual.

Other developmental researchers have expanded Perry's work to focus on gender differences in the various stages. For example, Baxter-Magolda (1992) has found that, in dualistic stages, men might prefer to engage in a game of displaying their knowledge in front of their peers whereas women might focus on helping each other master the material. In their study of women's intellectual development, Belenky and others (1986) found two parallel ways of knowing. For some women, studying something means isolating the issue from its context and focusing on deep analysis of one feature—which the researchers term *separate* knowing. For other women, studying something means asking questions such as "What does this mean for me? What are the implications for the community?"—which they term *connected* knowing. Of course, both ways of knowing can be found among men as well. Danielle, who is very comfortable limiting the discussion to only the figures in the readings, is an example of separate knowing, whereas Gloria, who cannot divorce the readings from her first-hand knowledge of illegal immigrants, is an example of connected knowing.

The research underlying these models clearly indicates that intellectual development takes time—it does not happen overnight and cannot be forced. Given the kind of development involved in the later stages, it is perhaps not surprising that Baxter-Magolda's research also shows many students leave college still in multiplistic stages, and that their development toward relativistic and committed stages continues well beyond college. This is good news if we consider that people who do not go to college tend to stay in dualistic stages, but it is also below the expectations that most instructors have for their students. Instructors, therefore, must make sure their expectations are reasonable given students' current level of intellectual development: what is reasonable for a graduating senior may not be for a first-year student, and vice versa. However, although development cannot be forced, it can be nurtured and encouraged by posing appropriate challenges and providing the support necessary to foster intellectual growth (Vygotsky, 1978). The strategies at the end of the chapter provide some suggestions in this direction.

Social Identity Development

Another developmental area that can affect learning is identity. The development of identity involves psychological changes that affect behaviors (such as social interactions), including those in the classroom. The basic premise of identity theory is that identity is not a given; instead, it needs to be achieved and continually negotiated as individuals try to balance developmental tensions and tasks throughout their lives (Erikson, 1950). For students, much of the work of identity development happens as they begin to question values and assumptions inculcated by parents and society, and start to develop their own values and priorities (Marcia, 1966).

One aspect of student identity development that is particularly salient for college students is that of social identity—the extent and nature of their identification with certain social groups, especially those groups that are often targets of prejudice and discrimination. Social identity has been studied extensively in relation to race/ethnicity, for example, the development of black identity (Cross, 1995), Asian American identity (Kim, 1981), Chicano identity (Hayes-Bautista, 1974), and Jewish identity (Kandel, 1986). All these models describe similar trajectories, which culminate with the establishment of a positive social identity as a member of a specific group (Adams et al., 1997). This general model also parallels the identity development process of members of other social groups, most notably gay and lesbian individuals (Cass, 1979) and individuals with disabilities (Onken & Slaten, 2000). Hardiman and Jackson (1992) have proposed a social identity development model that describes two developmental paths, one for minority groups and one for dominant groups. This model pulls the thread together from all the other models, highlighting the similar stages members of minority groups go through, but underscores the fact that for any given stage, members of majority groups have to deal with complementary developmental challenges. In our description of social identity development, we will use the Hardiman-Jackson model as our base model, occasionally highlighting pertinent insights from other models.

The first stage of the Hardiman-Jackson model corresponds to early childhood, where individuals start out in a *naïve* stage, devoid of any preconception or prejudice. They see differences in the people they observe, such as skin color, but they do not attach

167

value to those. It is only in a second stage that, through persistent and systematic societal reinforcement, conscious or unconscious *acceptance* of certain messages about different groups sets in—the socially constructed ideas about which groups are healthy, normal, beautiful, lazy, smart, sinful, and so on. For example, Kayla's perception that immigrants are "sucking this country dry" might come from this stage. Both dominant and minority groups at this second stage accept broader societal attitudes. For minority students, this can have several results. They may have negative attitudes about themselves—in other words, internalized racism, homophobia, sexism, and so on—and behave so as to conform to the dominant image. For example, gay students at this stage may use homophobic language and try to act "straight."

Many students stop here, unless their worldviews are challenged by more information, different perspectives, recognition of injustice, or meaningful work with people from different groups. If they are challenged, it can move them forward to a stage of *resistance.* In this stage, students are acutely aware of the ways in which "isms" affect their life and the world. In addition, members of dominant groups usually experience shame and guilt about the privilege resulting from their own membership in it. Conversely, members of minority groups tend to experience pride in their own identity, often valuing their group more than the socially dominant one, which is sometimes seen as the source of societal evils. These students tend to go through a phase of *immersion* (Cross, 1995), in which they prefer to socialize with members of their own group and withdraw from other groups. Fries-Britt (2000) documents the struggles of high-ability black students who are torn between identification with their academics and identification with their racial group, which might view their academic excellence as "acting white." In her book *Why Are All the Black Kids Sitting Together in the Cafeteria?* Beverly Daniel Tatum (1997) lucidly analyzes such racial dynamics. Moreover, she points out that racial minority students are usually aggressively questioning societal racism at the same developmental juncture when white students are feeling overwhelmed by the same accusations, a stage that Helms (1993) calls *disintegration*. The first story portrays one such tension. Gloria is very conscious of the racial subtext underpinning immigration debates, but Danielle sees it only as Gloria's pet peeve. The discussion is effectively stalled by Gloria's accusation of racism to Kayla. Analogous phenomena are true for other groups as well. For lesbian, gay, and bisexual students, a crucial step toward positive self-identity is coming out. D'Augelli (1994) points out that adopting a lesbian, gay, or bisexual (LGB) identity necessitates abandoning an implied heterosexual identity, with the consequent loss of all its attendant privileges. Rankin (2003) documents the feelings of lesbian, gay, bisexual, and transgendered (LGBT) students who, in response to marginalization experienced in their courses on the basis of their sexual orientation, report spending all their free time at the LGBT center on campus as a way to experience a positive environment for themselves, even at the cost of not spending enough time studying and struggling in those courses.

If students successfully move through this stage, they arrive at more sophisticated stages, those of *redefinition* and *internalization*. In these stages, students redefine their sense of self, moving beyond the dominant–minority dichotomy. These identities become one part of their make-up but not the defining feature. They no longer experience guilt or anger, but they might commit to work for justice in their spheres of influence.

Implications of This Research

Even though some of us might wish to conceptualize our classrooms as culturally neutral or might choose to ignore the cultural dimensions, students cannot check their sociocultural identities

169

at the door, nor can they instantly transcend their current level of development. Professor Battaglia knows that immigration is a loaded topic, but he thought students could consider the economic aspects alone. In fact, Gloria's and Kayla's identities as Hispanic and Polish-American, respectively, as well as their level of intellectual development and preferred ways of knowing, obviously influence their approach to the course topic, what aspects of the readings they focus on, how they make sense of the material, and what stances they take as a result. Therefore, it is important that the pedagogical strategies we employ in the classroom reflect an understanding of social identity development so that we can anticipate the tensions that might occur in the classroom and be proactive about them. The strategies at the end of the chapter explicitly link pedagogy and developmental considerations.

WHAT DOES THE RESEARCH TELL US ABOUT COURSE CLIMATE?

Just as we need to consider student development holistically, we also need to consider the various facets of course climate that influence student learning. By course climate we mean the intellectual, social, emotional, and physical environments in which our students learn. Climate is determined by a constellation of interacting factors that include faculty-student interaction, the tone instructors set, instances of stereotyping or tokenism, the course demographics (for example, relative size of racial and other social groups enrolled in the course), student-student interaction, and the range of perspectives represented in the course content and materials. All of these factors can operate outside as well as inside the classroom.

A common but simplistic way of thinking about climate is in binary terms: climate is either good (inclusive, productive) or bad (chilly, marginalizing). However, research suggests that it may be more accurate to think of climate as a continuum. In their study of the experiences of LGBT college students, DeSurra and Church (1994) asked those students to categorize the climate of their courses as either *marginalizing* or *centralizing,* depending on student perceptions of whether an LGBT perspective would be included and welcomed in the course or excluded and discouraged. In order to further categorize these perceptions, the students indicated whether the messages were *explicit* (evidenced by planned and stated attempts to include or to marginalize) or *implicit* (for example, inferred from the consistent absence of an LGBT perspective). This classification produced a continuum that we believe is useful for thinking about classroom climate in a broader sense than in relation to LGBT issues only.

At one end of the spectrum we find *explicitly marginalizing* climates. These are climates that are overtly hostile, discriminatory, or unwelcoming. In the second story, the TA's openly sexist comments and demeaning attitudes clearly demonstrate this kind of environment. Moving along the continuum, we find *implicitly marginalizing* climates. These are climates that exclude certain groups of people, but in subtle and indirect ways. These off-putting messages might even come from well-meaning instructors. For instance, Professor Guttman unintentionally created an implicitly marginalizing climate for women, even though he was trying to be welcoming and encouraging. In the story from the economics class, Danielle's request that racial lenses not be used for economic analysis also contributed to an implicitly marginalizing climate, by sending the message that discussions concerning race were not welcome.

Moving toward the more inclusive end of the continuum, we find *implicitly centralizing* climates. These climates are characterized by unplanned responses that validate alternative perspectives and experiences. Imagine, for instance, if after Danielle had asked

171

Gloria why she always has to bring up race, Professor Battaglia had stepped in to say, "Actually, Gloria might be on to something here, let's stay with her comment and dig deeper," and then went on to explore the applicability of Gloria's perspective to economic analysis. This comment would have validated the risk Gloria took with her remark and layered the content with additional meaning, promoting learning for everybody. It is important to recognize, however, that at this level the burden of raising a marginalized perspective still remains on the student. As such, it is often the case that the student has to take a risk because he does not know how his contribution will be received. When he does, however, in an implicitly centralizing climate, the instructor builds on the student's contribution in a productive and validating way.

At the most inclusive level of the continuum, we find *explicitly centralizing* climates. In courses with explicitly centralizing climates, marginalized perspectives are not only validated when students spontaneously bring them up, but they are intentionally and overtly integrated in the content. The climate here is characterized by obvious and planned attempts to include a variety of perspectives. Often, syllabi in these courses contain provisions (such as discussion ground rules and course policies) to foster sensitivity to the perspectives that students bring to the classroom.

It is important to remember that climate can be experienced differentially by different students: some students might feel unwelcome or discouraged whereas others might not. Also, students can experience the same environment negatively but for different reasons, as in Professor Guttman's course. Most of us would be likely to imagine that our courses fall on the inclusive end of the continuum. However, DeSurra and Church's research showed that implicitly marginalizing climates were most common across college classrooms.

Although DeSurra and Church's discussion focuses on marginalization based on sexual orientation, course climate has also been studied in relation to other characteristics. In particular, the earliest work on classroom climate, collectively known as the "chilly climate studies," documents marginalization on the basis of gender (Hall, 1982; Hall & Sandler, 1984; and Sandler & Hall, 1986). These studies suggested that course climate does not have to be blatantly exclusive or hostile in order to have a marginalizing effect on students and that, although each instance of subtle marginalization may be manageable on its own, the sum total of accumulated "micro-inequities" can have a profound negative impact on learning (Hall, 1982). Similar claims have been made about course climate in relation to race and ethnicity (for example, Watson et al., 2002, and Hurtado et al., 1999). These claims have been confirmed in later studies. Pascarella and others (1997) studied women in two-year colleges and concluded that perceptions of a negative climate had an inverse relationship with composite measures of cognitive development that included reading comprehension, mathematics, and critical thinking. Their study also found that perceptions of a marginalizing climate had a negative relationship with self-reported academic preparation for a career. In a follow-up longitudinal study, Whitt and others (1999) studied women students at twenty-three two- and four-year institutions in sixteen states and followed them through their junior year. They found that perception of a chilly climate was negatively associated with self-reported gains in writing and thinking skills, understanding science, academic preparation for a career, and understanding arts and humanities.

Even after establishing that climate does indeed have an impact on learning, a question remains: How? That is, what mechanisms operate to translate perceptions of inclusion or marginalization into gains or losses in learning or performance? This is a

173

complex question to answer, because many factors contribute to climate. For the purposes of this chapter, we focus on four basic areas of climate: stereotypes, tone, faculty-student and student-student interactions, and content. They are obviously interrelated, but we discuss them separately below, highlighting the mediating mechanisms by which they operate on student outcomes.

Stereotypes

Certain kinds of stereotypes are offensive and alienating and can produce a toxic classroom climate. What is less obvious is that the subtle activation of stereotypes can also influence learning and performance in profound ways, a phenomenon called "stereotype threat" (Steele & Aronson, 1995). Stereotype threat is a complex and nuanced phenomenon, but in simple terms it refers to the tension that arises in members of a stereotyped group when they fear being judged according to stereotypes. This sense of threat can negatively affect these individuals' performance on tasks (regardless of their ability), their level of preparation, their self-confidence, or their own belief in the stereotype. In their seminal study, Steele and Aronson (1995) focused on one stereotype of African Americans—that they perform poorly on standardized tests. They gave two groups of African American students a standardized test, asking one group to indicate their race prior to taking the test. The researchers found that simply by calling attention to race, a negative stereotype was activated in the minds of the African American participants. The activation of the stereotype in turn significantly depressed the performance of those African American students relative to other African American students for whom the stereotype was not activated. Similar studies have used common stereotypes about certain groups (for example, women are bad at math, older people are forgetful) and have demonstrated parallel findings. To date, we have results for

174

Hispanic (Gonzales, Blanton, & Williams, 2002) and Asian American students (Shih et al., 1999), women (Inzlicht & Ben-Zeev, 2000), older people (Levy, 1996), and students of low socio-economic status (Croizet & Claire, 1998).

The activation of a stereotype does not need to be intentional, and in fact seemingly innocuous comments can trigger stereotype threat. Subtle triggers include instructor comments and examples that convey certain assumptions about students. Problematic assumptions include those about the abilities or other qualities of members of certain groups or the extent to which students share the instructor's religion, upbringing, or socioeconomic status. Tokenism can be a trigger as well—instructors relying on minority students to represent the "minority point of view" rather than speaking for themselves. Professor Guttman is certainly conscious of the predicament of women in engineering, but the way he deals with it—refusing to call on women and insisting on giving them extra help—might trigger stereotype threat because it communicates problematic assumptions (that is, that women will be unprepared when he calls on them or that women need the extra help because of an ability deficiency). Regardless of whether the stereotype is activated blatantly or subtly, the effects on performance are similar.

How can stereotypes influence performance in students who do not even believe the stereotype? Steele and Aronson investigated two competing hypotheses. The first one attributed poor performance to lowered self-esteem and efficacy triggered by the stereotype. Measures of students' self-esteem failed to support this hypothesis. The second hypothesis, which their data confirmed, was that stereotypes have their impact by generating emotions that disrupt cognitive processes. In fact, students reported focusing on their anger at the stereotype or the instructor instead of on the test, not being able to think clearly, checking every answer multiple times only to run out of time for later questions, and so on (Steele & Aronson, 1995). In addition, as a coping mechanism to protect their self-concept against the self-fulfilling prophecy of their low performance, students might disidentify from their chosen discipline, deciding that that discipline was not good for them in the first place (Major et al., 1998). Thus, stereotype threat operates through two related mediating mechanisms, one cognitive and one motivational. Stereotype threat is an intriguing and complex phenomenon, and there are many nuances highlighted by this line of research that cannot be adequately addressed here. However, the one point we have tried to highlight is that the way we frame the material and the task matters—and it has implications for learning and performance. Fortunately, research shows that, just as easily as stereotype threat can be activated, it can also be removed (see "Strategies" section).

Tone

Course climate is not just about race, gender, minority status group membership, or the stereotypes associated with them. Course climate is also about how the instructor communicates with students, the level of hospitableness that students perceive, and the more general range of inclusion and comfort that students experience. For instance, Ishiyama and Hartlaub (2002) studied how the tone an instructor sets affects climate by manipulating course syllabi. They created two versions of the same syllabus, with policies identical in substance but one worded in a punitive tone, the other in an encouraging one. They discovered that the tone used influenced students' judgments about instructor approachability. In their study, students are less likely to seek help from the instructor who worded those policies in punitive language than from the instructor who worded the same policies in rewarding language. Rubin (1985) dubs those instructors "scolders"—those who word policies in boldface block letters and promise harsh punishments rather than offering a pedagogical rationale for the policy. Even though the study of tone was focused on syllabi, it is reasonable to assume that its impact is more pervasive. Other facets of tone include the kind of language used in the classroom (encouraging or demotivating), especially in the way negative feedback is offered (constructive and focused on the task or demeaning and focused on the person). In fact, in their study of why undergraduates leave the sciences, Seymour and Hewitt (1997) found that sarcasm, denigration, and ridicule by faculty were some of the reasons reported by students. The belittling tone of the TA in the second story makes him unapproachable to many students. The impact of tone extends even to classroom incivilities, such as tardiness, inappropriate cell phone and laptop use in class, and rudeness. Boice (1998) studied student incivilities and linked them to the absence of positive motivators, both in the instructor's speech and nonverbal signals. Thus we see that tone impacts learning and performance through motivational and socioemotional mechanisms (see Chapter Three).

Faculty-Student and Student-Student Interaction

Astin (1993) investigated the impact of personal and situational variables on several college outcomes; some of his findings naturally dealt with the relationship between climate and learning. In his study of more than 200,000 students and 25,000 faculty at 200 institutions, he identified several factors contributing to the college experience. The factor that relates to course climate the most is what he termed "Faculty Student Orientation," and includes items such as student perceptions of whether faculty are interested in students' academic problems, care about the concerns of minority groups, are approachable outside of class, and treat students as persons and not as numbers. He found that this factor positively impacts retention, the percentage of students who go on to graduate school, and self-reported critical thinking, analysis, and problem-solving skills. Seymour and Hewitt (1997) found that one of the reasons students switch from the sciences is faculty unavailability, and that, conversely, one of the variables that changed the minds of students who were thinking about switching was the intervention by a faculty member during a critical point in the student's academic or personal life. Similarly, Pascarella and Terenzini (1977) discovered that the absence of faculty contacts or the perception that those are largely formalistic exchanges is one of the determinants of student withdrawal from college. Just like tone, faculty-student interaction impacts learning and performance through motivational and socioemotional mediating mechanisms, influencing participation, risk-taking, and persistence. Of course, students also contribute to the classroom climate with their own behaviors, like Gloria and Kayla did in the first story, but the way the instructor responds to those behaviors is the final determinant of climate. If Professor Battaglia had been able to curtail the emotional responses by appealing to ground rules for discussion or by providing a strong rationale for the readings he chose or by changing course to explore Gloria's critique further, the discussion might have ended in a very different way.

Content

The climate variables explored thus far are all process variables— explicit and subtle speech and behaviors of faculty and students. But what about the content of our courses? Is there something inherent to *what* we teach—not *how*—that can influence climate? Marchesani and Adams (1992) describe a continuum of inclusion for course content from the Exclusive Curriculum, where only a dominant perspective is represented, to the Exceptional Outsider

178

stage, in which a token marginalized perspective is included only to comply with a requirement (for instance, one Native American poet in an American poetry course), to ever more inclusive stages, culminating with the Transformed Curriculum, where multiple perspectives are placed at the center. Although this classification is more germane to arts, humanities, and social science courses, our conception of content is relevant to climate in all courses. Course readings certainly fall in this category, but content is broader than that. It includes the examples and metaphors instructors use in class and the case studies and project topics we let our students choose. Just as important as those used are those omitted, because they all send messages about the field and who belongs in it. Again, if Professor Guttman had systematically highlighted the contributions of engineers who happen to be women, this would have communicated powerful messages about women in engineering. For students who are developing their sense of identity, purpose, and competence, some of these messages can translate into messages about their own power, identity, and agency and can influence engagement and persistence in the field. Astin's study (1993) identified a factor, which he called "Faculty Diversity Orientation," comprising items such as inclusion of readings on gender and racial issues in the curriculum. He found that this factor positively impacts student GPA. The realization that Professor Battaglia teaches economics in isolation from race might be very discouraging for students such as Gloria. In fact, Seymour and Hewitt (1997) found that many of the women and minority students who left the sciences transferred to fields where race and gender are legitimate lenses of analysis instead of "a dirty little secret over in the engineering school." In conclusion, content can affect learning through cognitive, motivational, and socioemotional mechanisms because it determines what is and is not learned and how meaningful the material and the field are to students.

Implications of This Research

What are the implications of the findings on climate for teaching and learning? The first is that learning doesn't happen in a vacuum but in a course and classroom context where intellectual pursuits interface with socioemotional issues. The second is that climate works in both blatant and subtle ways, and many well-intentioned or seemingly inconsequential decisions can have unintended negative effects with regard to climate. Finally, as instructors, we have a great deal of control over the climate we shape, and can leverage climate in the service of learning once we understand how and why it influences student learning. Because of the connections between classroom climate and student development, many of the strategies that help foster a productive climate also encourage student development. The next section offers many such strategies.

WHAT STRATEGIES DOES THE RESEARCH SUGGEST?

Here are a number of strategies that may help you encourage student development and create a productive classroom climate. Most of these strategies work toward both goals, reinforcing our claim that student development must be considered in the context of the course environment.

Strategies That Promote Student Development and Productive Climate

Make Uncertainty Safe   For those students who are comfortable in black and white worldviews, there can be an emotional resistance to intellectual development, and it might be important to support them in dealing with ambiguity. There are various ways to do this. Validate different viewpoints, even unpopular ones. Explicitly let students know that part of critical thinking is to embrace complexity rather than oversimplify matters. Explain that even though it might seem frustrating, the point of classroom discussions is not to reach consensus but to enrich everybody's thinking. Model this attitude in your disciplinary context.

Resist a Single Right Answer   Textbooks present information very linearly, but knowledge is generated and contested over time. If you want students to be in dialogue with the texts in your discipline, create a structure that can support it. You can ask students to generate multiple approaches to a problem or debate a devil's advocate position. Ask them to articulate their perspective before you volunteer yours so as not to bias them. When appropriate, use assignments with multiple correct solutions.

Incorporate Evidence into Performance and Grading Criteria   If you want students to support their opinions with evidence, use rubrics and other tools to scaffold this practice. You can educate students to use the rubric by asking them to read each other's work and circle the pieces of evidence to highlight them visually. Incorporating evidence in your grading scheme will also reduce "grade grubbing" based on the notion that personal opinions are subjective and cannot be graded fairly.

Examine Your Assumptions About Students   Because assumptions influence the way we interact with our students, which in turn impacts their learning, we need to uncover and at times question those assumptions. It is common for instructors to assume that students share our background and frames of reference (for example, historical or literary references). It is equally common to make assumptions about students' ability (for example, Asian

181

students will do better in math), identity and viewpoint (for example, students share your sexual orientation or political affiliation), and attributions (for example, tentative language indicates intellectual weakness). These assumptions can result in behaviors that are unintentionally alienating and can affect climate and students' developing sense of identity.

Be Mindful of Low-Ability Cues   In their efforts to help students, some instructors inadvertently send mixed messages based on assumptions (for example, "I'll be happy to help you with this because I know girls have trouble with math"). These cues encourage attributions focused on permanent, uncontrollable causes like gender, which diminish students' self-efficacy. Instead, it is more productive to focus on controllable causes, such as effort (for example, "the more you practice, the more you learn"). A "throw away" comment on an instructor's part can send an unintended but powerful message that may saddle students' identity with negative perceptions related to their group membership and influence their perception of the course climate.

Do Not Ask Individuals to Speak for an Entire Group Minority students often report either feeling invisible in class or sticking out like a sore thumb as the token minority. This experience is heightened when they are addressed as spokespeople for their whole group, and can have implications on performance (for example, if they become nonengaged, angry, or combative). These emotions can disrupt students' ability to think clearly, be logical, solve problems, and so on.

Reduce Anonymity   Creating an effective learning climate often includes making students feel recognized as individuals, both by the instructor and by peers. Making an effort to learn students' names, providing opportunities for students to learn each others' names, inviting students to office hours, going to a student's theater production or sports event, and so on, can help to break down the barriers created by large classes.

Model Inclusive Language, Behavior, and Attitudes   Just as instructors operate under a set of assumptions that may or may not be true, so do students. Addressing these assumptions (for example, that we all share a common heritage, set of experiences, or goals) by modeling inclusiveness can provide a powerful learning experience for all students. For instance, avoid using masculine pronouns for both males and females or, when you use American idioms, explain them for the benefit of non-native English speakers. These types of behaviors can "catch on" in a classroom and create a climate that is welcoming to all rather than demotivating to some who do not feel represented or validated. Feeling included and not marginalized is essential for the development of a positive sense of identity.

Use Multiple and Diverse Examples   Multiple examples are important if students are to understand that theories and concepts can operate in a variety of contexts and conditions, and they also increase the likelihood of students relating to at least some of them. So, for instance, plan examples that speak to both sexes, work across cultures, and relate to people from various socioeconomic statuses, traditional age as well as adult returning students. This simple strategy can help students feel connected to the content, that they belong in the course or field, and reinforce their developing sense of competence and purpose.

Establish and Reinforce Ground Rules for Interaction Ground rules can help to assure that peers are being inclusive and respectful in order to create an effective learning climate and promote students' development. To generate maximal buy-in for the ground rules, you can involve students in the process of establishing them. See Appendix E for an example of such a process. Of course, you will still need to occasionally reinforce the ground rules and correct students for the occasional noninclusive behavior or disrespectful comment.

Make Sure Course Content Does Not Marginalize Students
Think about whether certain perspectives are systematically unrepresented in your course materials (for example, a course on family focusing only on traditional families, or a course on public policy ignoring race issues). Neglecting some issues implies a value judgment, which can alienate certain groups of students, thus impeding their developing sense of identity.

Use the Syllabus and First Day of Class to Establish the Course Climate First impressions are incredibly important because they can be long-lasting. Your students will form impressions about you and the course on the first day, so set the tone that you want to permeate the semester. Think through how to introduce yourself and the course. How will you balance establishing your competence and authority with coming across as supportive and approachable? What kind of icebreaker can help students get to know each other and become comfortable with you and the course while engaging the content meaningfully?

Set Up Processes to Get Feedback on the Climate Because some alienating attitudes, behaviors, and language function under the surface (that is, they are subtle), it is not always easy to get a sense of whether everyone in the class feels equally valued, accepted, heard, and so on. You can continually monitor the climate—particularly in courses dealing with sensitive issues—by asking student representatives who meet with you on a regular basis to share feedback from the class, or through an early course evaluation that specifically asks about climate issues. You can also videotape yourself or ask a third party (a TA, a teaching center consultant, a colleague) to sit in on your class and collect data on your interactions with students. Indicators to monitor can include noticing which groups are called on, interrupted, asked less sophisticated questions, or given acknowledgment for their contributions more than other groups.

Anticipate and Prepare for Potentially Sensitive Issues We usually know from our own or our colleagues' past experiences what issues seem to be "hot topics" for some of our students. Preparing students to learn from these opportunities requires careful framing (for instance, an acknowledgment that the topic can have personal significance for many students and also an articulation of the expectations for the tone of the discussion), an explanation for why the course is dealing with the issue (for instance, the necessity to hear all sides of the debate to arrive at a multifaceted understanding), and ground rules (see above) that assure a civil discussion.

Address Tensions Early If you are closely monitoring the climate and it becomes apparent that you or others are inadvertently shutting people out, marginalizing others, "pressing someone's button," and so on, address the issue before it gets out of hand. This may mean apologizing for yourself or others, if warranted (for example, "I'm sorry if some of you interpreted my comment as ..."), taking a student aside after class to explain the impact of a comment, explicitly discussing the tension (for example, "Some people believe it racist to say ..."), or delving into the issue through a series of questions (for example, "What are other ways people might perceive that statement?"). Remember that college students are learning to manage their emotions and sometimes don't know how to express them appropriately. In these cases, you might want to discuss intent versus impact (for example, "You probably did not mean this, but some people might interpret your comments as sexist because ..."). This strategy protects students who make unsophisticated comments so that they do not shut down and foreclose further development, while acknowledging the frustration of the rest of the class.

Turn Discord and Tension into a Learning Opportunity
Students need to learn that debate, tension, discord, and cognitive dissonance are all opportunities to expand one's perspective, delve deeper into a topic, better understand opposing views, and so on; hence, we need not avoid them. However, because college students are still developing social and emotional skills, these can often overshadow intellect, logic, and rational thinking. As a result, we need to work to continually shape our classroom climate. So do not foreclose a discussion just because tensions are running high; rather, funnel those emotions into useful dialogue. For example, you might ask students to take on another perspective using a role play, take a time out (for example, write their reactions down so that they are more useful and constructive), or simply explain how and why discomfort and tension can be a valuable part of learning.

Facilitate Active Listening   Sometimes tensions arise because students are not hearing what others are saying. To build this important skill and enhance classroom interactions, you might ask students to paraphrase what someone has said, followed up by a series of questions as to whether their perception was inaccurate or incomplete. You can also model this skill yourself by paraphrasing a student's response and then asking whether you captured their perspective accurately.

SUMMARY

In this chapter, we have argued that we need to consider students holistically as intellectual, social, and emotional beings. We have reviewed the research that documents how students are still developing in all these areas and in their sense of identity, and we have documented how their level of development can influence learning and performance. Likewise, we have argued that we need to look at our classrooms not only as intellectual but also social and emotional environments, and we have shown that all these facets of the course climate interact with student development and impact learning and performance. We also have shown that although instructors can only encourage development, they can have a great impact on the course climate. Our hope is that instructors can be more intentional in how they shape their course's climate and, consequently, student learning.

CHAPTER 7

How Do Students Become Self-Directed Learners?

The "A" Student

I was exhausted from reading and grading twenty-five papers over the past weekend, but I was glad to be able to hand them back so quickly. It was the first big assignment in my freshman seminar on immigration, and it required students to state an argument and support it with evidence from course readings and supplemental documents. After class, one of the students, Melanie, approached me and insisted that she needed to talk with me immediately about her grade (not about her paper, mind you!). Hers was a typical first paper in this course—it lacked a clearly articulated argument, and there was only weak evidence to support what I inferred was her argument. As we walked across campus toward my office, she began explaining that she was a "gifted" writer who had always received As on her high school English papers. She made clear to me that there must be some mistake in this paper's grade because her mother, a high school English teacher, had read the paper over the weekend and thought it was wonderful. Melanie admitted that she had started this assignment the night before it was due, but insisted that she worked best under pressure, saying, "That's just how my creative juices flow."

Professor Sara Yang

The Hamster Wheel

After I saw John's grade on the second Modern Chemistry exam, I couldn't help but ask myself, "How can someone attend every single lecture—sitting attentively in the front row—and go to every recitation and lab, no less, and still do so poorly on my exams?" I had explicitly told the students that my exams are designed to test conceptual understanding, and yet John seemed to be thrown for a loop. His first exam score had also been pretty low, but he wasn't alone in that, given students' first-exam jitters. By this time, however, I thought he would have learned what to expect. I asked John what had happened, and he too seemed perplexed. "I studied for weeks," he said, flipping open his textbook. I could hardly believe how much of the text was highlighted. The pages practically glowed with neon yellow. He went on to describe how he had re-read the relevant chapters multiple times and then memorized various terms by writing their definitions on flashcards. I asked where he had learned this approach to studying, and he explained that it had always worked for him when he used to prepare for his science tests in high school.

Professor Gar Zeminsky

WHAT IS GOING ON IN THESE STORIES?

On the surface, these stories seem quite different: Melanie starts her history paper at the last minute, whereas John studies hard (and harder) for weeks before his chemistry exams. However, both students perform well below their expectations without understanding why. As we analyze the details of each story, other issues emerge. We see that John has a set of study strategies—mostly involving rote memorization of facts and definitions—that were

189

sufficient in his high school classes but that are proving to be ineffective for the intellectual demands of a college course. Rather than changing his approach after a poor performance on the first exam, however, John doggedly redoubles his efforts only to find that more of the same does not help. Melanie also enlists strategies that worked for her in the past, but she fails to recognize important differences—in both disciplinary approach and level of sophistication—between the kinds of writing valued in high school English classes and the kinds of writing expected in her college history course. Furthermore, she does not even acknowledge that she did poorly on the current assignment. Both Melanie and John are encountering new sets of intellectual challenges. Unfortunately, neither of them recognizes the shortcomings in their strategies, and they fail to develop new ones. To complicate matters, Melanie holds beliefs about her own abilities, based in part on past performance, that make her unwilling to admit that there is anything wrong with her current approach.

WHAT PRINCIPLE OF LEARNING IS AT WORK HERE?

Although these two students are struggling with different tasks in distinct courses, their difficulties point to similar shortcomings in *metacognition*. Metacognition refers to "the process of reflecting on and directing one's own thinking" (National Research Council, 2001, p. 78). Both Melanie and John have trouble accurately assessing their own learning and performance, and they fail to adapt their approaches to the current situation. As a result, both students' learning and performance suffer. In other words, when it comes to applying metacognitive skills to direct their own learning—the focus of this chapter—Melanie and John fall short.

190

Principle: To become self-directed learners, students must learn to assess the demands of the task, evaluate their own knowledge and skills, plan their approach, monitor their progress, and adjust their strategies as needed.

This principle lays out the key metacognitive skills that are critical to being an effective self-directed (also called "self-regulated" or "lifelong") learner. Such skills arguably become more and more important at higher levels of education and in professional life as one takes on more complex tasks and greater responsibility for one's own learning. For example, compared to high school, students in college are often required to complete larger, longer-term projects and must do so rather independently. Such projects often demand that students recognize what they already know that is relevant to completing the project, identify what they still need to learn, plan an approach to learn that material independently, potentially redefine the scope of the project so they can realistically accomplish it, and monitor and adjust their approach along the way. Given all this, it is not surprising that one of the major intellectual challenges students face upon entering college is managing their own learning (Pascarella & Terenzini, 2005).

Unfortunately, these metacognitive skills tend to fall outside the content area of most courses, and consequently they are often neglected in instruction. However, helping students to improve their metacognitive skills can hold enormous benefits. The benefits include not only intellectual habits that are valuable across disciplines (such as planning one's approach to a large project, considering alternatives, and evaluating one's own perspective), but also more flexible and usable discipline-specific knowledge. Imagine if John and Melanie had learned to evaluate

191

the demands of the tasks that they were given and had been able to adjust their approaches to learning accordingly. By the second exam, John might have shifted from highlighting his textbook and memorizing facts to concentrating on the conceptual underpinnings of chemistry, perhaps creating a concept map to test his understanding of key ideas and the causal relationships between them. Melanie might have switched to a new writing strategy that centered on articulating a clear argument and supporting it with evidence, rather than persisting with the descriptive approach she probably used in high school. In other words, better metacognitive skills would have helped both John and Melanie learn more, which would have been reflected in improved performance.

WHAT DOES THE RESEARCH ABOUT METACOGNITION TELL US?

Researchers have proposed various models to describe how learners would ideally apply metacognitive skills to learn and perform well (Brown et al., 1983; Butler, 1997; Pintrich, 2000; Winne & Hadwin, 1998). Although these models differ in their particulars, they share the notion that learners need to engage in a variety of processes to *monitor* and *control* their learning (Zimmerman, 2001). Moreover, because the processes of monitoring and controlling mutually affect each other, these models often take the form of a cycle. Figure 7.1 depicts a cycle of basic metacognitive processes in which learners

- Assess the task at hand, taking into consideration the task's goals and constraints
- Evaluate their own knowledge and skills, identifying strengths and weaknesses

192

- Plan their approach in a way that accounts for the current situation
- Apply various strategies to enact their plan, monitoring their progress along the way
- Reflect on the degree to which their current approach is working so that they can adjust and restart the cycle as needed

In addition to the many ways in which these processes can overlap and interact with each other, students' beliefs about intelligence and learning (such as whether intelligence is fixed or malleable and whether learning is quick and easy or slow and effortful) represent a factor that can influence the whole cycle in a variety of ways (see the center of Figure 7.1). In the sections

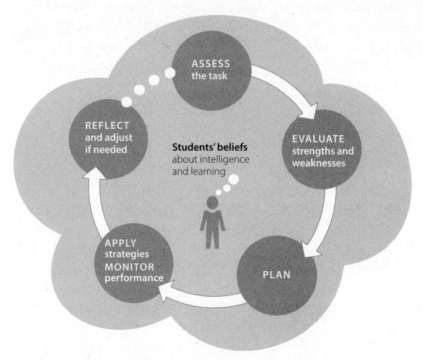

Figure 7.1. Cycle of Self-Directed Learning

below, we examine key research findings related to each process in this cycle, as well as to students' beliefs about intelligence and learning.

Assessing the Task at Hand

When students submit work that misses the point of an assignment, faculty often ask themselves in bewilderment: "Did they even read the assignment?" In fact, your students may *not* have or, if they did, they may have failed to accurately assess what they were supposed to do, perhaps making assumptions about the task based on their previous educational experiences. In one research study investigating students' difficulties with college writing assignments, Carey, Flower, Hayes, and others (1989) found that half of the college students they observed ignored the instructor's articulation of the writing assignment and instead used a generic writing-as-knowledge-telling strategy that they had used in high school. These students consequently presented everything that they knew about the paper's topic without regard to the specific goal or purpose of the assignment.

This research suggests that the first phase of metacognition—assessing the task—is not always a natural or easy one for students. We see this in the stories at the beginning of the chapter. Even though Professor Yang's assignment specified that students' papers should present an argument with supporting evidence, Melanie fell back on strategies that she had learned in her high school English class. John also ignored—or misunderstood—his professor's statement about the purpose of the exam (to test conceptual knowledge) and assumed that he knew how to study, based on his high school experiences (memorize facts rather than identify key ideas and their relationships). In both cases, the student inappropriately assessed the task despite the instructor's efforts toward giving clear directions.

194

Given that students can easily misassess the task at hand, it may not be sufficient simply to remind students to "read the assignment carefully." In fact, students may need to (1) learn *how* to assess the task, (2) practice incorporating this step into their planning before it will become a habit, and (3) receive feedback on the accuracy of their task assessment *before* they begin working on a given task.

Evaluating One's Own Strengths and Weaknesses

Even if students can adequately assess an assignment—that is, they manage to determine what needs to be done to effectively complete the assignment—there is still a question of how well prepared they are to meet the task at hand. Research has found that people in general have great difficulty recognizing their own strengths and weaknesses, and students appear to be especially poor judges of their own knowledge and skills. For example, when nursing students were asked about their proficiency in performing several basic procedures (such as inserting an IV), the majority of them *overestimated* their abilities relative to their actual performance. This phenomenon has been found in a variety of contexts (Dunning, 2007). Moreover, research suggests that the students with weaker knowledge and skills are less able to assess their abilities than students with stronger skills. For example, when asked to predict their performance both before and after completing a test, students in an undergraduate psychology course showed different levels of accuracy in their estimates, based on their *actual* performance: The highest-performing students were accurate in their predictions and postdictions (and became more accurate over subsequent tests), but the poor students grossly overestimated their performance both before and after taking the test and showed little improvement in their estimates over time (Hacker et al., 2000).

195

This tendency—especially among novices—to inaccurately assess one's knowledge and skill relative to a particular goal is particularly troubling because it has serious consequences for one's ability to achieve that goal. For example, a student who inaccurately assesses his or her skills for a particular task might seriously underestimate the time it will take to effectively complete the given assignment or the additional help and resources that will have to be acquired. This inability to self-assess is apparent in both stories from the beginning of the chapter. Melanie believes that she is a gifted writer and considers her strength to be writing under pressure. As a result of this overconfidence, she begins her history paper at the last minute. John, too, is proud of his meticulous reading and relentless highlighting of his chemistry textbook, but he confuses this diligence with successful learning of the key concepts. If these students had managed to evaluate their abilities more realistically, they might have engaged more appropriate strategies that, in turn, could have produced better outcomes.

Planning an Appropriate Approach

Given students' difficulties in assessing the task and their own abilities, it follows that their capacity to plan effectively would also be compromised. In the stories at the beginning of the chapter, we see two ways students' planning can go awry: (1) simply not planning enough, especially for a complex task and (2) planning inappropriately for the current situation. Melanie exemplifies the first problem by starting her paper the night before and spending little or no time thinking ahead about what (and how) she needs to write for this assignment. John definitely plans how he will study for his chemistry test; however, his plan is poorly suited to the kind of exam Professor Zeminsky gives. Research on students' planning behavior provides evidence for both of these planning problems.

Melanie's lack of planning is consistent with a body of research that shows students tend to spend too little time planning, especially when compared to more expert individuals. For example, in one study, physics experts (graduate students and faculty) and novices (students in introductory courses) were asked to solve various physics problems. Not surprisingly, the experts solved the problems more quickly and more accurately than the novices. However, the intriguing result was that the experts spent proportionately much more time than novices planning their approach. Novices, conversely, spent almost no time planning and instead started each problem by applying various equations to try to find a solution. This lack of planning led the novices to waste much of their time because they made false starts and took steps that ultimately did not lead to a correct solution (Chi et al., 1989). Similar effects have been found in other disciplines, such as math and writing (Hayes & Flower, 1986; Schoenfeld, 1987). In other words, even though planning one's approach to a task can increase the chances of success, students tend not to recognize the need for it.

Research also shows that when students do engage in planning, they often make plans that are not well matched to the task at hand. For example, one research study analyzed the planning behavior of experts (college writing teachers) and novices (students) and then used independent judges to rate the quality of the final written texts. Results showed that the novice—and less effective—writers were the ones who had planned less appropriately (Carey et al., 1989).

Applying Strategies and Monitoring Performance

Once students have a plan and begin to apply strategies that implement their plan, they need to monitor their performance. In other words, students need to ask themselves, "Is this strategy working, or would another one be more productive?" Without effectively monitoring their own progress, students like John in the story at the beginning of the chapter may continue to apply an ineffective strategy and consequently waste time and achieve poor outcomes.

Research on the effects of students' self-monitoring activities has highlighted two important findings. First, students who naturally monitor their own progress and try to explain to themselves what they are learning along the way generally show greater learning gains as compared to students who engage less often in self-monitoring and self-explanation activities. For example, in one study, students were asked to talk aloud while they studied an introductory science topic in a textbook. After studying, the students took a problem-solving test that measured how much they had learned. The researchers split the students into two groups according to their problem-solving performance—the good problem solvers and the poor problem solvers—and then looked to see whether there were any differences in how they studied the textbook from the talk-aloud protocols. A key difference they found was that the good problem solvers were far more likely to monitor their understanding while they studied, that is, to continually stop themselves as they were reading to ask whether they were understanding the concepts just presented (Chi et al., 1989).

Although this research shows a positive relationship between natural self-monitoring and learning effectiveness, the question of real interest for instructors is whether teaching students to self-monitor actually improves students' learning. Research in multiple science domains indicates that the answer is yes. Students who were taught or prompted to monitor their own understanding or to explain to themselves what they were learning had greater learning gains relative to students who were not given any monitoring instruction (Bielaczyc, Pirolli, & Brown, 1995; Chi et al.,

198

1994). In addition, research has shown that when students are taught to ask each other a series of comprehension-monitoring questions during reading, they learn to self-monitor more often and hence learn more from what they read (Palinscar & Brown, 1984).

Reflecting on and Adjusting One's Approach

Even when students monitor their performance and identify failures or shortcomings in their approach, there is no guarantee that they will adjust or try more effective alternatives. They may be resistant, for any number of reasons, to change their current method, or they may lack alternative strategies. Melanie, for example, is reluctant to deviate from a style of writing that won her praise in high school. But even if she *were* able to recognize deficits in her analytical writing, she might not know how to write differently. John, too, may not know any other ways to study for an exam.

Research has shown that good problem solvers will try new strategies if their current strategy is not working, whereas poor problem solvers will continue to use a strategy even after it has failed (National Research Council, 2001, p. 78). Similarly, good writers will evaluate their writing from their audience's perspective and revise the parts of their work that do not convey the desired meaning (Hayes & Flower, 1986). However, these kinds of adjustments tend not to occur if the perceived cost of switching to a new approach is too high. Such costs include the time and effort it takes to change one's habits as well as the fact that new approaches, even if better in the long run, tend to underperform more practiced approaches at first. So, busy or procrastination-prone students may be unwilling to put in an up-front investment in making a change. In fact, research shows that people will often continue to use a familiar strategy that works moderately

199

well rather than switch to a new strategy that would work better (Fu & Gray, 2004). This suggests that students will tend not to adopt newly learned strategies unless the perceived benefits clearly outweigh the perceived costs, especially the costs of effort and time.

Beliefs About Intelligence and Learning

At the beginning of this chapter, we indicated that students' beliefs about intelligence and learning can have a pervasive influence on metacognitive processes. Examples of such beliefs include whether students view learning as fast and easy or slow and difficult, and whether they perceive intelligence as fixed or malleable. Other examples include students' beliefs about their own abilities (in either direction) and their special talents.

Research shows that students' beliefs in these areas are associated with their learning-related behaviors and outcomes, including course grades and test scores (Schommer, 1994). For example, in one study, researchers collected a variety of measures, including students' beliefs about whether intelligence was fixed (there is nothing one can do to improve it) or incremental (one can work to develop greater intelligence), sense of self-efficacy, motivation, time spent studying, study strategies, and learning behaviors. By applying various statistical techniques to sort out the relationships among all these variables, the researchers found a pattern that linked students' beliefs about intelligence with their study strategies and learning behaviors (Henderson & Dweck, 1990). This connection makes intuitive sense in that students who believe intelligence is fixed have no reason to put in the time and effort to improve because they believe their effort will have little or no effect. Having put in relatively little effort, such students are less likely to learn and perform well. In contrast, students who believe that intelligence is incremental (that is, skills can be developed

200

that will lead to greater academic success) have a good reason to engage their time and effort in various study strategies because they believe this will improve their skills and hence their outcomes. Having put in relatively more effort—especially after facing difficulty—such students are more likely to learn and perform better.

Looking to the first story from the beginning of the chapter illustrates how beliefs about one's own abilities can also have an impact on metacognitive processes and learning. Melanie has beliefs about herself—"I'm a good writer" and "I always get As on my papers"—that influence her approach to Professor Yang's assignment. She starts her paper late, assuming that her innate talent for writing and her ability to work under pressure will carry her through. When the result—mainly her poor grade—does not match her beliefs and expectations, Melanie attributes the outcome to inaccurate grading rather than to her own conceptualization of the task, her skills, or the effort that she invested. If Melanie maintains these beliefs, it seems likely that she will not change her approach or try to refine her writing skills, even if she is given other opportunities to practice writing in this history course.

By the converse line of reasoning, a student who has *negative* beliefs about his or her abilities in particular contexts (for example, "I'm no good at math") may feel defeated from the outset and consequently not bother to plan or implement effortful strategies because of the belief that any time and effort expended will do little good. Unfortunately, therefore, a belief in one's own abilities in either direction—strong or weak—can seriously impede one's metacognitive processes and hence learning and development.

What can be done to help students acquire more productive beliefs about learning? Although a common finding is that beliefs and attitudes are difficult to change, new research offers some hope for modifying students' beliefs and consequently improving their learning. In a study of Stanford University students (Aronson, Fried, & Good, 2002), half of the students were given a short information session that promoted a belief in intelligence as "malleable," that is, something that develops with practice and hard work. The other half were told that intelligence comprised multiple components (for example, verbal, logical, interpersonal) and was "fixed" such that people simply needed to discover which of these fixed attributes was their particular talent in order to leverage their strengths. Both groups then participated in three sessions in which they were told to write letters to academically struggling high school students. In these letters, the study participants were encouraged to discuss the view of intelligence they had been taught in their information session as a means of encouraging their high school "pen pals" (who, in fact, did not exist). Follow-up assessments found that students in the "malleable" intelligence session showed more change in their views on intelligence and endorsed the "malleable" perspective more strongly than the "fixed" group and another control group. Over time, the malleable group showed an even stronger endorsement of the malleable position whereas the fixed and control groups did not. Perhaps most important, the "malleable" students rated their enjoyment of academics higher and showed a grade advantage the following quarter over the "fixed" group and control group.

Implications of This Research

Perhaps the simplest summary of the research presented in each of the preceding six sections is to say that students tend not to apply metacognitive skills as well or as often as they should. This implies that students will often need our support in learning, refining, and effectively applying basic metacognitive skills. To address these needs, then, requires us as instructors to consider the advantages these skills can offer students in the long run and then, as appropriate, to make the development of metacognitive skills part of our course goals.

In the case of assessing the task at hand and planning an appropriate approach, students not only tend to generate inappropriate assessments and plans but sometimes also completely fail to consider these critical steps. This suggests that students may need significant practice at task assessment and planning even to remember to apply those skills. In the case of monitoring one's progress and reflecting on one's overall success, research indicates that explicitly teaching students to engage in these processes is beneficial. Nevertheless, students will probably need considerable practice to apply these skills effectively.

Finally, some of the research—for example, on students' ability to evaluate their own strengths and weaknesses, their ability to adjust their strategies, and the impact of their beliefs about learning and intelligence—indicates somewhat large obstacles to be overcome. In these cases, the most natural implication may be to address these issues as directly as possible—by working to raise students' awareness of the challenges they face and by considering some of the interventions that helped students productively modify their beliefs about intelligence—and, at the same time, to set reasonable expectations for how much improvement is likely to occur.

WHAT STRATEGIES DOES THE RESEARCH SUGGEST?

In this section we list strategies for promoting each of the aspects of metacognition discussed in the chapter. In addition, we present two strategies that can be useful in helping students develop metacognitive skills in general.

Assessing the Task at Hand

Be More Explicit Than You May Think Necessary   Although it is natural to assume that a basic description of an assignment is sufficient, students may have assumptions about the nature of the task that are not in line with yours. For example, students in a design course might assume from previous experiences that the goal of any project is simply getting a finished product that they like. With this in mind, they might focus solely on the final design or presentation. However, if the instructor's objective is for students to develop more sophisticated *process* skills (for example, researching relevant design ideas to spur their creativity, recording their exploration of multiple concepts, and explaining their design choices and revisions along the way to a final product), it may be necessary not only to express these goals explicitly but also to articulate what students need to do to meet the assignment's objectives (for example, keeping a process journal in which they document their design iterations and explain their thought processes). It may also help to explain to students why these particular goals are important (for example, "Developing strong process skills will help you become more consistent and more able to handle complex tasks").

Tell Students What You Do *Not* Want   In addition to clearly articulating your goals for an assignment, it can be helpful to identify what you do *not* mean by referring to common misinterpretations students have shown in the past or by explaining why some pieces of work do not meet your assignment goals. For example, in the case of writing, it is often helpful to share writing samples that are annotated to highlight strong or weak features. Such samples can also be used to give students practice at recognizing some of the components you want them to include in their work (for example, identifying an argument and its supporting evidence).

Check Students' Understanding of the Task   To make sure that students are accurately assessing the task at hand, ask them what they think they need to do to complete an assignment or how they plan to prepare for an upcoming exam. Then give them feedback, including suggestions of alternatives if their strategies do not map onto the requirements of the task. For complex assignments, ask students to rewrite the main goal of the assignment *in their own words* and then describe the steps that they feel they need to take in order to complete that goal.

Provide Performance Criteria with the Assignment   When distributing an assignment, clearly articulate the criteria that will be used to evaluate students' work. This can be done as a checklist that highlights the assignment's key requirements, such as content, structural features, and formatting details. Encourage students to refer to the checklist as they work on the assignment, and require them to submit a signed copy of it with the final product. With further practice on similar assignments, such checklists can be phased out as students begin to check their work on their own.

Your criteria could also be communicated to students through a performance rubric that explicitly represents the component parts of the task along with the characteristics of each component at varying levels of mastery (see Appendix C). Distributing the rubric with the assignment description—instead of only with the graded assignment—helps students assess the task more accurately. In addition to helping students "size up" a particular assignment, rubrics can help students develop other metacognitive habits, such as evaluating their own work against

205

a set of criteria. Over time, these metacognitive skills should become internalized and automatic, and the need for rubrics will decrease.

Evaluating One's Own Strengths and Weaknesses

Give Early, Performance-Based Assessments   Provide students with ample practice and timely feedback to help them develop a more accurate assessment of their strengths and weaknesses. Do this early enough in the semester so that they have time to learn from your feedback and adjust as necessary. Identify the particular skills that questions and assignments target (for example, "These first five questions ask you to define terms and concepts while the second set of five requires a more sophisticated synthesis of theoretical approaches") so that students can see how well they do on a range of skills and can focus their energies on improving weaker skills. These formative assessments should help students detect the knowledge gaps they need to overcome.

Provide Opportunities for Self-Assessment   You can also give students opportunities to assess themselves without adding extra grading for yourself. For example, you might give students practice exams (or other assignments) that replicate the kinds of questions that they will see on real exams and then provide answer keys so that students can check their own work. When doing so, it is important to emphasize to students that the true benefits come from *doing* the activity—that is, writing answers to sample essay questions or solving problems—and reflecting on the experience rather than simply looking over the answers provided. This is important because looking at a solution or model answer without first working through the problem can lead students to believe that they know how to generate answers when they only know how to recognize a good answer when it is given to them. For more information on self-assessments, see Appendix A.

Planning an Appropriate Approach

Have Students Implement a Plan That You Provide For complex assignments, provide students with a set of interim deadlines or a time line for deliverables that reflects the way that you would plan the stages of work—in other words, a model for effective planning. For example, for a semester-long research paper, you could ask students to submit an annotated bibliography of the sources they anticipate using by week four, a draft of their thesis statement in week six, evidence supporting their thesis in week eight, a visual representation of their paper's structure in week ten, and a draft that has been reviewed by at least three peers and revised accordingly in week twelve. Although requiring students to follow a plan that you provide does not give them practice developing their own plan, it does help them think about the component parts of a complex task, as well as their logical sequencing. Remember that planning is extremely difficult for novices. As students gain experience, this kind of explicit modeling can be gradually removed and students can be required to develop and submit their own plan for approval.

Have Students Create Their Own Plan When students' planning skills have developed to a degree that they can make plans more independently, you can require them to submit a plan as the first "deliverable" in larger assignments. This could be in the form of a project proposal, an annotated bibliography, or a time line that identifies the key stages of work. Provide feedback on their plan, given that this is a skill that they should continue to refine. If students perceive that planning is a valued and assessed component of a task, they will be more likely to focus

207

time and effort on planning and, as a result, benefit from their investment.

Make Planning the Central Goal of the Assignment   If you wish to reinforce the value of planning and help students develop the skills of generating and revising their own plans, assign some tasks that focus *solely* on planning. For example, instead of solving or completing a task, students could be asked to plan a solution strategy for a set of problems that involves describing how they would solve each problem. Such assignments allow students to focus all of their energy on thinking the problem through and planning an appropriate approach. They also make students' thought processes explicit, rather than requiring you to intuit them from a final product. Follow-up assignments can require students to implement their plans and reflect on their strengths and deficiencies.

Applying Strategies and Monitoring Performance

Provide Simple Heuristics for Self-Correction   Teach students basic heuristics for quickly assessing their own work and identifying errors. For example, encourage students to ask themselves, "Is this a reasonable answer, given the problem?" If the answer is unreasonable—such as a negative number for a quantity measuring length—the student knows that he did something wrong and can reconsider his reasoning or recalculate. There are often disciplinary heuristics that students should also learn to apply. For example, in an anthropology class, students might ask themselves, "What assumptions am I making here, and to what extent are they appropriate for cross-cultural analysis?" Similarly, instructors can provide more practical guidelines for assignments, such as how long it should take to complete an assignment. If students find that they are taking far longer to complete the task than is reasonable, they know to either try a different approach or to seek help.

Have Students Do Guided Self-Assessments Require students to assess their own work against a set of criteria that you provide. Exercises in self-assessment can raise students' awareness of task requirements, hone their ability to recognize the qualities of good as well as poor work, and teach them how to monitor their own progress toward learning goals. However, students may not be able to accurately assess their own work without first seeing this skill demonstrated or getting some explicit instruction and practice. For example, some instructors find it helpful to share annotated samples of student work, in which good and poor qualities of the work are highlighted, before asking students to assess their own work.

Require Students to Reflect on and Annotate Their Own Work Require as a component of the assignment that students explain what they did and why, describe how they responded to various challenges, and so on. This can be done in various ways for different disciplines. For example, engineering students can annotate problem sets, sociology students can answer reflective questions about their methodological decisions or assumptions, and architecture students can keep "process logs" in which they record various iterations of a design and explain their choices. Requiring reflection or annotation helps students become more conscious of their own thought processes and work strategies and can lead them to make more appropriate adjustments.

Use Peer Review/Reader Response Have students analyze their classmates' work and provide feedback. Reviewing one another's work can help students evaluate and monitor their own work more effectively and then revise it accordingly. However,

209

peer review is generally only effective when you give student reviewers specific criteria about what to look for and comment on (for example, a set of questions to answer or a rubric to follow). For example, you might ask student reviewers to assess whether a peer's writing has a clearly articulated argument and corresponding evidence to support the argument. Similarly, you might ask students to document or evaluate how a classmate has solved a math problem and provide their own recommendations for a more effective strategy. For more information on peer review/reader response, see Appendix H.

Reflecting on and Adjusting One's Approach

Provide Activities That Require Students to Reflect on Their Performances   Include as a component of projects and assignments—or across projects and assignments—a formal requirement that students reflect on and analyze their own performance. For example, they may answer questions such as: What did you learn from doing this project? What skills do you need to work on? How would you prepare differently or approach the final assignment based on feedback across the semester? How have your skills evolved across the last three assignments? Requiring this self-reflective step can give students a valuable opportunity to stop and assess their own strengths and weaknesses and to build their metacognitive skills.

Prompt Students to Analyze the Effectiveness of Their Study Skills   When students learn to reflect on the effectiveness of their own approach, they are able to identify problems and make the necessary adjustments. A specific example of a self-reflective activity is an "exam wrapper." Exam wrappers are typically short handouts that students complete when an exam is returned to them; exam wrappers guide students through a brief analysis of their own performance on an exam and then ask students to relate their performance to various features of how they studied or prepared. For example, an exam wrapper might ask students (1) what types of errors they made (for example, mathematical versus conceptual), (2) how they studied (for example, "looked over" problems the night before versus worked out multiple problems a week prior to the exam), and (3) what they will do differently in preparation for the next exam (for example, rework problems from scratch rather than simply skim solutions). When students complete and submit exam wrappers after one exam, their responses can be returned to them before the next exam so they have a ready reminder of what they learned from their prior exam experience that can help them study more effectively. For more information on exam wrappers, see Appendix F.

Present Multiple Strategies   Show students multiple ways that a task or problem can be conceptualized, represented, or solved. One method for doing this in the arts is through public critiques in which students share different ways that they approached the problem, thus presenting one another with a range of possible solutions. In this way, students get exposure to multiple methods and can consider their pros and cons under a variety of circumstances. In other courses, students might be asked to solve problems in multiple ways and then discuss the advantages and disadvantages of the different methods. Exposing students to different approaches and analyzing their merits can highlight the value of critical exploration.

Create Assignments That Focus on Strategizing Rather Than Implementation   Have students propose a range of potential strategies and predict their advantages and disadvantages *rather than* actually choosing and carrying one through. For example, students might be asked to assess the applicability of different

211

formulas, methodologies, or artistic techniques for a given problem or task. By putting the emphasis of the assignment on thinking the problem through, rather than solving it, students get practice evaluating strategies in relation to their appropriate or fruitful application.

Beliefs About Intelligence and Learning

Address Students' Beliefs About Learning Directly   Even if it is not directly germane to the disciplinary content of your course, consider discussing the nature of learning and intelligence with your students to disabuse them of unproductive beliefs (for example, "I can't draw" or "I can't do math") and to highlight the positive effects of practice, effort, and adaptation. Some instructors like to point out that the brain is a muscle that requires exercise or to make the analogy between the ongoing practice and discipline required by musicians, dancers, and athletes and the mental discipline and practice necessary for developing intellectual skills.

Broaden Students' Understanding of Learning   Students often believe that "you either know something or you don't know it." In fact, learning and knowledge can operate on multiple levels, from the ability to recall a fact, concept, or theory (declarative knowledge) to knowing how to apply it (procedural knowledge) to knowing when to apply it (contextual knowledge) to knowing why it is appropriate in a particular situation (conceptual knowledge). In other words, you can know something at one level (recognize it) and still not *know* it (know how to use it). Consider introducing students to these various forms of knowledge so that they can more accurately assess a task (for example, "This calls for me to define x and explain when it is applicable"), assess their own strengths and weaknesses in relation to it (for example, "I can define x but I don't know when to use it"), and identify gaps in their education (for example, "I've never learned how to use x"). You might also point out to students that different kinds of knowledge are required for different tasks—for example, solving problems, writing poetry, designing products, and performing on stage. Asking students to consider diverse types and dimensions of knowledge can help expand their beliefs about intelligence and ability in ways that enhance their metacognitive development. (For more information on types of knowledge, see Chapter One and Appendix D.)

Help Students Set Realistic Expectations Give students realistic expectations for the time that it might take them to develop particular skills. It can be helpful to recall your own frustrations as a student and to describe how you (or famous figures in your field) overcame various obstacles. Seeing that intelligent and accomplished people sometimes struggle to gain mastery—and that learning does not happen magically or without effort—can prompt students to revise their own expectations about learning and their views of intelligence and to persevere when they encounter difficulty. It can also help students avoid unproductive and often inaccurate attributions about themselves (for example, "I can't do it; I must be dumb," "This is too hard; I'm not cut out for science") or the environment (for example, "I still haven't learned it; this instructor is no good," "I failed; the test was unfair") and instead focus on aspects of learning over which they have control: their effort, concentration, study habits, level of engagement, and so on.

General Strategies to Promote Metacognition

Beyond the strategies listed above that target individual processes of the metacognitive cycle, there are two additional strategies—

213

modeling and scaffolding—that are useful for supporting a variety of metacognitive skills. These strategies can be employed to promote the development of multiple metacognitive skills at once or to concentrate on a particular one.

Modeling Your Metacognitive Processes Show students how you yourself would approach an assignment and walk them through the various phases of *your* metacognitive process. Let them hear you "talk out loud" as you describe the way you would assess the task ("I like to begin by asking what the central problem is and considering the audience") and assess your own strengths and weaknesses in relation to the task ("I have a pretty good handle on the basic concepts, but I don't yet know what recent research has been done on the subject"). Then lay out your plan of action explicitly, articulating the various steps that you would undertake to complete the assignment ("I would start by browsing the relevant journals online, then create a set of exploratory sketches, then ..."). You could also include in your modeling some discussion of how you evaluate and monitor your progress—for example, by mentioning the kinds of questions you ask yourself to ensure that you are on the right path ("Could I be solving this problem more efficiently?" or "Am I making any questionable assumptions here?"). It is especially helpful for students to see that even experts—in fact, *especially* experts—constantly reassess and adjust as they go. Finally, you can show your students how you would evaluate the finished product ("I would revisit the original goal of the project and ask myself whether I satisfied it" or "I would ask a friend of mine with some knowledge of the subject matter to read my essay and point out logical inconsistencies").

A variation on, or potentially a second stage of, this modeling process is to lead students through a given task with a series of questions they can ask themselves each step of the way (for example, How would you begin? What step would you take next? How would you know if your strategy is working? Is there an alternative approach?).

Scaffold Students in Their Metacognitive Processes   Scaffolding refers to the process by which instructors provide students with cognitive supports early in their learning, and then gradually remove them as students develop greater mastery and sophistication. There are several forms of scaffolding that can help students develop stronger metacognitive skills. First, instructors can give students practice working on discrete phases of the metacognitive process in isolation before asking students to integrate them. (Some examples of this were discussed in relation to specific phases of metacognition.) Breaking down the process highlights the importance of particular stages, such as task assessment and planning, that students often undervalue or omit while giving them practice with and feedback on each skill individually. After giving students practice with particular skills in isolation, it is equally important to give students practice synthesizing skills and using them in combination. Ultimately, the goal of this form of scaffolding is to progress toward more complexity and integration.

A second form of scaffolding involves a progression from tasks with considerable instructor-provided structure to tasks that require greater or even complete student autonomy. For example, you might first assign a project in which students must follow a plan that *you* devise—perhaps including a breakdown of component tasks, a timetable, and interim deadlines for deliverables—and then in later projects relegate more of these planning and self-monitoring responsibilities to the students themselves.

SUMMARY

Faculty members almost invariably possess strong metacognitive skills themselves, even if they are not explicitly aware of using them. They may, as a result, assume that students also possess these skills or that they will develop them naturally and inevitably. Consequently, faculty may both overestimate their students' metacognitive abilities and underestimate the extent to which these skills and habits must be taught and reinforced through thoughtful instruction. Indeed, the research cited in this chapter suggests that metacognition does *not* necessarily develop on its own and that instructors can play a critical role in helping students develop the metacognitive skills that they need to succeed in college: assessing the task at hand, evaluating one's own strengths and weaknesses, planning, monitoring performance along the way, and reflecting on one's overall success.

Conclusion:
Applying the Seven
Principles to Ourselves

By now, the power of the principles described in the book should be apparent. These principles explain and predict a wide range of learning behaviors and phenomena and hence aid the design of courses and classroom pedagogy. Their interconnectedness should also be evident. Many of the problems students encounter when learning stem from an interaction of intellectual, social, and emotional factors. Therefore, their pedagogical solutions must address all these facets at once. This is achievable precisely because our principles work together to provide such solutions. It also means that the number of strategies we must master to be effective teachers is not infinite. In fact, although the specific strategies throughout this book vary from chapter to chapter, there are recurring themes among the strategies, such as collecting data about students, modeling expert practice, scaffolding complex tasks, and being explicit about objectives and expectations. These basic themes jointly address cognitive, motivational, and developmental goals. For instance, being explicit about one's learning objectives and grading criteria helps students see the component parts of a complex task and thus allows them to target their practice and move toward mastery. It also serves a motivational function because it increases students' expectations of success at the task, and it even impacts the learning climate by fostering a sense of fairness.

What is perhaps less evident is that these principles of learning apply to instructors as well because, when it comes to teaching, most of us are still learning. Teaching is a complex activity, and yet most of us have not received formal training in pedagogy. Furthermore, teaching is a highly contextualized activity because it is shaped by the students we have, advancements in our respective fields, changes in technology, and so on. Therefore, our teaching must constantly adapt to changing parameters. Although this realization can be overwhelming for some, it can also help us reframe our approach to improving our teaching because it means that we need not expect a static perfection, but a developing mastery of teaching. Learning to improve one's teaching is a process of progressive refinement, which, like other learning processes, is informed by the learning principles set forth in this book. This concluding chapter applies our seven learning principles to the process of learning about teaching. We highlight each principle's implications to learning about teaching. Just as in the previous chapters, we consider each principle individually for ease of exposition, but the ideas stemming from the seven principles together are all interrelated.

Like students, we possess a lot of *prior knowledge,* upon which we draw consciously and unconsciously when we teach, and this prior knowledge affects further learning and performance. But as we have seen, prior knowledge can be insufficient, inaccurate, or inappropriate, in which case it will hinder further learning. For instance, as experts in our respective fields, we possess a wealth of content knowledge, but this alone is insufficient for effective teaching. Some of us also possess the misconception that good teaching is all about entertainment and personality, and

218

that to be a good teacher one must be outgoing and funny. Not only is this notion inaccurate but it is also problematic because it locks both introvert and extrovert teachers in narrow and rigid roles without much room for growth. Finally, although it is helpful to be mindful of our own experiences as learners, it would be inappropriate to presume that all our students will share the same experiences we do and that therefore whatever teaching methods worked for us should work for our students as well. As pointed out repeatedly throughout this book, we are different from our students in many important ways. One of the recurring strategies emphasized in this book involves collecting data about students to help inform our teaching practice. Seen in this light, learning about our students is a way to build on our prior knowledge by learning more about the context and using this information to tailor our teaching to our audience.

Of course, in conjunction with the knowledge we possess about teaching, we need to think about the *organization* of that knowledge. Many of us started our careers without a rich, integrated, and flexible network of knowledge about teaching. For example, it is fairly common to keep one's knowledge of teaching compartmentalized by course: these are the kinds of assignments that work better for this course, these are the kinds of policies that are necessary when teaching first-year students, and so on. This organization is born out of experience, but it does not make for a flexible and systematic way to think about teaching because it centers on surface features of the course. The principles of learning presented in this book offer a deeper, more meaningful structure for organizing one's knowledge of teaching and learning and for building on that knowledge. This will help, for instance, when planning a new course for a new audience.

But refining our teaching is not only a cognitive process. It is also important to consider our *motivation* to learn (and continue to learn) about teaching. Given our other professional constraints,

219

what will sustain our efforts to improve our teaching? As we have seen, motivation is broadly determined by value and expectancy. One thing that most instructors value is efficiency. We are all busy and have demands on our time, and working on our teaching taxes that limited resource. Therefore, it is important that the time investment pays off. Several of the strategies we offer in this book require a time investment up front, but they yield time savings later on, especially for future iterations of the same course. For instance, creating a rubric can be time-consuming, especially if you have never created one, but it also saves time later by stream-lining the grading process and reducing student complaints—in addition to the learning benefits for students. On the expectation side, we are more likely to stay motivated if we set teaching goals for ourselves that are realistic, so that we are more likely to main-tain confidence in our ability to achieve those goals. This may, for example, mean that we should concentrate on improving one or two aspects of our teaching in a given semester, rather than trying to address everything simultaneously. It also might mean that instead of making radical changes to a course, we attempt more incremental changes, reflecting on them as we go. Many success-ful, experienced instructors maintain that it takes at the very least three years of progressive refinement to build an effective course.

Realistic expectations are especially important because teach-ing is a complex skill. To develop *mastery* in teaching, we need to acquire its component skills, integrate them, and apply them appropriately. Of course, this requires that we first unpack the multifaceted task of teaching. For example, the ability to facilitate productive and engaging discussions requires several subskills: the ability to pose appropriate questions, listen empathetically, maintain flow, respectfully correct misconceptions, manage time effectively, and many more. Putting all these skills together is the ultimate multitask. That is why we need to acquire fluency in each of them so that we develop enough automaticity to reduce the cognitive load that any one of them requires. Moreover, as with the development of mastery in any other domain, teaching requires learning when and where various teaching strategies and instructional approaches are applicable; for example, when one's learning objectives would be best served by group projects or case studies and when they would not, or when a multiple choice test is warranted and when it is not. In other words, refining our teaching practice requires that we transfer what we learn about teaching from one context to another, making adjustments as our courses, our students, our fields—and, indeed, ourselves—change.

Developing mastery in teaching is a learning process, and as such it requires the coupling of *practice and feedback*. As we have seen, for practice to be maximally effective, it should be focused on clear goals. In order to set appropriate goals for our teaching, we can be guided by timely and frequent feedback on what aspects of our courses are and are not working. Most institutions mandate end-of-semester evaluations in which students can give instructors feedback about their teaching, but that kind of feedback is not the most useful for direct improvement of our teaching practice because it happens at the end of the term. The best feedback is formative feedback throughout the semester. This feedback can come from sources such as early course evaluations, student management teams, colleagues, and teaching center staff. So, for instance, if students raise concerns about the organization of our lectures, this can help us focus our efforts on a particular goal to help us improve. Just as many of our students do not think of the homework as practicing specific skills, most of us do not think of our teaching as "practice." However, like our students, we learn most efficiently when we target the skills we most need to develop. If we think of teaching as deliberate, focused practice, in the hypothetical situation above we could decide to follow specific practices such as having an agenda for every lecture or making transitions between subtopics more explicit.

221

Thinking of teaching as progressive refinement raises the notion of *development,* which happens in the context of a given *climate.* What does this developmental process look like? First, instructors—like students—go through a process of intellectual development. We might begin at a stage where we are looking for the "right answer," the pedagogical magic bullet that will, say, achieve full student participation during classroom discussion. At some other stages, we might regard teaching solely as a matter of personal style and believe there is no better or worse way to go about it. At later stages we might realize that teaching is highly contextualized and think about the many decisions we need to make as educators in terms of student learning. Second, our identity as instructors also goes through developmental stages. We have to work to develop a sense of competence and autonomy in teaching, integrity, and purpose as educators, a productive way to relate to the students, and appropriate ways to express our emotions in the classroom. In advanced stages of intellectual and identity development, we might develop trust in our own style while being open to improvement. Because this developmental process involves us intellectually as well as socially and emotionally, the broader climate in which we learn about teaching matters. For instance, being in a department that really values teaching can be energizing. Conversely, the climate can be demoralizing in a department that does not adequately support efforts to improve teaching. As we have discussed, the climate will have an impact on us whether we realize it or not. However, if we realize that our immediate climate is affecting us negatively, we have a number of options. We can branch out and seek a more supportive climate by broadening our reach to colleagues in other departments, to the education section of the various professional associations, or to the teaching center on campus.

In this chapter, we have highlighted various aspects of learning about teaching using the learning principles as lenses of analysis. In general, all these principles can help us be more reflective—that is, metacognitive—about our teaching. As shown in this book, *self-directed learning* (metacognition) requires engaging in a cyclical process with several phases. Specifically, we need to carefully consider our own strengths and weaknesses in relation to our teaching, not only so we can play to our strengths but also so we can challenge ourselves to develop in areas in which we may need work. Moreover, since the task of teaching constantly changes (as our student population changes, as we teach new courses, as we revise old courses to include new material, as we try new approaches), we must continually reassess the task, plan an effective approach, monitor our progress, evaluate, and adjust. Just as many students do not naturally think of planning before they get started on a task, many instructors do the same with their courses. For instance, they construct the assessments for a course as an afterthought, instead of planning them to be in alignment with the course's learning objectives and instructional strategies from the beginning. Knowing that we are likely to skip some of the steps in the metacognitive cycle can help us be mindful of this tendency and compensate for it.

Finally, refining our teaching practice requires being aware of our core beliefs about teaching and learning. For instance, what do we believe is the purpose of our teaching? What do we believe about intelligence, ability, and learning? All these beliefs will impact our metacognitive cycle. For instance, if we think of teaching skill as a talent that one either has or lacks, we may not engage in the kinds of behaviors (for example, self-reflection, comparing strategies with colleagues, seeking professional development, and reading this book!) that might help us improve. Conversely, if we think of teaching as a set of skills one can develop and refine, it makes sense to engage in progressive refinement and in the whole metacognitive cycle. This book is a start in that process and an invitation to keep thinking and learning about teaching, as we hope that the ideas presented here will be generative of more insights and more strategies as they are applied and refined over time.

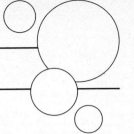

APPENDIX A

What Is Student Self-Assessment and How Can We Use It?

One way to gather feedback on students' prior knowledge and skills is to ask them to assess their own level of knowledge or skill. The objective is to get an idea of the range of abilities and experience of the class as a whole, not to evaluate individuals. Questions can focus on knowledge, skills, or experiences that you assume students have acquired and are prerequisites to your course, things that you believe are valuable to know but not essential, and topics and skills that you plan to address in the course. Students' responses to such questions can help you calibrate your course appropriately or help you direct students to supplemental materials that will help them fill in gaps or weaknesses in their existing skill or knowledge base that may hinder their progress. The questions also help students focus on the most important knowledge and skills addressed by your course and access information from prior courses or experiences that apply to your course.

The advantage of a self-assessment instrument is that it is relatively easy to construct and score and, because it can be administered anonymously, it is low-anxiety for the student. The weakness of the method is that students may not be able to accurately assess their abilities. Generally, people tend to overestimate their knowledge and skills. However, accuracy improves when the response options are clear and tied to specific concepts or behaviors that students can reflect on or even mentally simulate, such as being able to define a term, explain a concept, or recall specific kinds and qualities of experience, such as building or writing or performing in a specific context.

Exhibit A.1 presents some examples of questions and response items.

Exhibit A.1. Sample Self-Assessments

How familiar are you with "Karnaugh maps"?

a. I have never heard of them or I have heard of them but don't know what they are.
b. I have some idea of what they are but don't know when or how to use them.
c. I have a clear idea of what they are but haven't used them.
d. I can explain what they are and what they do, and I have used them.

Have you designed or built a digital logic circuit?

a. I have neither designed nor built one.
b. I have designed one but have never built one.
c. I have built one but have not designed one.
d. I have both designed and built a digital logic circuit.

How familiar are you with a "t-test"?

a. I have never heard of it.
b. I have heard of it but don't remember what it is.
c. I have some idea of what it is, but am not too clear.
d. I know what it is and could explain what it's for.
e. I know what it is and when to use it and could use it to analyze data.

How familiar are you with Photoshop?

a. I have never used it, or I have tried it but couldn't really do anything with it.

b. I can do simple edits using preset options to manipulate single images (e.g., standard color, orientation, and size manipulations).
c. I can manipulate multiple images using preset editing features to create desired effects.
d. I can easily use precision editing tools to manipulate multiple images for professional quality output.

For each of the following Shakespearean plays, place a check mark in the cells that describe your experience.

Play	Have seen a TV or movie production	Have seen a live performance	Have read it	Have written a college-level paper on it
Hamlet				
King Lear				
Henry IV				
Othello				

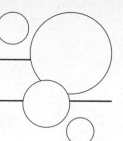

APPENDIX B

What Are Concept Maps and How Can We Use Them?

Concept maps are graphical tools for organizing and representing knowledge (Novak & Cañas, 2008). They are drawn as nodes and links in a network structure in which nodes represent concepts, usually enclosed in circles or boxes, and links represent relationships, usually indicated by lines drawn between two associate nodes. Words on the line, referred to as linking words or linking phrases, specify the relationship between the two concepts.

Both your students and you can benefit from the construction of concept maps. You can ask students to draw concept maps to get insight into what they already know and how they represent their knowledge. You can then use that information to direct your teaching. You can also use concept maps to see students' developing understanding and knowledge over time. For example, you can have students create maps several times throughout a course (at the beginning, middle, and end of the course), compare and contrast earlier and later maps, and discuss how their understanding of the course material has changed over the semester.

It is best for students to construct concept maps with reference to some particular question they seek to answer, which is called a focus question. The concept map may pertain to some

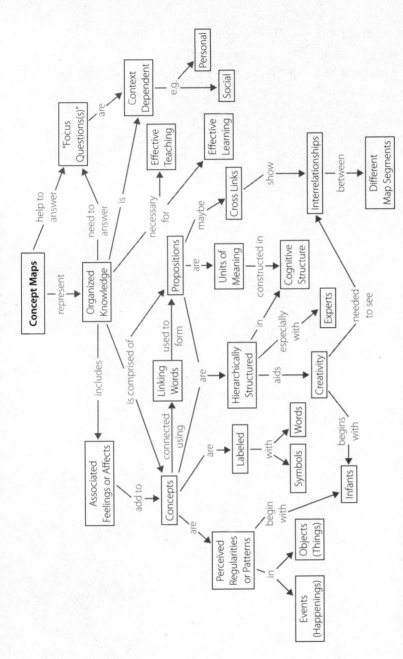

Figure B.1. Sample Concept Map

Reproduced from Novak, J. D., & Cañas, A. J. (2008), "The Theory Underlying Concept Maps and How to Construct Them." (Technical Report IHMC CmapTools 2006-01 Rev 2008-01). Pensacola, FL: Institute for Human and Machine Cognition. Retrieved March 26, 2009, from http://cmap.ihmc.us/Publications/ResearchPapers/ TheoryUnderlyingConceptMaps.pdf.

situation or event that we are trying to understand through the organization of knowledge in the form of a concept map, thus providing the context for the concept map. For example, you could ask students to answer the question "What are the reasons for the 2008–2009 financial crisis?" via a concept map.

For an example of a concept map that visually addresses the question "What are concept maps?" see Figure B.1. For more information on how to create and use concept maps, see Novak (1998).

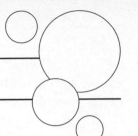

APPENDIX C

What Are Rubrics and How Can We Use Them?

A rubric is a scoring tool that explicitly represents the instructor's performance expectations for an assignment or piece of work. A rubric divides the assigned work into component parts and provides clear descriptions of different levels of quality associated with each component. Rubrics can be used for a wide array of assignments: papers, projects, oral presentations, artistic performances, group projects, and so on. Rubrics can be used as scoring or grading guides, and to provide formative feedback to support and guide ongoing learning efforts.

Using a rubric provides several advantages to both instructors and students. Grading according to an explicit and descriptive set of criteria (designed to reflect the weighted importance of the objectives of the assignment) helps ensure that the instructor's grading standards remain consistent across a given assignment. Furthermore, although they initially take time to develop, rubrics can reduce the time spent grading by reducing uncertainty and by allowing instructors to refer to the rubric description rather than having to write long comments. Finally, grading rubrics are invaluable in large courses that have multiple graders (other instructors, teaching assistants, and so on) because they can help ensure consistency across graders.

Used more formatively, rubrics can help instructors get a clearer picture of the strengths and weaknesses of their students as a group. By recording the component scores and tallying up the number of students scoring below an acceptable level on each component, instructors can identify those skills or concepts that need more instructional time and student effort.

When rubrics are given to students with the assignment description, they can help students monitor and assess their progress as they work toward clearly indicated goals. When assignments are scored and returned with the rubric, students can more easily recognize the strengths and weaknesses of their work and direct their efforts accordingly.

For sample rubrics, see Exhibits C.1, C.2, C.3, and C.4. For detailed information on how to construct a rubric, see Stevens and Levi (2005).

Exhibit C.1. Rubric for Class Participation

	A (Exemplary)	B (Competent)	C (Developing)	D/R
Frequency and Quality	Attends class regularly and *always contributes* to the discussion by raising thoughtful questions, analyzing relevant issues, building on others' ideas, synthesizing across readings and discussions, expanding the class' perspective, and appropriately challenging assumptions and perspectives	Attends class regularly and *sometimes contributes* to the discussion in the aforementioned ways.	Attends class regularly but *rarely contributes* to the discussion in the aforementioned ways.	Attends class regularly but *never contributes* to the discussion in the aforementioned ways.

SOURCE: Eberly Center for Teaching Excellence, Carnegie Mellon University.

Exhibit C.2. Rubric for Oral Exams

Dimensions	A (18–20 points) Exemplary	B (16–17 points) Competent	C (14–15 points) Developing	D/R
Overall Understanding	Shows a deep/robust understanding of the topic with a fully developed argument per the categories below	Shows a limited understanding of the topic, not quite a fully developed argument per the categories below	Shows a superficial understanding of the topic, argument not developed enough per the categories below	Shows no understanding of the topic and no argument per the categories below
Argument	Clearly articulates a position or argument	Articulates a position or argument that is incomplete or limited in scope	Articulates a position or argument that is unfocused or ambiguous	Does not articulate a position or argument
Evidence	Presents evidence that is *relevant and accurate* Presents *sufficient* amount of evidence to support argument	Presents evidence that is *mostly relevant and/or mostly accurate* Presents *limited* evidence to support argument	Presents evidence that is *somewhat inaccurate and/or irrelevant, but* corrects when prompted Does *not* present *enough* evidence to support argument, but augments when prompted	Presents *a lot of inaccurate and/or irrelevant evidence* Doesn't present enough evidence to support argument, even when prompted repeatedly

Implications	Fully discusses the major implications of the argument or position	Adequately discusses some of the major implications of the position	Discusses minor implications (missing the major ones) *or* does not discuss major implications adequately	Doesn't discuss the implications of the argument or position
Structure	There is logic in the progression of ideas	There are a few areas of disjointedness or intermittent lack of logical progression of ideas	Ideas are somewhat disjointed and/or do not always flow logically, making it a bit difficult to follow	Ideas are disjointed and/or do not flow logically, hence argument is very difficult to follow
Prompting	Did not have to prompt with probing questions at all	Prompted minimally (one or two probing questions)	Prompted a lot (a series of probing questions)	

SOURCE: Eberly Center for Teaching Excellence, Carnegie Mellon University.

Exhibit C.3. Rubric for Papers

	Excellent	Competent	Not Yet Competent	Poor
Creativity and Originality	You exceed the parameters of the assignment, with original insights or a particularly engaging style.	You meet all the parameters of the assignment.	You meet most of the parameters of the assignment.	You do not meet the parameters of the assignment.
Argument	Your central argument is clear, interesting, and demonstrable (i.e., based on evidence, not opinion). The claims made in the body of your paper clearly and obviously support your central argument. Your arguments and claims reflect a robust and nuanced understanding of key ideas from this course.	Your central argument is clear and demonstrable. The claims made in the body of your paper support your central argument. Your arguments and claims reflect a solid understanding of key ideas from this course.	Your central argument is demonstrable but not entirely clear. A few of the claims made in the body of your paper do not clearly support your central argument. Your arguments and claims reflect some understanding of key ideas from this course.	Your central argument is unclear or it is not demonstrable. The claims made in the body of your paper do not support your central argument. Your arguments and claims reflect little understanding of key ideas from this course.

Evidence	The evidence you use is specific, rich, varied, and unambiguously supports your claims. Quotations and illustrations are framed effectively and explicated appropriately in the text.	The evidence you use supports your claims. Quotations and illustrations are framed reasonably effectively and explicated appropriately in the text.	Some of the evidence you use does not support your claims. Some of the quotations and illustrations are not framed effectively or explicated appropriately in the text.	Little of the evidence you use supports your claims. Few of the quotations and illustrations are framed effectively or explicated appropriately in the text.
Structure	Your ideas are presented in a logical and coherent manner throughout the paper, with strong topic sentences to guide the reader. The reader can effortlessly follow the structure of your argument.	The reader can follow the structure of your argument with very little effort.	The reader cannot always follow the structure of your argument.	The reader cannot follow the structure of your argument.

(Continued)

Exhibit C.3. (*Continued*)

	Excellent	Competent	Not Yet Competent	Poor
Clarity	Your sentences are concise and well crafted, and the vocabulary is precise; the reader can effortlessly discern your meaning.	The reader can discern your meaning with very little effort.	The reader cannot always discern your meaning.	The reader cannot discern your meaning.
Mechanics	There are no distracting spelling, punctuation, or grammatical errors, and quotations are all properly cited.	There are few distracting spelling, punctuation, and/or grammatical errors, and quotations are all properly cited.	There are some distracting spelling, punctuation, and/or grammatical errors, and/or some of the quotations are not properly cited.	There are significant and distracting spelling, punctuation, or grammatical errors, and/or the quotations are improperly cited.

SOURCE: Eberly Center for Teaching Excellence, Carnegie Mellon University.

Exhibit C.4. Senior Design Project Rubric

Component	Sophisticated	Competent	Not Yet Competent
Research & Design			
Identifies project objectives based on general description and client requirements	All important major and minor objectives are identified and appropriately prioritized.	All major objectives are identified but one or two minor ones are missing or priorities are not established.	Many major objectives are not identified.
Identifies relevant and valid information to support decision-making.	All relevant information is obtained and information sources are valid. Design recommendations are well supported by the information.	Sufficient information is obtained and most sources are valid. Design recommendations are mostly supported by the information.	Insufficient information is obtained and/or sources lack validity. Design recommendations are not supported by information collected.
Generation and analysis of alternatives.	Three or more alternatives are considered. Each alternative is appropriately and correctly analyzed for technical feasibility.	At least three alternatives are considered. Appropriate analyses are selected but analyses include some minor procedural errors.	Only one or two alternatives are considered. Inappropriate analyses are selected and/or major procedural and conceptual errors are made.

(Continued)

Exhibit C.4. (*Continued*)

Component	Sophisticated	Competent	Not Yet Competent
Identifies relevant constraints (economic, environmental/safety, sustainability, etc.)	All relevant constraints are identified and accurately analyzed.	Most constraints are identified; some are not adequately addressed or accurately analyzed.	Few or no constraints are identified or some constraints are identified but not accurately analyzed.
Generates valid conclusions/decisions	Recommended solution is based on stated criteria, analysis, and constraints.	Solution/decision is reasonable; further analysis of some of the alternatives or constraints may have led to different recommendation.	Only one solution is considered or other solutions were ignored or incompletely analyzed. Many constraints and criteria were ignored.
Communication Presentation Visual aids Oral presentation Body language	Slides are error-free and logically present the main components of the process and recommendations. Material is readable and the graphics highlight and support the main ideas.	Slides are error-free and logically present the main components of the process and recommendations. Material is mostly readable and graphics reiterate the main ideas.	Slides contain errors and lack a logical progression. Major aspects of the analysis or recommendations are absent. Diagrams or graphics are absent or confuse the audience.

Speakers are audible and fluent on their topic, and do not rely on notes to present or respond. Speakers respond accurately and appropriately to audience questions and comments.	Speakers are mostly audible and fluent on their topic, and require minimal referral to notes. Speakers respond to most questions accurately and appropriately.	Speakers are often inaudible or hesitant, often speaking in incomplete sentences. Speakers rely heavily on notes. Speakers have difficulty responding clearly and accurately to audience questions.
Body language, as indicated by appropriate and meaningful gestures (e.g., drawing hands inward to convey contraction, moving arms up to convey lift, etc.), eye contact with audience, and movement, demonstrates a high level of comfort and connection with the audience.	Body language, as indicated by a slight tendency to repetitive and distracting gestures (e.g., tapping a pen, wringing hands, waving arms, clenching fists, etc.) and breaking eye contact with audience, demonstrates a slight discomfort with the audience.	Body language, as indicated by frequent, repetitive, and distracting gestures, little or no audience eye-contact, and/or stiff posture and movement, indicate a high degree of discomfort interacting with audience.

(Continued)

Exhibit C.4. (*Continued*)

Component	Sophisticated	Competent	Not Yet Competent
Team Work (Based on peer evaluation, observations of group meetings, and presentation)			
Delegation and fulfillment of responsibilities	Responsibilities delegated fairly. Each member contributes in a valuable way to the project. All members always attended meetings and met deadlines for deliverables.	Some minor inequities in the delegation of responsibilities. Some members contribute more heavily than others but all members meet their responsibilities. Members regularly attended meetings with only a few absences, and deadlines for deliverables were met.	Major inequities in delegation of responsibilities. Group has obvious freeloaders who fail to meet their responsibilities or members who dominate and prevent others from contributing. Members would often miss meetings, and/or deadlines were often missed.

Team morale and cohesiveness	Team worked well together to achieve objectives. Members enjoyed interacting with each other and learned from each other. All data sources indicated a high level of mutual respect and collaboration.	Team worked well together most of the time, with only a few occurrences of communication breakdown or failure to collaborate when appropriate. Members were mostly respectful of each other.	Team did not collaborate or communicate well. Some members would work independently, without regard to objectives or priorities. A lack of respect and regard was frequently noted.

Used by permission of Dr. John Oyler.

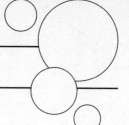

APPENDIX D

What Are Learning Objectives and How Can We Use Them?

Learning objectives articulate the knowledge and skills you want students to acquire by the end of the course or after completing a particular assignment. There are numerous benefits to clearly stating your objectives, for both you and your students. First, learning objectives communicate your intentions to students, and they give students information to better direct their learning efforts and monitor their own progress. Objectives also provide you with a framework for selecting and organizing course content, and they can guide your decisions about appropriate assessment and evaluation methods. Finally, objectives provide a framework for selecting appropriate teaching and learning activities (Miller, 1987).

What makes a learning objective clear and helpful? There are four elements. First, learning objectives should be *student-centered*; for example, stated as "Students should be able to _____." Second, they should *break down the task* and focus on specific cognitive processes. Many activities that faculty believe require a single skill (for example, writing or problem solving) actually involve a synthesis of many component skills. To master these complex skills, students must practice and gain proficiency in the discrete component skills. For example, writing may involve identifying an argument, enlisting appropriate evidence, organizing paragraphs, and so on, whereas problem solving may require defining the parameters of the problem, choosing appropriate formulas, and so on. Third, clear objectives should *use action verbs* to focus on concrete actions and behaviors that allow us to make student learning explicit, and communicate to students the kind of intellectual effort we expect of them. Furthermore, using action verbs reduces ambiguity in what it means to "understand." Finally, clear objectives should be *measurable*. We should be able to easily check (that is, assess) whether students have mastered a skill (for example, asking students to *state* a given theorem, *solve* a textbook problem, or *identify* the appropriate principle).

Determining the action verbs for learning objectives is made easier as a result of the work of Benjamin Bloom, who created a taxonomy of educational objectives (1956) that, with slight revision (Anderson & Krathwohl, 2001), is still used today by educators around the world. This taxonomy represents six levels of intellectual behavior, from the simple recall of facts to the creation of new knowledge. These levels, combined with verbs that represent the intellectual activity at each level, can help faculty members articulate their course objectives and hence focus both their and their students' attention and effort.

For examples of action verbs, see Table D.1, and for sample objectives, see Exhibit D.1.

Table D.1. Sample Verbs for Bloom's Taxonomy

Remember	Understand	Apply	Analyze	Evaluate	Create
Arrange	Associate	Calculate	Break down	Appraise	Assemble
Define	Classify	Construct	Combine	Argue	Build
Describe	Compare	Demonstrate	Compare	Assess	Compose
Duplicate	Contrast	Develop	Contrast	Check	Construct
Identify	Describe	Employ	Debate	Conclude	Design
Label	Differentiate	Estimate	Diagram	Critique	Formulate
List	Discuss	Examine	Examine	Detect	Generate
Locate	Exemplify	Execute	Experiment	Judge	Integrate
Name	Explain	Formulate	Extrapolate	Justify	Produce
Recall	Infer	Implement	Formulate	Monitor	Propose
Recite	Interpret	Modify	Illustrate	Rank	Rearrange
Recognize	Paraphrase	Sketch	Organize	Rate	Set up
Reproduce	Restate	Solve	Predict	Recommend	Transform
Select	Summarize	Use	Question	Select	
State	Translate			Test	
				Weigh	

Exhibit D.1. Sample Learning Objectives

By the end of the course students should be able to

- Articulate and debunk common myths about Mexican immigration (History)
- Discuss features and limitations of various sampling procedures and research methodologies (Statistics)
- Design an experimental study, carry out an appropriate statistical analysis of the data, and properly interpret and communicate the analyses (Decision Sciences)
- Analyze simple circuits that include resistors and capacitors (Engineering)
- Execute different choreographic styles (Dance)
- Sketch and/or prototype scenarios of use to bring opportunity areas to life (Design)
- Analyze any vocal music score and prepare the same score individually for any audition, rehearsal, or performance (Musical Theater)

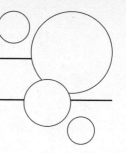

What Are Ground Rules and How Can We Use Them?

Ground rules help to maintain a productive classroom climate by clearly articulating a set of expected behaviors for classroom conduct, especially for discussions. Ground rules can be set by the instructor or created by the students themselves (some people believe that students adhere more to ground rules they have played a role in creating). Ground rules should reflect the objectives of the course. For example, if an objective of the course is for students to enlist evidence to support an opinion, a ground rule could reinforce that goal; if a goal is for students to connect content material to personal experiences, then ground rules that protect privacy and create a safe environment for sharing personal information are important.

Ground rules should be established at the beginning of a course, and the instructor should explain the purpose they serve (for example, to ensure that discussions are spirited and passionate without descending into argumentation, that everyone is heard, and that participants work together toward greater understanding rather than contribute disjointed pieces). Some instructors ask students to sign a contract based on the ground rules; others simply discuss and agree to the ground rules informally. It is important for instructors to remind students of these ground rules periodically, particularly if problems occur (for example, students cutting one another off in discussion or making inappropriate personal comments). Instructors should also be sure to hold students accountable to these rules, for example, by exacting a small penalty for infractions (this can be done in a lighthearted way, perhaps by asking students who violate the rules to contribute a dollar to a class party fund), by factoring conduct during discussions into a participation grade for the course, or by pulling aside and talking to students whose conduct violates the agreed-upon rules.

For sample ground rules, see Exhibit E.1, and for a method for helping students create their own ground rules, see Exhibit E.2.

Exhibit E.1. Sample Ground Rules

For Discussions

Listen actively and attentively.
Ask for clarification if you are confused.
Do not interrupt one another.
Challenge one another, but do so respectfully.
Critique ideas, not people.
Do not offer opinions without supporting evidence.
Avoid put-downs (even humorous ones).
Take responsibility for the quality of the discussion.
Build on one another's comments; work toward shared understanding.
Always have your book or readings in front of you.
Do not monopolize discussion.
Speak from your own experience, without generalizing.
If you are offended by anything said during discussion, acknowledge it immediately.
Consider anything that is said in class strictly confidential.

For Lectures

Arrive on time.
Turn your cell phone off.

Use laptops only for legitimate class activities (note-taking, assigned tasks).

Do not leave class early without okaying it with the instructor in advance.

Ask questions if you are confused.

Try not to distract or annoy your classmates.

Exhibit E.2. A Method for Helping Students Create Their Own Ground Rules

---

1. Ask students to think about the best group discussions in which they have participated and reflect on what made these discussions so satisfying.
2. Next, ask students to think about the worst group discussions in which they have participated and reflect on what made these discussions so unsatisfactory.
3. For each of the positive characteristics identified, ask students to suggest three things the group could do to ensure that these characteristics are present.
4. For each of the negative characteristics identified, ask students to suggest three things the group could do to ensure that these characteristics are not present.
5. Use students' suggestions to draft a set of ground rules to which you all agree, and distribute them in writing.
6. Periodically ask the class to reflect on whether the ground rules established at the beginning of the semester are working, and make adjustments as necessary.

SOURCE: Brookfield & Preskill (2005).

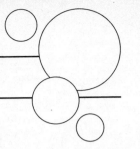

APPENDIX F

What Are Exam Wrappers and How Can We Use Them?

All too often when students receive back a graded exam, they focus on a single feature—the score they earned. Although this focus on "the grade" is understandable, it can lead students to miss out on several learning opportunities that such an assessment can provide:

- Identifying their own individual areas of strength and weakness to guide further study
- Reflecting on the adequacy of their preparation time and the appropriateness of their study strategies
- Characterizing the nature of their errors to find any recurring patterns that could be addressed

So to encourage students to process their graded exams more deeply, instructors can use *exam wrappers*, short handouts that students complete when an exam is turned back to them. Exam wrappers direct students to review and analyze their performance (and the instructor's feedback) with an eye toward adapting their future learning.

One way to use exam wrappers is to ask students to complete the handout when they get back their graded exams. This way, students are immediately encouraged to think through *why* they earned the score they did (what kinds of errors they made, how their performance might relate to their approach to studying) and how they might do better next time. Once students complete the exam wrappers, they should be collected, both for review by the instructional team and for safe keeping (because they will be used before the next exam, see next paragraph). In terms of reviewing the completed exam wrappers, the instructor, teaching assistants, or both should skim students' responses to see whether there are patterns either in how students analyzed their strengths and weaknesses or in how students described their approach to studying for the exam. These patterns may give the instructor some insights into students' patterns of performance and what advice might help students perform better on the next exam (for example, if students only reread their notes but did not do any practice problems for a problem-oriented exam, the instructor could advise students to actually solve problems from sample exams).

Then, a week or so before the next exam, the exam wrappers are returned to students, either in a recitation section or in some other setting where there is opportunity for structured discussion. Students can then be asked to reread their own exam wrapper responses from the previous exam and reflect on how they might implement their own advice or the instructor's advice for trying a better approach to studying for the upcoming exam. A structured class discussion can also be useful at this point to engage students in sharing effective study strategies and getting input and encouragement from the instructional team.

For a sample exam wrapper from a physics course, see Exhibit F.1.

Exhibit F.1. Sample Exam Wrapper

Physics Post-Exam Reflection   Name: _____

   This activity is designed to give you a chance to reflect on your exam performance and, more important, on the effectiveness of your exam preparation. Please answer the questions sincerely. Your responses will be collected to inform the instructional team regarding students' experiences surrounding this exam and how we can best support your learning. We will hand back your completed sheet in advance of the next exam to inform and guide your preparation for that exam.

1. Approximately how much time did you spend preparing for this exam? _____

2. What percentage of your test-preparation time was spent in each of these activities?

    a. Reading textbook section(s) for the first time _____
    b. Rereading textbook section(s) _____
    c. Reviewing homework solutions _____
    d. Solving problems for practice _____
    e. Reviewing your own notes _____
    f. Reviewing materials from course website _____
        (What materials? _____)
    g. Other _____
        (Please specify: _____)

3. Now that you have looked over your graded exam, estimate the percentage of points you lost due to each of the following (make sure the percentages add up to 100):

    a. Trouble with vectors and vector notation _____
    b. Algebra or arithmetic errors _____
    c. Lack of understanding of the concept _____
    d. Not knowing how to approach the problem _____
    e. Careless mistakes _____
    f. Other _____
    (Please specify: _____)

4. Based on your responses to the questions above, name at least three things you plan to do differently in preparing for the next

253

exam. For instance, will you just spend more time studying, change a specific study habit or try a new one (if so, name it), make math more automatic so it does not get in the way of physics, try to sharpen some other skill (if so, name it), solve more practice problems, or something else?

5. What can we do to help support your learning and your preparation for the next exam?

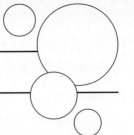

APPENDIX G

What Are Checklists and How Can We Use Them?

Checklists help instructors make their expectations for an activity or assignment explicit to students. This is often quite helpful because students do not always fully understand our expectations, and they may be guided by disciplinary or cultural conventions, or even the expectations of other instructors, that mismatch with what we expect for the current activity or assignment. In addition, checklists raise students' awareness of the required elements of complex tasks and thus can help students develop a more complete appreciation for the steps involved in effectively completing a given assignment.

Checklists should be distributed to students in advance of an assignment's due date, and students should be informed that it is their responsibility to fill out the checklist—making changes to their work, as necessary—and then staple the completed checklist to their assignment for submission. This increases the likelihood that certain basic criteria are met and avoids some annoying student tendencies (such as submitting multiple pages without stapling them together). For a sample checklist for a paper assignment, see Exhibit G.1.

Exhibit G.1. Sample Paper Checklist

Name:

Note: Please complete this checklist and staple it to each paper you submit for this course.

____ I have addressed all parts of the assignment.

____ My argument would be clear and unambiguous to any reader.

____ My paragraphs are organized logically and help advance my argument.

____ I use a variety of evidence (for example, quotes, examples, facts, illustrations) to reinforce my argument(s).

____ My conclusion summarizes my argument and explores its implications; it does not simply restate the topic paragraph.

____ I have revised my paper ___ times to improve its organization, argument, sentence structure, and style.

____ I have proofread my paper carefully, not relying on my computer to do it for me.

____ My name is at the top of the paper.

____ The paper is stapled.

____ The paper is double-spaced.

____ I have not used anyone else's work, ideas, or language without citing them appropriately.

____ All my sources are in my bibliography, which is properly formatted in APA style.

____ I have read the plagiarism statement in the syllabus, understand it, and agree to abide by the definitions and penalties described there.

Student Signature: _____ Date: _____

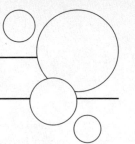

APPENDIX H

What Is Reader Response/Peer Review and How Can We Use It?

Reader response (often called peer review) is a process in which students read and comment on each others' work as a way to improve their peers' (and their own) writing. In order for students to be able to engage in this process effectively, the reviewers need a structure to guide their reading and feedback, the writers need reviews from several readers, and the writers need sufficient time to implement feedback and revise their work. Consequently, the instructor must plan assignment dates accordingly and create an instrument to direct the process.

Reader response/peer review offers advantages to readers, writers, and instructors alike. The advantage to the writer is that the process provides targeted feedback to direct revisions of the paper. The advantage to instructors is that students engage in the revision process before instructors ever see the paper, thus, one hopes, resulting in a better final product. Some empirical research has shown that if students get focused feedback from four peers, their revisions are better than those students who received feedback from their professors only. And the expectation for readers/

257

reviewers is that by analyzing others' strengths and weaknesses, they can become better at recognizing and addressing their own weaknesses.

Following in Exhibit H.1 is an example of an instrument that one instructor provides to her students for a basic academic argument paper. Notice that the instructions are geared toward helping reviewers identify the gist of the paper first, then locate the meaningful components of the argument, and then provide feedback. As with any instruments instructors use in their classes, the instructions make the most sense when they are grounded within the course context.

Exhibit H.1. Sample Reader Response/Peer Review Instrument

To the reviewer: The purpose of the peer review is to provide targeted feedback to the writer about what is working in the paper and what is not.

I. Please read the paper through the first time without making any markings on it in order to familiarize yourself with the paper.

II. During the second read, please do the following:
- Underline the main argument of the paper
- Put a check mark in the left column next to pieces of evidence that support the argument
- Circle the conclusion

III. Once you have done this, read the paper for the third and final time, and respond briefly to the following questions:
- Does the first paragraph present the writer's argument and the approach the writer is taking in presenting that argument? If not, which piece is missing, unclear, understated, and so forth?
- Does the argument progress clearly from one paragraph to the next (for example, is the sequencing/organization logical)? Does each paragraph add to the argument (that is, link the evidence to the main purpose of the paper)? If not, where does the structure break down, and/or which paragraph is problematic and why?

258

- Does the writer support the argument with evidence? Please indicate where there is a paragraph weak on evidence, evidence not supporting the argument, and so on.
- Does the conclusion draw together the strands of the argument? If not, what is missing?
- What is the best part of the paper?
- Which area(s) of the paper needs most improvement (e.g., the argument, the organization, sentence structure or word choice, evidence)? Be specific so that the writer knows where to focus his or her energy.

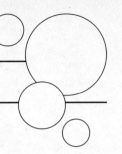

REFERENCES

Adams, M., Bell, L. A., & Griffin, P. (Eds.) (1997). *Teaching for diversity and social justice: A sourcebook*. New York: Routledge.

Ahmed, L. (1993). *Women and gender in Islam: Historical roots of a modern debate*. New Haven: Yale University Press.

Alexander, L., Frankiewicz, R. G., & Williams, R. E. (1979). Facilitation of learning and retention of oral instruction using advance and post organizers. *Journal of Educational Psychology, 71*, 701–707.

Alexander, P., Schallert, D., & Hare, V. (1991). Coming to terms: How researchers in learning and literacy talk about knowledge. *Review of Educational Research, 61*, 315–343.

Alibali, M. W. (1999). How children change their minds: Strategy change can be gradual or abrupt. *Developmental Psychology, 35*, 27–145.

Allport, G. (1954). *The nature of prejudice*. Cambridge, MA: Addison-Wesley.

Alvermann, D., Smith, I. C., & Readance, J. E. (1985). Prior knowledge activation and the comprehension of compatible and incompatible text. *Reading Research Quarterly, 20*, 420–436.

Ambrose, S. A., Dunkle, K. L., Lazarus, B. B., Nair, I., & Harkus, D. A. (1997). *Journeys of women in science and engineering: No universal constants*. Philadelphia: Temple University Press.

American Psychological Society (2008). 25 Principles of Learning. Retrieved May 15, 2009, from http://www.psyc.memphis.edu/learning/whatweknow/index.shtml

Ames, C. (1990). Motivation: What teachers need to know. *Teachers College Record, 91*, 409–472.

Anderson, J. R. (1983). *The architecture of cognition.* Cambridge, MA: Harvard University Press.

Anderson, J. R. (1992). Automaticity and the ACT theory. *American Journal of Psychology, 105,* 165–180.

Anderson, J. R., Conrad, F. G., & Corbett, A. T. (1989). Skill acquisition and the LISP tutor. *Cognitive Science, 13*(4), 467–505.

Anderson, J. R., Corbett, A. T., Koedinger, K. R., & Pelletier, R. (1995). Cognitive tutors: Lessons learned. *Journal of the Learning Sciences, 4,* 167–207.

Anderson, L. W., & Krathwohl, D. R. (Eds.) (2001). *A taxonomy for learning, teaching, and assessing: A revision of Bloom's taxonomy of educational objectives.* New York: Longman.

Aronson, J., Fried, C. B., & Good, C. (2002). Reducing the effects of stereotype threat on African American college students by shaping theories of intelligence. *Journal of Experimental Social Psychology, 38*(2), 113–125.

Astin, A. W. (1993). *What matters in college? Four critical years revisited.* San Francisco: Jossey-Bass.

Atkinson, J. (1964). *An introduction to motivation.* Princeton, NJ: Van Nostrand.

Atkinson, J. W. (1957). Motivational determinants of risk taking behavior. *Psychological Review, 64,* 369–372.

Ausubel, D. P. (1960). The use of advance organizers in the learning and retention of meaningful verbal material. *Journal of Educational Psychology, 51,* 267–272.

Ausubel, D. P. (1978). In defense of advance organizers: A reply to the critics. *Review of Educational Research, 48,* 251–257.

Ausubel, D. P., & Fitzgerald, D. (1962). Organizer, general background, and antecedent learning variables in sequential verbal learning. *Journal of Educational Psychology, 53,* 243–249.

Balzer, W. K., Doherty, M. E., & O'Connor, R. (1989). Effects of cognitive feedback on performance. *Psychological Bulletin, 106,* 410–433.

Bandura, A. (1997). *Self-efficacy: The exercise of control*. New York: Freeman.

Barnett, S. M., & Ceci, S. J. (2002). When and where do we apply what we learn? A taxonomy for far transfer. *Psychological Bulletin, 128*(4), 612–637.

Barron, K., & Harackiewicz, J. (2001). Achievement goals and optimal motivation: Testing multiple goal models. *Journal of Personality and Social Psychology, 80*, 706–722.

Bartlett, F. C. (1932). *Remembering: A study in experimental and social psychology*. Cambridge: Cambridge University Press.

Bassok, M. (1990). Transfer of domain-specific problem-solving procedures. *Journal of Experimental Psychology: Learning, Memory, and Cognition, 16*(3), 522–533.

Baxter-Magolda, M. (1992). *Knowing and reasoning in college: Gender-related patterns in students' intellectual development*. San Francisco: Jossey-Bass.

Beaufort, A. (2007). *College writing and beyond: A new framework for university writing instruction*. Logan, UT: Utah State University Press.

Beilock, S. L., Wierenga, S. A., & Carr, T. H. (2002). Expertise, attention and memory in sensorimotor skill execution: Impact of novel task constraints on dual-task performance and episodic memory. *The Quarterly Journal of Experimental Psychology A: Human Experimental Psychology, 55A*(1211–1240).

Belenky, M., Clinchy, B., Goldberger, N., & Tarule, J. (1986). *Women's ways of knowing: The development of self, voice, and mind*. New York: Basic Books.

Bereiter, C., & Scardamalia, M. (1987). *The psychology of written composition*. Hillsdale, NJ: Erlbaum.

Berry, D. C., & Broadbent, D. E. (1988). Interactive tasks and the implicit-explicit distinction. *British Journal of Psychology, 79*, 251–272.

Biederman, I., & Shiffrar, M. M. (1987). Sexing day-old chicks: A case study and expert systems analysis of a difficult perceptual-learning task. *Journal of Experimental Psychology: Learning, Memory, and Cognition, 13*(4), 640–645.

263

Bielaczyc, K., Pirolli, P. L., & Brown, A. L. (1995). Training in self-explanation and self-regulation strategies: Investigating the effects of knowledge acquisition activities on problem solving. *Cognition and Instruction, 13*(2), 221–252.

Black, P., & William, D. (1998). Assessment and classroom learning. *Assessment in Education, 5,* 7–74.

Blessing, S. B., & Anderson, J. R. (1996). How people learn to skip steps. *Journal of Experimental Psychology: Learning, Memory, and Cognition, 22,* 576–598.

Bloom, B. S. (Ed.) (1956). *A taxonomy of educational objectives: Handbook I: Cognitive domain.* New York: David McKay.

Bloom, B. S. (1984). The 2-sigma problem: The search for methods of group instruction as effective as one-to-one tutoring. *Educational Researcher 13,* 4–6.

Boice, R. (1998). Classroom incivilities. In K. A. Feldman & M. B. Paulson (Eds.), *Teaching and learning in the college classroom.* Needham Heights, MA: Simon & Schuster Custom Publications.

Boster, J. S., & Johnson, J. C. (1989). Form or function: A comparison of expert and novice judgments of similarity among fish. *American Anthropologist, 91,* 866–889.

Bower, G. H., Clark, M. C., Lesgold, A. M., & Winzenz, D. (1969). Hierarchical retrieval schemes in recall of categorical word lists. *Journal of Verbal Learning and Verbal Behavior, 8,* 323–343.

Bradshaw, G. L., & Anderson, J. R. (1982). Elaborative encoding as an explanation of levels of processing. *Journal of Verbal Learning and Verbal Behavior, 21,* 165–174.

Bransford, J. D., & Johnson, M. K. (1972). Contextual prerequisites for understanding: Some investigations of comprehension and recall. *Journal of Verbal Learning and Verbal Behavior, 11,* 717–726.

Brewer, M. B. (1988). A dual process model of impression formation. In T. K. Srull & R. S. Wyer, Jr. (Eds.), *Advances in Social Cognition, 1* (pp. 1–36). Hillsdale, NJ: Erlbaum.

264

Brewer, W. F., & Lambert, B. L. (2000, November). *The theory-ladenness of observation and the theory-ladenness of the rest of the scientific process.* Paper presented at the Seventeenth Biennial Meeting of the Philosophy of Science Association, Vancouver, British Columbia, Canada.

Brookfield, S. D., & Preskill, S. (2005). *Discussion as a way of teaching: Tools and techniques for democratic classrooms* (2nd ed.). San Francisco: Jossey-Bass.

Broughton, S. H., Sinatra, G. M., & Reynolds, R. E. (2007). *The refutation text effect: Influence on learning and attention.* Paper presented at the Annual Meetings of the American Educational Researchers Association, Chicago, Illinois.

Brown, A. L., Bransford, J. D., Ferrara, R. A., & Campione, J. C. (1983). Learning, remembering, and understanding. In *Handbook of child psychology* (pp. 77–166). New York: Wiley.

Brown, A. L., & Kane, M. J. (1988). Preschool students can learn to transfer. Learning to learn and learning from example. *Cognitive Psychology, 20,* 493–523.

Brown, D. (1992). Using examples to remediate misconceptions in physics: Factors influencing conceptual change. *Journal of Research in Science Teaching, 29,* 17–34.

Brown, D., & Clement, J. (1989). Overcoming misconceptions via analogical reasoning: Factors influencing understanding in a teaching experiment. *Instructional Science, 18,* 237–261.

Brown, L. T. (1983). Some more misconceptions about psychology among introductory psychology students. *Teaching of Psychology, 10,* 207–210.

Butler, D. (1997). *The roles of goal setting and self-monitoring in students self-regulated engagement of tasks.* Paper presented at the annual meeting of the American Educational Research Association, Chicago, IL.

Cardelle, M., & Corno, L. (1981). Effects on second language learning of variations in written feedback on homework assignments. *TESOL Quarterly, 15,* 251–261.

Carey, L. J., & Flower, L. (1989). *Foundations for creativity in the writing process: Rhetorical representations of ill-defined problems* (Technical Report No. 32). Center for the Study of Writing at University of California at Berkeley and Carnegie Mellon University.

Carey, L. J., Flower, L., Hayes, J., Shriver, K. A., & Haas, C. (1989). *Differences in writers' initial task representations* (Technical Report No. 34). Center for the Study of Writing at University of California at Berkeley and Carnegie Mellon University.

Carver, C. S., & Scheier, M. F. (1998). *On the self-regulation of behavior.* Cambridge: Cambridge University Press.

Cass, V. (1979). Homosexual identity formation: A theoretical model. *Journal of Homosexuality, 4,* 219–235.

Catrambone, R. (1995). Aiding subgoal learning: Effects on transfer. *Journal of Educational Psychology, 87,* 5–17.

Catrambone, R. (1998). The subgoal learning model: Creating better examples so that students can solve novel problems. *Journal of Experimental Psychology: General, 127,* 355–376.

Catrambone, R., & Holyoak, K. J. (1989). Overcoming contextual limitations on problem solving transfer. *Journal of Experimental Psychology, 15*(6), 1147–1156.

Chase, W. G., & Ericsson, K. A. (1982). Skill and working memory. In G. H. Bower (Ed.), *The psychology of learning and motivation* (Vol. 16, pp. 1–58). New York: Academic Press.

Chase, W. G., & Simon, H. A. (1973a). Perception in chess. *Cognitive Psychology, 1,* 31–81.

Chase, W. G., & Simon, H. A. (1973b). The mind's eye in chess. In W. G. Chase (Ed.), *Visual information processing.* New York: Academic Press.

Chi, M.T.H. (2008). Three types of conceptual change: Belief revision, mental model transformation, and categorical shift. In S. Vosniadou (Ed.), *Handbook of research on conceptual change* (pp. 61–82). Hillsdale, NJ: Erlbaum.

Chi, M.T.H., Bassok, M., Lewis, M. W., Reimann, P., & Glaser, R. (1989). Self-explanations: How students study and use examples in learning to solve problems. *Cognitive Science, 13,* 145–182.

266

Chi, M.T.H., DeLeeuw, N., Chiu, M.-H., & LaVancher, C. (1994). Eliciting self-explanations improves understanding. *Cognitive Science, 18,* 439–477.

Chi, M.T.H., Feltovich, P. J., & Glaser, R. (1981). Categorization and representation of physics problems by experts and novices. *Cognitive Science, 5,* 121–152.

Chi, M.T.H., & Roscoe, R. D. (2002). The processes and challenges of conceptual change. In M. Limon & L. Mason (Eds.), *Reconsidering conceptual change: Issues in theory and practice* (pp. 3–27). The Netherlands: Kluwer.

Chi, M.T.H., & VanLehn, K. (1991). The content of physics self-explanations. *Journal of the Learning Sciences, 1,* 69–105.

Chickering, A. (1969). *Education and identity.* San Francisco: Jossey-Bass.

Chickering, A., & Reisser, L. (1993). *Education and identity* (2nd ed.). San Francisco: Jossey-Bass.

Chinn, C. A., & Malhotra, B. A. (2002). Children's responses to anomalous scientific data: How is conceptual change impeded? *Journal of Educational Psychology, 94,* 327–343.

Clarke, T. A., Ayres, P. L., & Sweller, J. (2005). The impact of sequencing and prior knowledge on learning mathematics through spreadsheet applications. *Educational Technology Research and Development, 53,* 15–24.

Clement, J. (1993). Using bridging analogies and anchoring intuitions to deal with students' misconceptions in physics. *Journal of Research in Science Teaching, 30,* 1241–1257.

Clement, J. J. (1982). Students' preconceptions in introductory mechanics. *American Journal of Physics, 50,* 66–71.

Cognition and Technology Group at Vanderbilt (1994). From visual word problems to learning communities: Changing conceptions of cognitive research. In K. McGilly (Ed.), *Classroom lessons: Integrating cognitive theory and classroom practice* (pp. 157–200). Cambridge, MA: MIT Press/Bradford Books.

Confrey, J. (1990). A review of the research on student conceptions in mathematics, science, and programming. In C. B. Cazden (Ed.),

267

Review of Research in Education. Washington, DC: American Educational Research Association.

Cooper, G., & Sweller, J. (1987). The effects of schema acquisition and rule automation on mathematical problem-solving transfer. *Journal of Educational Psychology, 79,* 347–362.

Croizet, J. C., & Claire, T. (1998). Extending the concept of stereotype threat to social class: The intellectual underperformance of students from low socio-economic backgrounds. *Personality and Social Psychology Bulletin, 24,* 588–594.

Cross, W. (1995). The psychology of nigrescence: Revisiting the cross model. In J. Ponterotto, J. Casas, L. Suzuki, & C. Alexander (Eds.), *Handbook of multicultural counseling* (pp. 93–122). Thousand Oaks, CA: Sage.

Csikszentmihalyi, M. (1991). *Flow: The psychology of optimal experience.* New York: Harper Collins.

Cury, F., Elliot, A. J., Da Fonseca, D., & Moller, A. C. (2006). The social-cognitive model of achievement motivation and the 2 × 2 achievement framework. *Journal of Personality and Social Psychology, 90*(4), 666–679.

D'Augelli, A. R. (1994). Identity development and sexual orientation: Toward a model of lesbian, gay, and bisexual development. In E. Trickett, R. Watts, & D. Birman (Eds.), *Human diversity: Perspectives on people in context* (pp. 312–333). San Francisco: Jossey-Bass.

Dean, R. S., & Enemoh, P. A. C. (1983). Pictorial organization in prose learning. *Contemporary Educational Psychology, 8,* 20–27.

DeGroot, A. (1965). *Thought and choice in chess.* New York: Mouton.

DeJong, T., & Ferguson-Hessler, M. (1996). Types and qualities of knowledge. *Educational Psychologist, 31,* 105–113.

Del Mas, R. C., & Liu, Y. (2007). Students' conceptual understanding of the standard deviation. In M. C. Lovett & P. Shah (Eds.), *Thinking with data* (pp. 87–116). New York: Erlbaum.

DeSurra, C., & Church, K. A. (1994). *Unlocking the classroom closet: Privileging the marginalized voices of gay/lesbian college students.* Paper presented at the Annual Meeting of the Speech Communication Association.

DiSessa, A. A. (1982). Unlearning Aristotelian physics: A study of knowledge-based learning. *Cognitive Science, 6*, 37–75.

Dooling, D. J., & Lachman, R. (1971). Effects of comprehension on retention of prose. *Journal of Experimental Psychology, 88*, 216–22.

Dunbar, K. N., Fugelsang, J. A., & Stein, C. (2007). Do naïve theories ever go away? Using brain and behavior to understand changes in concepts. In M.C. Lovett & P. Shah (Eds.), *Thinking with data*. New York: Lawrence Erlbaum.

Dunning, D. (2007). *Self-insight: Roadblocks and detours on the path to knowing thyself.* New York: Taylor & Francis.

Dweck, C., & Leggett, E. (1988). A social-cognitive approach to motivation and personality. *Psychological Review, 95*, 256–273.

Egan, D. E., & Schwartz, B. J. (1979). Chunking in recall of symbolic drawings. *Memory & Cognition, 7*, 149–158.

El Guindi, F. (1999). *Veil: Modesty, privacy, and resistance.* New York: Berg Publishers.

Elliot, A. J. (1999). Approach and avoidance motivation and achievement goals. *Educational Psychologist, 34*, 169–189.

Elliot, A. J., & Fryer, J. W. (2008). The goal construct in psychology. In J. Y. Shah & W. L. Gardner (Eds.), *Handbook of motivation science* (pp. 235–250). New York, NY: Guilford Press.

Elliot, A. J., & McGregor, H. A. (2001). A 2 × 2 achievement goal framework. *Journal of Personality and Social Psychology, 80*(3), 501–519.

Ericsson, K. A., & Charness, N. (1994). Expert performance: Its structure and acquisition. *American Psychologist, 49*, 725–747.

Ericsson, K. A., Chase, W. G., & Faloon, S. (1980). Acquisition of a memory skill. *Science, 208*, 1181–1182.

Ericsson, K. A., Krampe, R. T., & Tescher-Romer, C. (2003). The role of deliberate practice in the acquisition of expert performance. *Psychological Review, 100*, 363–406.

Ericsson, K. A., & Lehmann, A. C. (1996). Expert and exceptional performance: Evidence on maximal adaptations on task constraints. *Annual Review of Psychology, 47*, 273–305.

Ericsson, K. A., & Smith, J. (1991). *Toward a general theory of expertise: Prospects and limits*. Cambridge: Cambridge University Press.

Ericsson, K. A., & Staszewski, J. J. (1989). Skilled memory and expertise: Mechanisms of exceptional performance (pp. 235–267). In D. Klahr, & K. Kotovsky (Eds.), *Complex information processing: The impact of Herbert A. Simon*. Hillsdale, NJ: Erlbaum.

Erikson, E. (1950). *Childhood and society*. New York: Norton.

Evans, N., Forney, D., & Guido-DiBrito, F. (1998). *Student development in college: Theory, research, and practice*. San Francisco: Jossey-Bass.

Eylon, B., & Reif, F. (1984). Effects of knowledge organization on task performance. *Cognition and Instruction, 1*, 5–44.

Finucane, M. L., Alhakami, A., Slovic, P., & Johnson, S. M. (2000). The affect heuristic in judgments of risks and benefits. *Journal of Behavioral Decision Making, 13*, 1–17.

Fiske, S. T., & Taylor, S. E. (1991). *Social cognition*. New York: McGraw-Hill.

Ford, M. E. (1992). *Motivating humans: Goals, emotions and personal agency beliefs*. Newbury Park, CA: Sage Publications, Inc.

Fries-Britt, S. (2000). Identity development of high-ability black collegians. In M. Baxter-Magolda (Ed.), *Teaching to promote intellectual and personal maturity: Incorporating students' worldviews and identities into the learning process* (Vol. *82*). San Francisco: Jossey-Bass.

Fu, W. T., & Gray, W. D. (2004). Resolving the paradox of the active user: Stable suboptimal performance in interactive tasks. *Cognitive Science, 28*(6), 901–935.

Gardner, R. M., & Dalsing, S. (1986). Misconceptions about psychology among college students. *Teaching of Psychology, 13*, 32–34.

Garfield, J., del Mas, R. C., & Chance, B. (2007). Using students' informal notions of variability to develop an understanding of formal measures of variability. In M. C. Lovett & P. Shah (Eds.), *Thinking with data* (pp. 117–147). New York: Erlbaum.

Gentner, D., Holyoak, K. J., & Kokinov, B. N. (2001). *The analogical mind*. Cambridge, MA: MIT Press.

270

Gentner, D., Loewenstein, J., & Thompson, L. (2003). Learning and transfer: A general role for analogical encoding. *Journal of Educational Psychology, 95,* 393–405.

Gick, M. L., & Holyoak, K. J. (1980). Analogical problem solving. *Cognitive Psychology, 12,* 306–355.

Gick, M. L., & Holyoak, K. J. (1983). Schema induction and analogical transfer. *Cognitive Psychology, 15,* 1–38.

Gilligan, C. (1977). In a different voice: Women's conception of self and morality. *Harvard Educational Review, 47,* 481–517.

Gobet, F., & Charness, N. (2006). Expertise in chess. In K. A. Ericsson et al. (Eds.), *The Cambridge handbook of expertise and expert performance* (pp. 523–538). New York: Cambridge University Press.

Gonzales, P. M., Blanton, H., & Williams, K. J. (2002). The effects of stereotype threat and double-minority status on the test performance of Latino women. *Personality and Social Psychology Bulletin, 28*(5), 659–670.

Goodrich Andrade, H. (2001). The effects of instructional rubrics on learning to write. *Current Issues in Education [On-line], 4.* Available: http://cie.ed.asu.edu/volume4/number4/.

Gutman, A. (1979). Misconceptions of psychology and performance in the introductory course. *Teaching of Psychology, 6,* 159–161.

Guzetti, B. J., Snyder, T. E., Glass, G. V., & Gamas, W. S. (1993). Meta-analysis of instructional interventions from reading education and science education to promote conceptual change in science. *Reading Research Quarterly, 28,* 116–161.

Hacker, D. J., Bol, L., Horgan, D. D., & Rakow, E. A. (2000). Test prediction and performance in a classroom context. *Journal of Educational Psychology, 92,* 160–170.

Hall, R. (1982). *A classroom climate: A chilly one for women?* Washington, DC: Association of American Colleges.

Hall, R., & Sandler, B. (1984). *Out of the classroom: A chilly campus climate for women.* Washington, DC: Association of American Colleges.

Hansen, D. (1989). Lesson evading and dissembling: Ego strategies in the classroom. *American Journal of Education, 97,* 184–208.

271

Harackiewicz, J., Barron, K., Taucer, J., Carter, S., & Elliot, A. (2000). Short-term and long-term consequences of achievement goals: Predicting interest and performance over time. *Journal of Educational Psychology, 92*, 316–330.

Hardiman, R., & Jackson, B. (1992). Racial identity development: Understanding racial dynamics in college classrooms and on campus. In M. Adams (Ed.), *Promoting diversity in college classrooms: Innovative responses for the curriculum, faculty and institutions.* (Vol. 52, pp. 21–37). San Francisco: Jossey-Bass.

Hattie, J., & Timperley, H. (2007). The power of feedback. *Review of Educational Research, 77*, 81–112.

Hayes, J. R., & Flower, L. S. (1986). Writing research and the writer. *American Psychologist Special Issue: Psychological Science and Education, 41*, 1106–1113.

Hayes-Baustista, D. (1974). Becoming Chicano: A "dis-assimilation" theory of transformation of ethnic identity. Unpublished doctoral dissertation. University of California.

Healy, A. F., Clawson, D. M., & McNamara, D. S. (1993). The long-term retention of knowledge and skills. In D.L. Medin (Ed.), *The psychology of learning and motivation* (pp. 135–164). San Diego, CA: Academic Press.

Helms, J. (1993). Toward a model of white racial identity development. In J. Helms (Ed.), *Black and white racial identity: Theory, research and practice*. Westport, CT: Praeger.

Henderson, V. L., & Dweck, C. S. (1990). Motivation and achievement. In S. S. Feldman & G. R. Elliott (Eds.), *At the threshold: The developing adolescent* (pp. 308–329). Cambridge, MA: Harvard University Press.

Hidi, S., & Renninger, K. A. (2006). The four-phase model of interest development. *Educational Psychologist, 41*(2), 111–127.

Hinds, P. J. (1999). The curse of expertise: The effects of expertise and debiasing methods on predictions of novice performance. *Journal of Experimental Psychology: Applied, 5*(2), 205–221.

Hinsley, D. A., Hayes, J. R., & Simon, H. A. (1977). From words to equations: Meaning and representation in algebra word problems. In

M. A. Just & P. S. Carpenter (Eds.), *Cognitive processes in comprehension*. Hillsdale, NJ: Erlbaum.

Holyoak, K. J., & Koh, K. (1987). Surface and structural similarity in analogical transfer. *Memory & Cognition, 15*, 332–340.

Howe, N., & Strauss, W. (2000). *Millennials rising: The next great generation*. New York: Vintage.

Hurtado, S., Milem, J., Clayton-Pedersen, A., & Allen, W. (1999). *Enacting diverse learning environments: Improving the climate for racial/ethnic diversity in higher education*. Washington, DC: The George Washington University.

Inzlicht, M., & Ben-Zeev, T. (2000). A threatening intellectual environment: Why females are susceptible to experience problem-solving deficits in the presence of males. *Psychological Science, 11*(5), 365–371.

Ishiyama, J., & Hartlaub, S. (2002). Does the wording of syllabi affect student course assessment in introductory political science classes? *PS: Political Science and Politics*, 567–570. Retrieved from http://www.apsanet.org/imgtest/WordingSyllabiAssessment-Ishiyama.pdf.

Judd, C. H. (1908). The relation of special training to general intelligence. *Educational Review, 36*, 28–42.

Kahnemann, D. (1973). *Attention and effort*. Englewood Cliffs, NJ: Prentice-Hall.

Kahnemann, D., & Frederick, S. (2002). Representativeness revisited: Attribute substitution in intuitive judgment. In T. Gilovich, D. Griffin, & D. Kahnemann (Eds.), *Heuristics and biases: The psychology of intuitive judgment*. New York: Cambridge University Press.

Kaiser, M. K., McCloskey, M., & Proffitt, D. R. (1986). Development of intuitive theories of motion: Curvilinear motion in the absence of external forces. *Developmental Psychology, 22*, 67–71.

Kalyuga, S., Ayres, P., Chandler, P., & Sweller, J. (2003). Expertise reversal effect. *Educational Psychologist, 38*, 23–31.

Kandel, A. (1986). *Processes of Jewish American identity development: Perceptions of Conservative Jewish women*. Unpublished Doctoral Dissertation. University of Massachusetts at Amherst.

Kaplan, J., Fisher, D., & Rogness, N. (2009). Lexical ambiguity in statistics: What do students know about the words: association, average, confidence, random and spread? *Journal of Statistics Education, 17*(3).

Kim, J. (1981). Processes of Asian American identity development: A study of Japanese American women's perceptions of their struggle to achieve positive identities as Americans of Asian ancestry. Unpublished doctoral dissertation. University of Massachusetts.

Klahr, D., & Carver, S. M. (1988). Cognitive objectives in a LOGO debugging curriculum: instruction, learning, and transfer. *Cognitive Psychology, 20,* 362–404.

Koedinger, K. R., & Anderson, J. R. (1990). Abstract planning and perceptual chunks: Elements of expertise in geometry. *Cognitive Science, 14*(4), 511–550.

Koedinger, K. R., & Anderson, J. R. (1993). Reifying implicit planning in geometry: Guidelines for model-based intelligent tutoring system design. In S. Lajoie & S. Derry (Eds.), *Computers as cognitive tools.* Hillsdale, NJ: Erlbaum.

Kohlberg, L. (1976). Moral stages and moralization: The cognitive-developmental approach. In T. Lickona (Ed.), *Moral development and behavior: Theory, research, and social issues* (pp. 31–53). New York: Holt, Rinehart & Winston.

Kole, J. A., & Healy, A. (2007). Using prior knowledge to minimize interference when learning large amounts of information. *Memory & Cognition, 35,* 124–137.

Lamburg, W. (1980). Self-provided and peer-provided feedback. *College Composition and Communication, 31*(1), 63–69.

Lansdown, T. C. (2002). Individual differences during driver secondary task performance: Verbal protocol and visual allocation findings. *Accident Analysis & Prevention, 23,* 655–662.

Larkin, J., McDermott, J., Simon, D. P., & Simon, H. (1980). Expert and novice performance in solving physics problems. *Science, 208*(4450), 1335–1342.

Lesgold, A., et al. (1988). Expertise in a complex skill: Diagnosing x-ray pictures. In M.T.H. Chi & R. Glaser (Eds.), *The nature of expertise* (pp. 311–342). Hillsdale, NJ: Erlbaum.

Levi-Strauss, C. (1969). *The elementary structures of kinship*. Boston: Beacon Press.

Levy, B. (1996). Improving memory in old age through implicit self-stereotyping. *Journal of Personality and Social Psychology, 71*(6), 1092–1107.

Loewenstein, J., Thompson, L., & Gentner, D. (2003). Analogical learning in negotiation teams: Comparing cases promotes learning and transfer. *Academy of Management Learning and Education, 2*(2), 119–127.

Lovett, M. C. (2001). A collaborative convergence on studying reasoning processes: A case study in statistics. In S. Carver & D. Klahr (Eds.), *Cognition and instruction: Twenty-five years of progress* (pp. 347–384). Mahwah, NJ: Erlbaum.

Maehr, M., & Meyer, H. (1997). Understanding motivation and schooling: Where we've been, where we are, and where we need to go. *Educational Psychology Review, 9*, 371–409.

Major, B., Spencer, S., Schmader, T., Wolfe, C., & Crocker, J. (1998). Coping with negative stereotypes about intellectual performance: The role of psychological disengagement. *Personality and Social Psychology Bulletin 24*(1), 34–50.

Marchesani, L., & Adams, M. (1992). Dynamics of diversity in the teaching–learning process: A faculty development model for analysis and action. In M. Adams (Ed.), *Promoting diversity in college classrooms: Innovative responses for the curriculum, faculty, and institutions* (Vol. 52, pp. 9–20). San Francisco: Jossey-Bass.

Marcia, J. (1966). Development and validation of ego identity status. *Journal of Personality and Social Psychology, 5*, 551–558.

Martin, F., Klein, J. D., & Sullivan, H. (2007). The impact of instructional elements in computer-based instruction. *British Journal of Educational Technology, 38*, 623–636.

275

Martin, V. L., & Pressley, M. (1991). Elaborative-interrogation effects depend on the nature of the question. *Journal of Educational Psychology, 83,* 113–119.

Mason Spencer, R., & Weisberg, R. W. (1986). Context-dependent effects on analogical transfer. *Memory and Cognition, 14*(5), 442–449.

Mathan, S. A., & Koedinger, K. R. (2005). Fostering the intelligent novice: Learning from errors with metacognitive tutoring. *Educational Psychologist, 40*(4), 257–265.

Mayer, R. E. (2002). *The promise of educational psychology, volume 2: Teaching for meaningful learning.* Upper Saddle River, NJ: Merrill Prentice Hall.

McCloskey, M. (1983). Naïve theories of motion. In D. Gentner and A. Stevens (Eds.), *Mental models* (pp. 289–324), Hillsdale, NJ: Erlbaum.

McCloskey, M., Caramazza, A., & Green, B. (1980). Curvilinear motion in the absence of external forces: Naïve beliefs about the motion of objects. *Science, 210,* 1139–1141.

McDaniel, M. A., & Donnelly, C. M. (1996). Learning with analogy and elaborative interrogation. *Journal of Educational Psychology, 88,* 508–519.

McGregor, H., & Elliot, A. (2002). Achievement goals as predictors of achievement-relevant processes prior to task engagement. *Journal of Educational Psychology, 94,* 381–395.

McKendree, J. (1990). Effective feedback content for tutoring complex skills. *Human-Computer Interaction, 5*(4), 381–413.

McKeough, A., Lupart, J., & Marini, A. (1995). *Teaching for transfer: Fostering generalization in learning.* Mahwah, NJ: Erlbaum.

Meece, J., & Holt, K. (1993). A pattern analysis of student's achievement goals. *Education Psychology, 85,* 582–590.

Merrill, D. C., Reiser, B. J., Ranney, M., & Trafton, G. J. (1992). Effective tutoring techniques: A comparison of human tutors and intelligent tutoring systems. *Journal of the Learning Sciences, 2*(3), 277–305.

Miller, A. H. (1987). *Course design for university lecturers.* New York: Nichols Publishing.

Miller, R., Greene, B., Montalvo, G., Ravindran, B., & Nichols, J. (1996). Engagement in academic work: The role of learning goals, future consequences, pleasing others and perceived ability. *Contemporary Educational Psychology, 21*, 388–422.

Minstrell, J. A. (1989). Teaching science for understanding. In L. B. Resnick & L. E. Klopfer, (Eds.), *Toward the thinking curriculum: Current cognitive research*. Alexandria: ASCD Books.

Minstrell, J. A. (1992). Facets of students' knowledge and relevant instruction. In R. Duit, F. Goldberg, & H. Niedderer (Eds.), *Proceedings of the International Workshop on Research in Physics Education: Theoretical Issues and Empirical Studies* (pp. 110–128). Kiel, Germany: Institut fur die Padagogik der Naturwissenshaften.

Mitchell, T. R. (1982). Motivation: New directions for theory, research, and practice. *Academy of Management Review, 7*, 80–88.

Monteith, M. J., & Mark, A. Y. (2005). Changing one's prejudiced ways: Awareness, affect, and self-regulation. *European Review of Social Psychology, 16*, 113–154.

Monteith, M. J., Sherman, J. W., & Devine, P. G. (1998). Suppression as a stereotype control strategy. *Personality and Social Psychology Review, 2*, 63–82.

Morris, P. E., Gruneberg, M. M., Sykes, R. N., & Merrick, A. (1981). Football knowledge and the acquisition of new results. *British Journal of Psychology, 72*, 479–483.

Nathan, M. J., & Koedinger, K. R. (2000). An investigation of teachers' beliefs of students' algebra development. *Journal of Cognition and Instruction, 18*(2), 209–237.

Nathan, M. J., & Petrosino, A. (2003). Expert blind spot among preservice teachers. *American Educational Research Journal, 40*(4), 905–928.

National Research Council (2000). *How people learn: Brain, mind, experience, and school*. Washington, D.C.: National Academy Press.

National Research Council (2001). *Knowing what students know: The science and design of educational assessment*. Washington, DC: National Academy Press.

Navon, D., & Gopher, D. (1979). On the economy of the human-processing system. *Psychological Review, 86,* 214–255.

Naylor, J. C., & Briggs, G. E. (1963). Effects of task complexity and task organization on the relative efficiency of part and whole training methods. *Journal of Experimental Psychology, 65*(2), 217–224.

Nelson, J. (1990). "This was an easy assignment": Examining how students interpret academic writing tasks. *Research in the Teaching of English, 24*(4), 362–396.

Nickerson, R. (1999). How we know—and sometimes misjudge—what others know: Imputing one's own knowledge to others. *Psychological Bulletin, 125*(6), 737–759.

Novak, J. (1998). *Learning, creating, and using knowledge: Concept maps as facilitative tools in schools and corporations.* Mahwah, NJ: Erlbaum.

Novak, J. D. & Cañas, A. J. (2008). "The theory underlying concept maps and how to construct them." (Technical Report IHMC CmapTools 2006-01 Rev 2008-01). Pensacola, FL: Institute for Human and Machine Cognition. Retrieved March 26, 2009, from http://cmap.ihmc.us/Publications/ResearchPapers/TheoryUnderlyingConceptMaps.pdf.

Onken, S., & Slaten, E. (2000). Disability identity formation and affirmation: The experiences of persons with severe mental illness. *Sociological Practice: A Journal of Clinical and Applied Sociology, 2*(2), 99–111.

Paas, F., Renkl, A., & Sweller, J. (2003). Cognitive load theory and instructional design: Recent developments. *Educational Psychologist, 38*(1), 1–4.

Paas, F., Renkl, A., & Sweller, J. (2004). Cognitive load theory: Instructional implications of the interaction between information structures and cognitive architecture. *Instructional Science, 32,* 1–8.

Paas, F., & van Merrienboer, J. (1994). Variability of worked examples and transfer of geometrical problem solving skills: A cognitive-load approach. *Journal of Educational Psychology, 86*(122–133).

278

Palinscar, A. S., & Brown, A. L. (1984). Reciprocal teaching of comprehension-fostering and comprehension-monitoring activities. *Cognition & Instruction, 1*, 117–175.

Pascarella, E., & Terenzini, P. (1977). Patterns of student-faculty informal interaction beyond the classroom and voluntary freshman attrition. *Journal of Higher Education, 5*, 540–552.

Pascarella, E., & Terenzini, P. (1991). *How college affects students: Findings and insights from twenty years of research.* San Francisco: Jossey-Bass.

Pascarella, E. T., & Terenzini, P. T. (2005). *How college affects students: A third decade of research.* San Francisco: Jossey-Bass.

Pascarella, E., Whitt, E., Edison, M., & Nora, A. (1997). Women's perceptions of a "chilly climate" and their cognitive outcomes during the first year of college. *Journal of College Student Development, 38*(2), 109–124.

Peeck, J., Van Den Bosch, A. B., & Kruepeling, W. (1982). The effect of mobilizing prior knowledge on learning from text. *Journal of Educational Psychology, 74*, 771–777.

Perfetto, G. A., Bransford, J. D., & Franks, J. J. (1983). Constraints on access in a problem-solving context. *Memory and Cognition, 11*, 24–31.

Perry, W. (1968). *Forms of intellectual and ethical development in the college years: A scheme.* New York: Holt, Rinehart & Winston.

Pintrich, P. R. (2000). The role of goal orientation in self-regulated learning. In M. Boekaerts, P. R. Pintrich, & M. Zeider (Eds.), *Handbook of self-regulation* (pp. 451–502). San Diego Academic Press.

Pittsburgh Science of Learning Center. (2009). Instructional principles and hypotheses. Retrieved May 15, 2009, from http://www.learnlab.org/research/wiki/index.php/InstructionalPrinciples.

Ram, A., Nersessian, N. J., & Keil, F. C. (1997). Special issue: Conceptual change. *The Journal of the Learning Sciences, 6*, 1–91.

Rankin, S. (2003). *Campus climate for gay, lesbian, bisexual, and transgender people: A national perspective.* New York: The National Gay and Lesbian Task Force Policy Institute.

279

Reber, P. J., & Kotovsky, K. (1997). Implicit learning in problem solving: The role of working memory capacity. *Journal of Experimental Psychology: General, 126*, 178–203.

Reder, L. M., & Anderson, J. R. (1980). A partial resolution of the paradox of interference: The role of integrating knowledge. *Cognitive Psychology, 12*, 447–472.

Reed, S. K., Ernst, G. W., & Banerji, R. (1974). The role of analogy in transfer between similar problem states. *Cognitive Psychology, 6*, 436–450.

Resnick, L. B. (1976). Task analysis in instructional design: Some cases from mathematics. In D. Klahr (Ed.), *Cognition and Instruction* (pp. 51–80). Hillsdale, NJ: Erlbaum.

Resnick, L. B. (1983). Mathematics and science learning. *Science, 220*, 477–478.

Ritter, S., Anderson, J. R., Koedinger, K. R., & Corbett, A. (2007). Cognitive tutor: Applied research in mathematics education. *Psychonomic Bulletin & Review, 14*(2), 249–255.

Ross, B. H. (1987). This is like that: The use of earlier problems and the separation of similarity effects. *Journal of Experimental Psychology: Learning, Memory, and Cognition, 13*, 629–639.

Ross, B. H. (1989). Distinguishing types of superficial similarity: Different effects on the access and use of earlier problems. *Journal of Experimental Psychology: Learning, Memory, and Cognition, 15*, 456–468.

Rothkopf, E. Z., & Billington, M. J. (1979). Goal-guided learning from text: Inferring a descriptive processing model from inspection times and eye movements. *Journal of Educational Psychology, 71*, 310–327.

Rubin, S. (1985). Professors, students, and the syllabus. (1985, August 7). *The Chronicle of Higher Education*, p. 56.

Ryan, T. A. (1970). *Intentional Behavior*. New York: Ronal Press.

Salden, R.J.C.M., Paas, F., & van Merrienboer, J.J.G. (2006). A comparison of approaches to learning task selection in the training of complex cognitive skills. *Computers in Human Behavior, 22*, 321–333.

Sandler, B., & Hall, R. (1986). *The campus climate revisited: Chilly for women faculty, administrators, and graduate students.* Washington, DC: Association of American Colleges.

Schoenfeld, A. H. (1987). What's all the fuss about metacognition? In A. H. Schoenfeld (Ed.), *Cognitive Science and Mathematics Education* (pp. 189–215). Hillsdale, NJ: Erlbaum.

Schommer, M. (1994). An emerging conceptualization of epistemological beliefs and their role in learning. In R. Barner & P. Alexander (Eds.), *Beliefs about text and instruction with text* (pp. 25–40). Hillsdale, NJ: Erlbaum.

Schwartz, D. L., & Bransford, J. D. (1998). A time for telling. *Cognition and Instruction, 16,* 475–522.

Schwartz, D. L., Lin, X., Brophy, S., & Bransford, J. D. (1999). Toward the development of flexibly adaptive instructional designs. In C. M. Reigelut (Ed.), *Instructional design theories and models: Volume 2.* Hillsdale, NJ: Erlbaum.

Seymour, E., & Hewitt, N. (1997). *Talking about leaving: Why undergraduates leave the sciences.* Boulder, CO: Westview Press.

Shih, M., Pittinsky, T., & Ambady, N. (1999). Stereotype susceptibility: Identity salience and shifts in quantitative performance. *Psychological Science, 10,* 80–83.

Shuman, R. E. (1979). How to grade student writing. In G. Stanford (Ed.), *Classroom practices in teaching English 1979–1980: How to handle the paper load.* Urbana, IL: National Council of Teachers of English.

Singley, M. K. (1995). Promoting transfer through model tracing. In A. McKeough, J. Lupart, & A. Marini (Eds.), *Teaching for transfer.* Mahwah, NJ: Lawrence Erlbaum Associates.

Singley, M. K., & Anderson, J. R. (1989). *The transfer of cognitive skill.* Cambridge, MA: Harvard University Press.

Smith, E. E., Adams, N., & Schorr, D. (1978). Fact retrieval and the paradox of interference. *Cognitive Psychology, 10,* 438–464.

Smith, M. D., & Chamberlin, C. J. (1992). Effect of adding cognitively demanding tasks on soccer skill performance. *Perceptual and Motor Skills, 75,* 955–961.

281

Soloway, E., Adelson, B., & Ehrlich, K. (1988). Knowledge and processes in the comprehension of computer programs. In M.T.H. Chi & R. Glaser (Eds.), *The nature of expertise* (pp. 129–152). Hillsdale, NJ: Erlbaum.

Somuncuoglu, Y., & Yildirim, A. (1999). Relationship between achievement goal orientations and use of learning strategies. *Journal of Educational Research, 92,* 267–277.

Spiro, R. J., Feltovich, P. J., Coulson, R. L., & Anderson, D. K. (1989). Multiple analogies for complex concepts: Antidotes for analogy-induced misconception in advanced knowledge acquisition. In S. Vosniadou & A. Ortony (Eds.), *Similarity and analogical reasoning* (pp. 498–531). New York: Cambridge University Press.

Sprague, J., & Stuart, D. (2000). *The speaker's handbook.* Fort Worth, TX: Harcourt College Publishers.

Steele, C. M., & Aronson, J. R. (1995). Stereotype threat and the intellectual test performance of African Americans. *Journal of Personality and Social Psychology, 69*(5), 797–811.

Stevens, D. D., & Levi, A. J. (2005). *Introduction to rubrics: An assessment tool to save grading time, convey effective feedback and promote student learning.* Sterling, VA: Stylus.

Stone, L. (2000). *Kinship and gender: An introduction.* Boulder, CO: Westview Press.

Strayer, D. L., & Johnston, W. A. (2001). Driven to distraction: Dual-task studies of simulated driving and conversing on a cellular telephone. *Psychological Science, 12*(6), 462–466.

Sun, R., Merrill, E., & Peterson, T. (2001). From implicit skills to explicit knowledge: A bottom-up model of skill learning. *Cognitive Science, 25,* 203–244.

Sweller, J., & Cooper, G. A. (1985). The use of worked examples as a substitute for problem-solving in learning algebra. *Cognition and Instruction, 2,* 59–89.

Tatum, B. D. (1997). *Why are all the black kids sitting together in the cafeteria? And other conversations about race.* New York: Basic Books.

Taylor, A. K. & Kowalski, P. (2004), Naïve psychological science: The prevalence, strength, and sources of misconceptions. *The Psychological Record, 54.*

Teague, R. C., Gittelman, S. S., & Park, O.-C. (1994). *A review of the literature on part-task and whole-task training and context dependency* (Report No. 1010). Army Research Institute for the Behavioral and Social Sciences.

Thonis, E. (1981). *Schooling and language minority students: A theoretical framework.* Los Angeles, CA: Evaluation, Dissemination and Assessment Center, California State University.

Thorndike, E. L., & Woodworth, R. S. (1901). The influence of improvement in one mental function upon the efficiency of other functions. *Psychological Review, 8*(3), 247–261.

Traxler, M. J., & Gernsbacher, M. A. (1992). Improving written communication through minimal feedback. *Language and Cognitive Processes, 7,* 1–22.

Valle, A., Cabanach, R., Nunez, J., Gonzales-Pienda, J., Rodriguez, S., & Piñeiro, I. (2003). Multiple goals, motivation and academic learning. *British Journal of Educational Psychology, 73,* 71–87.

Vosniadou, S., & Brewer, W. F. (1987). Theories of knowledge restructuring in development. *Review of Educational Research, 57,* 51–67.

Vygotsky, L. S. (1978). *Mind in society: The development of the higher psychological processes.* Cambridge, MA: The Harvard University Press (Originally published 1930, New York: Oxford University Press.)

Watson, L. W., Terrell, M. C., & Wright, D. J. (2002). *How minority students experience college: Implications for planning and policy.* Sterling, VA: Stylus.

Weiner, B. (1986). *An attributional theory of motivation and emotion.* New York: Springer-Verlag.

White, B. Y., & Frederickson, J. R. (1990). Causal models progressions as a foundation for intelligent learning environments. *Artificial Intelligence, 42,* 99–157.

Whitt, E., Nora, A., Edison, M., Terenzini, P., & Pascarella, E. (1999). Women's perceptions of a "chilly climate" and cognitive outcomes in college: Additional evidence. *Journal of College Student Development, 40*(2), 163–177.

Wickens, C. D. (1991). Processing resources and attention. In D. L. Damos (Ed.), *Multiple task performance* (pp. 3–34). London: Taler & Francis, Ltd.

Wigfield, A., & Eccles, J. (1992). The development of achievement task values: A theoretical analysis. *Developmental Review, 12*, 265–310.

Wigfield, A., & Eccles, J. (2000). Expectancy-value theory of achievement motivation. *Contemporary Educational Psychology, 25*, 68–81.

Wightman, D. C., & Lintern, G. (1985). Part-task training for tracking and manual control. *Human Factors, 27*(3), 267–283.

Wikan, U. (1982). *Behind the veil in Arabia: Women in Oman.* Chicago: University of Chicago Press.

Winne, P. H., & Hadwin, A. F. (1998). Studying as self-regulated learning. In D. Hacker, J. Dunlosky & A. Graesser (Eds.), *Metacognition in educational theory and practice.* Mahwah, NJ: Erlbaum.

Woloshyn, V. E., Paivio, A., & Pressley, M. (1994). Use of elaborative interrogation to help students acquire information consistent with prior knowledge and information inconsistent with prior knowledge. *Journal of Educational Psychology, 86*, 79–89.

Zimmerman, B. J. (2001). Theories of self-regulated learning and academic achievement: An overview and analysis. In B. J. Zimmerman & D. H. Schunk (Eds.), *Self-regulated learning and academic achievement* (2nd ed., pp. 1–38). Hillsdale, NJ: Erlbaum.

NAME INDEX

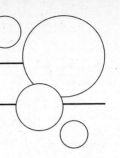

SUBJECT INDEX

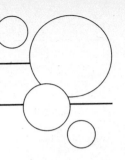

A

Ability, 181–182

Active listening, 186

Advance organizers, 53

Affective goals, 73

American Psychological Association, 7

Analogies: connecting students with prior knowledge, 33; illustrating limits of, 20–21, 36–37

Application of skills, 107–112

Assessments: administering diagnostic, 28–29; aligning for course, 85; diagnosing weak or missing component skills, 114–115; finding appropriate challenge levels with, 145; of prior knowledge, 19–20; providing performance-based, 206. *See also* Self-assessments

Assignments: checking student understanding of, 205; creating appropriately challenging, 86; defining unacceptable, 204–205; focusing on strategies solving, 211–212; including planning in, 191, 207–208; peer reviews and feedback of, 209–210; presenting multiple solutions for, 211; providing performance criteria with, 205–206; rubrics for, 231–232

Attainment value, 75, 76

Autonomy of students, 161

B

Brainstorming, 29–30

C

Centralizing course climate, 171–173

Challenge: adjusting with instructional scaffolding, 132–133, 146–147; assessing level of, 130–133, 136, 145; setting for students, 85–86

Change: guiding process of conceptual, 27; involved in learning, 3

Checklists, 255–256

Chickering model of student development, 160–163

Chunking, 52

Class participation rubric, 233

Classes. *See* Course climate; Large classes

Clickers, 31

Climate. *See* Course climate

Cognitive load, 103–107, 116

Cognitive structures: expert and novice, 45–58; supplying students with, 53